Clive Oxenden
Christina Latham-Koenig

New
ENGLISH FILE

Intermediate
Student's Book

OXFORD
UNIVERSITY PRESS

Contents

Look out for `Study Link`
This shows you where to find extra material for more practice and revision.

1 A

G present simple and continuous; action and non-action verbs
V food and restaurants
P /ʊ/ and /uː/, understanding phonetics

Food: fuel or pleasure?

1 READING & SPEAKING

a What kind of food or dishes do you associate with these countries?

The United States	China	France
Italy	Japan	Mexico

b Read the interviews with **Alice** and **Jacqueline**. Match the questions with their answers.

We talk to women around the world about their relationship with food.

1 Is food a pleasure for you?
2 What do you normally eat in a typical day?
3 Do you ever cook?
4 Do you ever eat 'unhealthy' food? How do you feel about it?
5 Are you trying to cut down on anything at the moment?
6 Are people's diets in your country getting better or worse?

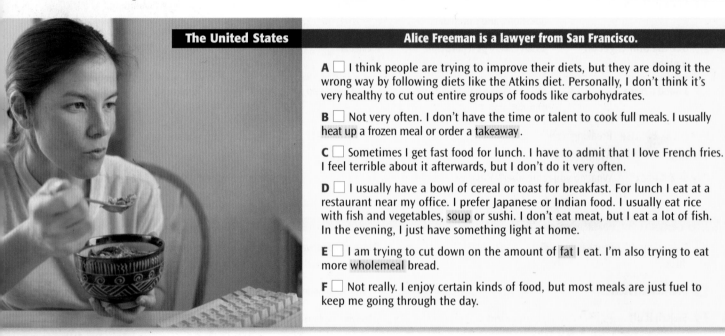

The United States | **Alice Freeman is a lawyer from San Francisco.**

A ☐ I think people are trying to improve their diets, but they are doing it the wrong way by following diets like the Atkins diet. Personally, I don't think it's very healthy to cut out entire groups of foods like carbohydrates.

B ☐ Not very often. I don't have the time or talent to cook full meals. I usually heat up a frozen meal or order a takeaway.

C ☐ Sometimes I get fast food for lunch. I have to admit that I love French fries. I feel terrible about it afterwards, but I don't do it very often.

D ☐ I usually have a bowl of cereal or toast for breakfast. For lunch I eat at a restaurant near my office. I prefer Japanese or Indian food. I usually eat rice with fish and vegetables, soup or sushi. I don't eat meat, but I eat a lot of fish. In the evening, I just have something light at home.

E ☐ I am trying to cut down on the amount of fat I eat. I'm also trying to eat more wholemeal bread.

F ☐ Not really. I enjoy certain kinds of food, but most meals are just fuel to keep me going through the day.

France | **Jacqueline Fabre is an IT consultant from Lyons.**

A ☐ Yes, I cook every evening for my family. I often make soup or traditional French dishes like 'boeuf bourguignon', which is a kind of beef and red wine stew, and then we have cheese and salad. It may seem a lot but we don't eat big portions. What's important for me is quality, not quantity.

B ☐ Yes, I'm trying to eat less chocolate.

C ☐ I think people's diets are getting worse and worse. It's quite strange because we have a lot of information now about how bad fast food is for you. I'm afraid it's a problem in a lot of European countries.

D ☐ Not at home. I think most of the food I cook is healthy, but occasionally when I eat out I have something unhealthy, but it doesn't worry me.

E ☐ Yes, definitely. For me good meals with the family make me happy!

F ☐ I'm quite traditional and I have three main meals a day. For breakfast, I like hot chocolate, and bread and butter with honey or jam. For lunch, I often eat in a restaurant with my colleagues. I usually have vegetables and meat or fish but I love pasta and rice too. In the afternoon, I have fruit with biscuits or a piece of chocolate. In the evening, I have a proper meal with my family.

Adapted from the British press

c Read the interviews again and answer the questions below. Write A (*Alice*), J (*Jacqueline*), or B (*both of them*).

Who...?

1 often eats in restaurants   _____
2 eats quite a lot of sweet things   _____
3 eats ready-prepared food   _____
4 cooks big meals at home   _____
5 enjoys eating   _____
6 feels bad when she eats unhealthily _____
7 is trying to eat less of something   _____
8 prefers having good food to having a lot of food   _____
9 is negative about eating habits in her country   _____

d Match the highlighted words or phrases with the definitions.

1 _____ to have a meal in a restaurant, not at home
2 _____ a sweet food made by bees, which people often eat on bread
3 _____ the quantity you eat of a kind of food during a meal
4 _____ to make cold food hot
5 _____ food you buy from a restaurant to eat at home
6 _____ food from animals or plants used for cooking, e.g. oil, butter, etc.
7 _____ food prepared in a particular way, e.g. sushi, lasagne, etc.
8 _____ made from brown flour
9 _____ a liquid food, often made of vegetables, e.g. tomatoes, onions
10 _____ meat cooked for a long time in liquid, usually with vegetables

e Which of the two women do you think has the healthier diet? Why?

f Now interview each other with the questions from **1b**. How similar are your eating habits?

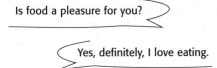

Is food a pleasure for you?

Yes, definitely, I love eating.

2 GRAMMAR present simple and continuous, action and non-action verbs

Rumiko Yasuda is a magazine editor from Tokyo.   **Japan**

a **1.1** Listen to **Rumiko** answering questions 2–6 from the interviews. Do you think food for her is fuel or pleasure? Why?

b Listen again and answer the questions.

1 What does she usually have in the morning?
2 Where does she usually have lunch and dinner?
3 Why doesn't she often cook?
4 Does she eat or drink anything unhealthy?
5 Is she cutting down on anything at the moment? Why (not)?
6 What's happening to the Japanese diet at the moment?
7 Does she think this is a completely bad thing?

c Look at some of the things Rumiko said. Circle the correct form. Then compare with a partner and say why the other form is wrong.

1 *I don't usually have / I'm not having* breakfast at work.
2 I used to go to fast food restaurants, but now *I prefer / I am preferring* eating something healthier.
3 *I am drinking / I drink* a lot of coffee every day.
4 I think Japanese people *get / are getting* fatter.
5 *I like / I'm liking* the fact that there are more different kinds of food and restaurants now.

d ⟳ **p.130 Grammar Bank 1A.** Read the rules and do the exercises.

e Make questions to ask your partner with the present simple or continuous. Ask for more information.

What / usually have for breakfast?
How many cups of coffee / drink a day?
Where / usually have lunch?
How often / eat out a week?
/ prefer eating at home or eating out?
/ need to buy any food today?
/ you hungry? / want something to eat?
/ take any vitamins or food supplements at the moment?
/ try to eat healthily at the moment?

3 VOCABULARY food and restaurants

a Do the quiz in pairs.

Food Quiz
Can you think of …?

ONE **red** fruit, ONE **yellow** fruit, ONE **green** fruit

TWO things that a strict vegetarian doesn't eat

THREE kinds of food which are made from milk

FOUR things people have for breakfast

FIVE things people eat between meals

SIX vegetables you can put in a salad

SEVEN things which are usually on a table in a restaurant

b ➲ **p.144 Vocabulary Bank** *Food and restaurants.*

c Ask and answer the questions below with a partner.

Food and eating

1 How often do you eat…?
  a takeaway food   b ready-cooked meals
  c low-fat food   d home-made food

2 What's your favourite…?
  a fruit   b vegetable   c snack
  d home-made dish

3 What food do you like eating…?
  a when the weather's very cold
  b when you're feeling a bit down
  c for Sunday lunch

4 Is there any kind of food you <u>can't</u> eat?

Restaurants

5 What's your favourite…?
  a kind of restaurant (French, Italian, etc.)
  b restaurant dish   c takeaway food

6 How important are these things to you in a restaurant?
  Number 1–4 (1 = the most important)
  the food ☐   the service ☐
  the atmosphere ☐   the price ☐

7 How do you prefer these things to be cooked?
  (grilled, boiled, etc.)
  chicken   fish   eggs   potatoes

8 If you eat steak, how do you like it cooked?
  (rare, medium, well done)

4 PRONUNCIATION /ʊ/ and /uː/, understanding phonetics

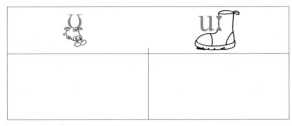

a Look at the sound pictures. How do you pronounce them?

b Put the words in the correct column.

butcher	cook	food	fruit	good
juice	mousse	soup	spoon	sugar

c ⬤ 1.2 Listen and check.

d ➲ **p.157 Sound Bank.** Look at the typical spellings for /ʊ/ and /uː/.

e Look at the information box. How do phonetic symbols in a dictionary help you pronounce words correctly?

> **⚠ Pronouncing difficult words**
>
> Some words are difficult to pronounce because
> 1 they have a 'silent' syllable or letter, e.g. *vegetables* /ˈvedʒtəblz/
> 2 some letters are pronounced in an unusual way e.g. *steak* /steɪk/
> 3 you aren't sure where the stress is, e.g. *dessert* /dɪzˈɜːt/

f ⬤ 1.3 Look at some more food words which are difficult to pronounce. Use the phonetics to practise saying them correctly. Then listen and check.

1	knife	/naɪf/
	biscuit	/ˈbɪskɪt/
	salmon	/ˈsæmən/
2	sausages	/ˈsɒsɪdʒɪz/
	lettuce	/ˈletɪs/
	sugar	/ˈʃʊgə/
3	yoghurt	/ˈjɒgət/
	menu	/ˈmenjuː/
	diet	/ˈdaɪət/

g ⬤ 1.4 Listen and repeat the sentences.

1 The first course on the menu is lettuce soup.
2 What vegetables would you like with your steak?
3 Do you want yoghurt or chocolate mousse for dessert?
4 I take two spoonfuls of sugar in my coffee.
5 Sausages and biscuits aren't very good for you.
6 Would you like a fruit juice?

5 LISTENING

a Have you ever tried English food? What did you think of it?

b **1.5** Kevin Poulter, an English chef, has just opened a restaurant in Santiago, the capital of Chile. Listen to an interview with him and number the photos 1–5 in the order he mentions them.

c Listen again and answer the questions.

1 Why did he decide to open a restaurant in Chile?

2 Why did he call it Frederick's?

3 Why were Chilean people surprised when he opened his restaurant?

4 What English dishes does he serve in his restaurant? Are they popular?

5 Where does he recommend tourists eat in England? Why?

6 How many women work in his kitchen? Why does he think there are so few women in restaurant kitchens?

7 What English food does he miss most?

d Do you think an English restaurant would be a success if it opened in your town? Why (not)? What food from your country would you miss most if you went to live abroad?

6 SPEAKING

a Work in groups of three A, B, and C. First read sentences 1–6 and decide (individually) whether you agree or disagree. Think about examples you can use to support your point of view.

1 Women worry more about their diet than men.
2 Young people today eat less healthily than ten years ago.
3 Men cook as a hobby, women cook because they have to.
4 Vegetarians are healthier than people who eat a lot of meat.
5 You can often eat better in cheap restaurants than in expensive ones.
6 Every country thinks that their cooking is the best.

b Now A say what you think about sentence 1. B and C listen and then agree or disagree with A. Then B say what you think about sentence 2, etc. Try to use the expressions in **Useful language**.

Useful language

For example…   I agree.   I don't agree.   I think it's true.   I don't think it's true.   (I think) it depends.

1
B

G past tenses: simple, continuous, perfect
V sport
P /ɔː/ and /ɜː/

If you really want to win, cheat

1 GRAMMAR past tenses: simple, continuous, perfect

a In which sports are there most cases of cheating? How do people cheat in these sports?

b Read the article and find out how the people cheated.

Famous (cheating) moments in sport

Divine intervention?

With a little help from my friends

Dishonischenko!

Adapted from the British press

1 FOOTBALL

Argentina were playing England in the quarter-finals of the 1986 World Cup in Mexico. In the 52nd minute the Argentinian captain, Diego Maradona, scored a goal. The English players protested but the referee gave the goal. However, TV cameras showed that Maradona had scored the goal with his hand! Maradona said the next day, 'It was partly the hand of Maradona, and partly the hand of God.'

Later in the game Maradona scored another goal and Argentina won 2-1. They went on to win the World Cup.

2 ATHLETICS

Fred Lorz, from New York, won the marathon at the St Louis Olympic Games in 1904. He finished the race in three hours 13 minutes.

After the race Fred was waiting to get his medal and the spectators were cheering him loudly. Alice Roosevelt, the daughter of the US President, was in the crowd, and some journalists took a photo of Fred with her. But then suddenly somebody started shouting 'cheat' and soon everybody was shouting the same thing. It was true. Fred had travelled 18 of the 42 kilometres in a friend's car! Fred didn't win the gold medal and he was banned from athletics.

3 FENCING

Boris Onischenko, an army officer from the Soviet Union, was competing against Jim Fox from Britain in the 1976 Montreal Olympics. Boris was winning and the electronic scoreboard was showing 'hit' after 'hit' for him. Jim Fox protested to the referee. Fox said that Boris was scoring points without hitting him. Olympic officials examined Boris's sword and they made a shocking discovery. Boris had changed the electronic part of his sword. He could turn on the 'hit' light on the scoreboard even when he hadn't hit Fox. Boris went home, in disgrace, the next day. The British newspapers called him 'Dishonischenko'.

c Look at the highlighted verbs in text 1. What three tenses are they? Underline an example of each tense in the other two texts.

d Which of the three tenses in **c** do we use for…?

1 completed actions in the past _____

2 an action in progress at a particular moment in the past _____

3 an action that happened *before* the past time we are talking about _____

e ⊙ **p.130 Grammar Bank 1B.** Read the rules and do the exercises.

f Cover the texts. In pairs, retell the three stories using the correct tenses.

Text 1	Text 2	Text 3
England (play) Argentina.	Fred Lorz (win) the marathon in 1904.	Boris Onischenko (compete) against Jim Fox.
Maradona (score) a goal.	He (wait) to get his medal.	Boris (win) but Jim Fox (protest).
The English players (protest) but the referee (give) the goal.	The spectators (cheer).	The Olympic officials (examine) Boris's sword.
The TV cameras (show) that Maradona (score) the goal with his hand.	Everybody (start) shouting 'cheat'.	They (discover) that he (change) the electronic part of his sword.
	Fred (travel) 18 km by car!	

2 SPEAKING

a You are going to tell an anecdote. Choose one of the topics below and plan what you are going to say. Ask your teacher for any words you need.

Tell your partner about…

a time you cheated (in an exam or in a sport / game)

What were you doing?
Where? When?
Why did you cheat?
What happened?

a really exciting sports event you saw

Where and when was it?
Who was playing?
What happened?
Why was it so exciting?

a time you had an accident or got a sports injury

What were you doing? How did the accident happen? What part of your body did you hurt? What happened next? How long did it take you to recover?

a time you saw or met a celebrity

Where were you? What was the celebrity doing? What was he / she wearing? Did you speak to him / her? What happened in the end?

b In pairs, tell each other your stories. Ask for more details.

3 LISTENING

a Can you think of two disadvantages of being a professional football referee?

b ⬤ 1.6 You're going to hear an interview with an ex-Champions League referee from Spain. Listen and choose a, b, or c.

Juan Antonio Marín
refereed 200 league and
50 international matches

1 What was the most exciting match he ever refereed?
   a His first professional match.
   b He can't choose just one.
   c Real Madrid against Barcelona.

2 Why does he mention Mauro Silva?
   a Because he was the best player he ever saw.
   b Because he was a great person.
   c Because he was a very good footballer and a good person.

3 The worst experience he ever had as a referee was…
   a when a player hit him during a match.
   b when a woman with a child tried to attack him.
   c when a 16-year-old boy attacked him.

4 Why does he think there is more cheating in football today?
   a Because football is big business.
   b Because the referees are worse.
   c Because footballers are better at cheating.

5 How does he say footballers cheat?
   a They fall over when nobody has touched them.
   b They accept money to lose matches.
   c They touch the ball with their hands.

6 What's the most difficult thing for him about being a referee?
   a Players who cheat.
   b Making decisions.
   c The rules are too complicated.

7 Does he think fair play still exists?
   a Yes.
   b No.
   c He doesn't say.

c Listen again for more information. Do you agree with him that there is more cheating in football than before?

4 VOCABULARY sport

a In pairs, do the quiz.

Sports Quiz

1 How long does a football match last?
2 How many referees are there in a basketball match?
3 How many players are there in a volleyball team?
4 How often are the World Athletics Championships held?
5 How long is a marathon?
6 How many holes are there on a golf course?
7 How long is one lap of an athletics track?

b ● p.145 Vocabulary Bank *Sport*.

c In pairs, think of a sports team in your town / country and answer the questions.

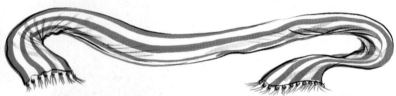

- ⚽ What's the name of the team?
- 🏐 What sport do they play?
- 🏀 Where do they play? (in a stadium, sports hall, etc.)
- ⚽ Who is...?
  a the coach
  b the captain
  c the best player in the team
- 🏐 How many spectators watch their matches?
- 🏀 What happened in their last match?

5 PRONUNCIATION /ɔː/ and /ɜː/

a Write the words in the correct column. Be careful with *or* (there are two possible pronunciations).

| ball serve caught world draw fought hurt |
| score sport shirt warm up worse court |

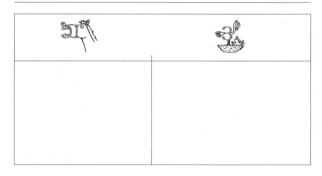

b **1.7** Listen and check.

c ● p.157 **Sound Bank.** Look at the typical spellings for these sounds.

d **1.8** Practise saying these sentences. Listen and check.

1 I got hurt when I caught the ball.
2 Her serve's worse than the other girl's.
3 It was a draw – the score was four all.
4 It's the worst sport in the world.
5 We warmed up on the court.
6 They wore red shirts and white shorts.

6 SPEAKING

In pairs, interview your partner about sport using the questionnaire. Ask for more information.

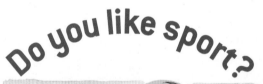

Do you like sport?

YES

What sport(s) do you play?
▼
Have you ever won a cup or a trophy?
▼
Have you ever been injured doing sport?
▼
Do you prefer doing sport or being a spectator?
▼
Do you prefer watching individual or team sports?
▼
Do you go to watch a local sports team?
▼
Are there good sports facilities in your town?
▼
Is there any sport you'd like to learn to play well?
▼
How many hours do you spend a week watching sport on TV?

NO

What sports do / did you have to do at school?
▼
Do / did you enjoy it?
▼
Do you do any sport in your free time?
▼
Do you think you're fit? Would you like to get fitter?
▼
Do your family and friends like sport?
▼
Is there any sport you don't mind watching on TV?
▼
What sport do you hate watching most on TV?
▼
Have you ever been to a big sporting occasion?
▼
Do you think physical education should be optional at school?

When you hear the final whistle

1 **F** *One of the hardest things for any sportsperson to do is to know when to retire.* Do you retire when you are at your physical 'peak' or do you wait until your body (or your coach) tells you that it's time to go? But even harder is finding the answer to the question 'What am I going to do with the rest of my life?'

2 _____. 'There's a high risk of depression and people often find adjusting to a new way of life difficult', says Ian Cockerill, a sports psychologist. 'For sportspeople, there's an extra trauma – the loss of status, the loss of recognition, and the loss of the glamour. That's the hardest part.' As Eddie Acaro, the US jockey says, 'When a jockey retires, he becomes just another little man.'

3 _____. Perhaps they just can't stand life without the 'high' of playing professional sport. Michael Jordan, the greatest basketball player of all time, retired three times. He retired once from the Chicago Bulls, made a successful comeback with the Bulls, then retired again. His second comeback with an inferior team ended in failure and he retired for ever at the age of 38. Jordan said, 'There will never be anything I do that will fulfil me as much as competing did.'

4 _____. Muhammad Ali needed the money, but his comeback fight, at the age of 39, against Trevor Berbick, was one of the saddest spectacles in modern sport. After losing to Berbick, Ali retired permanently. Three years later he developed Parkinson's disease.

5 _____. As Jimmy Greaves, an ex-England international footballer said, 'I think that a lot of players would prefer to be shot once their career is over.' Many of them spend their retirement in a continual battle against depression, alcohol, or drugs.

6 _____. Franz Beckenbauer is a classic example of a footballer who won everything with his club, Bayern Munich. After retiring he became a successful coach with Bayern and finally president of the club. John McEnroe, the infamous 'bad boy' of tennis, is now a highly respected and highly paid TV commentator. But sadly, for most sportspeople these cases are the exceptions.

Adapted from the British press

Muhammad Ali, former US boxer

Franz Beckenbauer, former German footballer

John McEnroe, former US tennis player

Michael Jordan, former US basketball player

a Look at the photos. In pairs, answer the questions.

Have you ever seen any of these people playing sport?
At what age do you think people reach their 'peak' in these sports?
Do you know what these people do now?

b Read the article once. Do most sportspeople find it easy or difficult to retire?

c Complete the article with sentences A–F below.

A For some people the pain of saying goodbye never leaves them.
B Others can't resist the chance of one last 'pay day'.
C Some sportspeople go on playing too long.
D But for the lucky few, retirement can mean a successful new career.
E Retirement for people in general is traumatic.
F ~~One of the hardest things for any sportsperson to do is to know when to retire.~~

d Can you remember these words? If not, check with the text. Underline the stressed syllable.

1 adjective: *depressed*   noun: *depression*
2 adjective: *glamorous*   noun: _____
3 verb: *lose*   noun: _____
4 verb: *recognize*   noun: _____
5 verb: *fail*   noun: _____
6 verb: *retire*   noun: _____

e Think of a sportsperson from your country who has retired. What is he / she doing now? Do you think he / she retired at the right time?

G future forms: *going to*, present continuous, *will / shall*
V family, personality
P prefixes and suffixes

1 C We are family

1 VOCABULARY & SPEAKING family

a Look at the two pictures. Which one do you think shows the typical family of the future?

Read the first paragraph of the article and find out.

Families have a great-great future

Twenty years ago, the typical extended family was 'wide'. It usually consisted of two or three generations, with many children in each 'nuclear family'. People had lots of aunts and uncles but often didn't know their grandparents. However, according to a new study by the British research group Mintel, the family is changing shape. The family groups of the future will be 'long and thin', with three or four small generations.

Here are some of their predictions:

1 Most children will know their great-grandparents (and even great-great-grandparents) because people are living longer.

2 Very few children will have brothers or sisters, and it will be common to be an only child. As a result, future generations will not have many cousins either.

3 Many children will grow up isolated from other children and young adults. This will make them more selfish and introverted.

4 More couples will divorce and re-marry, some more than once. They may have children with their new partners, so many children will have a stepmother or stepfather and half-brothers or sisters.

5 There will be many 'boomerang children'. These are children who leave home to get married, but then divorce and return to live with their parents.

6 There will be more single-parent families.

7 Because houses are now so expensive, different generations may decide to live together, so parents, grandparents, and adult children may co-own their houses, and many couples will have to live with their in-laws.

b Now read the whole article. Match the highlighted words with the definitions.

1 _____ your grandparents' parents
2 _____ a child who doesn't have any brothers or sisters
3 _____ families where the mother or father is bringing up the children on his / her own
4 _____ your uncle's or aunt's children
5 _____ the family of your husband / wife
6 _____ all your relatives including aunts, grandparents, etc.
7 _____ your grandparents' grandparents
8 _____ boys who have (for example) the same father as you but a different mother
9 _____ the new wife of your father
10 _____ people who are having a relationship

c Read the seven predictions again. In pairs or small groups, answer the questions for each prediction.

1 Is this already happening in your country?
2 Do you think it will happen in the future?
3 Do you think it will be a good thing or a bad thing?

Useful language

I think so.   I don't think so.   Maybe.   Perhaps.

Probably.   I'm sure it will.

2 GRAMMAR future forms

a 🔊 1.9 Listen to three dialogues between different family members. Who is talking to who (e.g. brother to sister)? What are they talking about?

b Listen again and match two sentences with each dialogue (1–3). Write 1, 2, or 3 in each box.

A Shall I make you a cup of tea? ☐   C Are you going to go to university? ☐   E I'll be really careful. ☐
B You'll crash it again. ☐   D I'm staying at Mum's tonight. ☐   F It's going to be cold tonight. ☐

c With a partner, decide which sentence(s) A–F refer(s) to…

a plan or intention   ☐
an arrangement   ☐
a prediction   ☐☐
a promise   ☐
an offer   ☐

d ⊙ **p.130 Grammar Bank 1C.** Read the rules and do the exercises.

e Move around the class, ask other students questions, and complete the table.

Find someone who…	name	more details
is seeing a relative this weekend.		
isn't having dinner with their family tonight.		
is getting married soon.		
is going out with their brother or sister on Saturday night.		
is going to have a new nephew or niece soon.		
is going to leave home in the near future.		
is going to have a big family reunion soon.		
isn't going to go on holiday with their family this year.		

3 READING

a In a family with two children, do you think it's better to be the older or the younger brother or sister? Why?

b You're going to read an article about two sisters, Wendy (the younger sister) and Carnie (the older sister). Before you read, predict the answers to the questions below. Write W (Wendy) or C (Carnie).

Who do you think…?

1 had a more eccentric hairstyle

2 admired her sister

3 didn't want to be with her sister

4 followed her sister everywhere

5 tried to compete with her sister

6 wasn't a good student

7 told her parents when her sister did something wrong

8 used to hurt her sister physically

9 was jealous of her sister

10 always defended the other sister

c Now read the article and check your answers.

d Look at the highlighted words and phrases. In pairs, choose the right meaning, a or b.

1 a boring
  b fashionable

2 a children
  b adults

3 a age difference
  b the time they weren't together

4 a become friends again
  b stop speaking

5 a kiss
  b hurt with your fingers

6 a say bad things about
  b say good things about

7 a we got on very well
  b we got on very badly

8 a ask for help
  b say that somebody is responsible for something bad

e Do you think their relationship is typical of brothers and sisters?

We are family…

Two sisters tell the truth about themselves – and each other…

Wendy Wilson and her older sister Carnie are the daughters of the Beach Boys founder, Brian Wilson. They formed the band Wilson Philips (with the daughter of Michelle Philips of The Mamas and Papas) and their first album was a worldwide hit. Today they are both married and live in Los Angeles. Here they talk about their relationship.

Wendy

Carnie

Wendy, the younger sister says:

I always thought Carnie was really ¹cool. Especially when she was a teenager and had bright red spiky hair. But, like most older sisters, she wasn't at all interested in her younger sister. I desperately wanted to be with her and her friends, and sometimes I used to follow them, but she hated that.

When we were ²kids we both had a lot of material things like toys and clothes, but even then we knew that Mom and Dad weren't happy. We used to talk about it all the time, and after a while they separated and we stayed with my Mom. We didn't see Dad for quite a few years, which really hurt us. But it's also the thing that brought me and Carnie closer together. When I was 16 or 17 the one and a half year ³age gap between us didn't matter any more, and we started to get on with each other and to write songs together.

Being in a band – or working at anything – with a member of your family can be difficult, but it also has advantages. If we have a big argument about a song, after a while we remember that we are sisters and we ⁴make it up. Nothing is going to stop us from being sisters.

Carnie, the older sister says:

I sometimes think that poor Wendy has spent all her life competing with me. She was a very quiet, shy child, while I was incredibly talkative and demanding – I was awful! I wasn't interested in studying, all I wanted to do was go to parties, and Wendy used to tell my parents. So I was horrible to her – I used to ⁵pinch her and bite her.

I was very jealous of Wendy also because she was more attractive than me. But she always defended me when other people ⁶criticized me, and sometimes it seemed as if she was the older sister and I was the younger one. Although we were complete opposites, ⁷we were also very close and had a lot of fun together. We still do.

I think I suffered a lot because of my father leaving us when we were small, but Wendy helped me to understand that Dad loved us too, but in a different way. She also taught me that you can't ⁸blame other people for your problems, you have to look at yourself.

HOW WORDS WORK...

Look at two sentences from the *We are family* text.

'We started to get on with each other.'

'You have to look at yourself.'

- Use *each other* when A does an action to B and B does the same action to A
  We love each other = I love you and you love me.
- Use a reflexive pronoun (*myself, yourself, himself, herself, itself, ourselves, yourselves, themselves*) when the subject of the verb is the same as the object.
  I cut myself. She looked at herself in the mirror.
- You can also use a reflexive pronoun for emphasis.
  Nobody helped me. I did it all myself.

Complete the sentences with *each other* or a reflexive pronoun.

1 After the argument they didn't speak to _____ for a week.
2 This light is automatic. It turns _____ on and off.
3 We built the house _____. It took three years.
4 We only see _____ once a month.
5 They argue a lot. They don't understand _____.
6 I blame _____ for the accident. It was my fault.

4 VOCABULARY personality

a Can you remember? What do you call a person who…?

1 talks a lot _____
2 doesn't talk very much _____
3 feels uncomfortable and nervous when he / she meets new people _____
4 thinks someone loves another person more than him / her _____

b 🔵 p.146 Vocabulary Bank *Personality*.

c Write down the first **three** adjectives of personality that you can remember from the Vocabulary Bank. Don't show them to your partner. Your teacher will tell you what they say about you.

5 PRONUNCIATION prefixes and suffixes

a Underline the stressed syllable.

1 jealous   ambitious   generous
2 sociable   reliable
3 responsible   sensible
4 competitive   talkative   aggressive   sensitive
5 unfriendly   insecure   impatient

b 🔊 **1.10** Listen and check. Are *-ous* / *-able* / *-ible* / *-ive* stressed? Are *un-* / *in-* / *im-* stressed?

c Practise saying the adjectives.

6 LISTENING & SPEAKING

a What's your position in the family? Are you the oldest child, a middle child, the youngest child, or an only child?

b 🔊 **1.11** Listen to a psychologist talking about the influence your position in the family has on your personality. Complete the chart by writing four more adjectives of personality in each column.

Oldest children	Middle children	Youngest children	Only children
self-confident	*independent*	*charming*	*spoilt*

c Compare with a partner. Then listen to the four sections again and check your answers. Can you remember any more details?

d Look at the completed chart above. In pairs, say
– if you think it is true for you – if not, why not.
– if you think it is true for your brothers and sisters or your friends.

7 🔊 **1.12** SONG ♫ *We are family*

THE STORY SO FAR

1.13 Listen to the story of Mark and Allie. Mark the sentences T (true) or F (false).

1 Mark met Allie in London two years ago.
2 He's American and she's British.
3 They work for MTV.
4 He invited her to San Francisco for a holiday.
5 They both got jobs in the new Paris office.
6 Mark is going to be Allie's boss.
7 They are both in Paris now.

Mark	_____. I'm Mark Ryder.
Nicole	Ah, you're the new marketing director.
Mark	That's right.
Nicole	I'm Nicole Delacroix. I'm Allie's personal assistant. _____ to Paris!
Mark	Thank you.
Nicole	I'll just tell Allie you're here. Allie? Mark Ryder's here. OK. You're from San Francisco, _____ you?
Mark	Yes, I am.
Allie	Hello, Mark.
Mark	Allie. It's _____ to see you again. How are you?
Allie	Very well. Did you have a good _____?
Mark	Yes, fine, no problems.
Allie	Let me _____ you to the team. You've _____ Nicole, my personal assistant?
Mark	Yes, we've said hello.
Allie	_____ is Jacques Lemaître, our PR director.
Jacques	How _____ you do?
Mark	Mark Ryder. How do you do?
Allie	And this is Ben Watts, our designer.
Ben	Hi, Mark.
Mark	Great to _____ you, Ben.
Ben	We've _____ a lot about you.
Mark	Really? All good, I hope.
Allie	OK. Shall we go to my office?

MEETING PEOPLE

a **1.14** Cover the dialogue and listen. What do the people in the Paris office do?

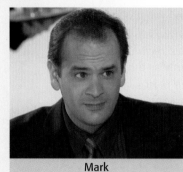
Mark

Allie

Jacques

Ben

Nicole

b Read the dialogue. In pairs, what do you think the missing words are? **Don't write them in yet.**

c Listen again and complete the dialogue.

d Look at the highlighted phrases. Which is the most formal way to greet someone?

e **1.15** Listen and repeat the highlighted phrases. Copy the rhythm.

f Move round the class in pairs, introducing your partner to other students. Use the highlighted phrases.

SOCIAL ENGLISH It's a secret

a **1.16** Listen. What do Mark and Allie want to keep secret?

b Listen again. Answer with M (Mark), A (Allie), or B (both).
1 Who thinks it's strange that they're together now?
2 Who missed the other person a lot?
3 Who thinks Nicole is very friendly?
4 Who thinks it's going to be hard to keep their secret?
5 Who wants to find a flat?
6 Who's thinking about work?

c **1.17** Complete the USEFUL PHRASES. Listen and check.

d **1.17** Listen again and repeat the phrases. How do you say them in your language?

USEFUL PHRASES
What a l_____ view!
Why d_____ we sit down?
I h_____ to find an apartment.
Don't worry. It won't t_____ you long.
I was w_____ (what kind of a boss…).
W_____, you'll find out tomorrow.

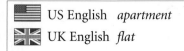
US English *apartment*
UK English *flat*

Study Link MultiROM

a Read the two emails once and answer the questions.

   1 Why has Stephanie written to Claudia?
   2 Does Claudia recommend her friend?

b The computer has found <u>five spelling mistakes</u> in Claudia's email. Can you correct them?

c Read Claudia's email again. Then cover it and answer the questions from memory.

   1 Which ⊞ adjectives describe Christelle's personality?
   2 What does she like doing in her free time?
   3 What negative things does Claudia say about Christelle?

d Look at the highlighted expressions we use to modify adjectives. Put them in the right place in the chart.

Anna is	very / _____	untidy.
	_____	
	_____	

Useful language: describing a person

He's quite / very, etc. + adjective
   (e.g. *friendly, extrovert*, etc.)
She's a bit + negative adjective (e.g. *untidy, shy*, etc.)
He likes / loves / doesn't mind + verb + *-ing*
He's good at + verb + *-ing*

Imagine you received Stephanie's email asking about a friend of yours.

WRITE an email to answer it.

PLAN what you're going to write using the paragraph summaries below. Use the **Useful language** box and **Vocabulary Bank p.146** *Personality* to help you.

Paragraph 1	age, family, work / study
Paragraph 2	personality (good side)
Paragraph 3	hobbies and interests
Paragraph 4	any negative things?

CHECK the email for mistakes (grammar , punctuation , and spelling).

From: Stephanie
   To: Claudia
Subject: Hi from Scotland

Dear Claudia,

I hope you're well.

I've just had an email from your friend Christelle. She wants to rent a room in my house this summer. Could you tell me a bit about her (age, personality, etc. and what she likes doing) so that I can see if she would fit in with the family? Please be honest!

Send my regards to your family and I hope to hear from you soon.

Best wishes

Stephanie

From: Claudia
   To: Stephanie
Subject: Hi from Switzerland

Hi Stephanie,

Thanks for your email.

Of course I can tell you about Christelle. She's 21, and she's studing law with me.

I think she's quite extrovert and very sociable – she has lots of freinds. She's also very good with children. She has a young step-brother and several young cousins, and I know she likes playing with them. She's incredibly hard-working and responsable – she passed all her exams last year, which is more than I did!

She likes going out, seeing films, and listening to music, but not rock or heavy metal – so don't worry about noise! And she's happy to do things on her own – she's very independent, so you won't really have to look after her. Her parents are divorced and she lives with her mother and stepfather, but she also sees her father regularly.

The only negative things I can think of are that she's a bit untidy – her room is usualy in a mess – and that her English is, well, not brilliant. But I'm sure she'll learn fast! I think she's really nice and that you and the family will get on well with her.

I hope that's useful. Let me know if you need any more information about her.

Love
Claudia

PS I attach a photo of the two of us.

GRAMMAR

Put the verbs in the correct tense.

A Wow. _Is_ that your new car? (be)

B Yes.

A When [1]_____ it? (you / get)

B I [2]_____ (buy) it last month.
[3]_____ it? (you / like)

A Yes, it's great. What happened to your front light?

B I [4]_____ (hit) another car when I [5]_____ (drive) to work. I thought the traffic lights [6]_____ (change), but they hadn't. Would you like to go for a drive?

A I can't just now because I [7]_____ (meet) a friend in ten minutes. How about tomorrow evening? It's Wednesday and I usually [8]_____ (finish) work early.

B OK. I [9]_____ (pick you up) at 7. 00. You [10]_____ (love) it, I know.

A I'm sure I will. See you tomorrow then.

[10]

VOCABULARY

a Word groups. <u>Underline</u> the word that is different. Say why.

1	fresh	seafood	frozen	home-made
2	fried	chicken	duck	sausages
3	knife	roast	fork	spoon
4	referee	coach	captain	pitch
5	pool	track	beat	court
6	aggressive	jealous	bossy	affectionate
7	charming	sensible	sociable	moody
8	cousin	family	mother-in-law	grandfather

b Write words for the definitions.

1 It's an adjective for food that is hot, e.g. curry or chilli.
   s_____

2 It's what you have before the main course.
   s_____.

3 It means when two teams finish a match with the same score.
   d_____

4 It means to hurt yourself in an accident or doing a sport.
   get i_____

5 Your mother's second husband is your **s**_____.

6 It's an adjective for a person who always thinks about him / herself.
   s_____

7 It's an adjective. It's the opposite of generous.
   m_____

c Fill each gap with one word.

1 I always ask _____ steak when we eat _____.
2 What do you usually have _____ lunch?
3 It's a good idea to warm _____ before you start running.
4 Who do you get _____ with best in your family?

[20]

PRONUNCIATION

a <u>Underline</u> the word with a different sound.

1	u:	pool	tuna	fruit	course
2	ʊ	cook	food	look	football
3	ɔː	court	ball	roast	prawns
4	ʌ	couple	draw	cousin	duck
5	ɒ	sausage	bossy	frozen	golf

b <u>Underline</u> the stressed syllable.

menu   referee   impatient   sociable   irresponsible   [10]

What can you do?

REVISE & CHECK

CAN YOU UNDERSTAND THIS TEXT?

Jam today, tomorrow, yesterday...

Craig Flatman is every nutritionist's nightmare – a fifteen-year-old who never eats anything except bread and jam but, unbelievably, is perfectly healthy! Although his diet contains hardly any protein and is 60% sugar, he is 1.84m tall, weighs 69kg, and his parents say he has never been seriously ill apart from typical childhood illnesses.

Craig, or 'Jam boy', as his friends have nicknamed him, rejects any form of meat, fish, fresh fruit, or vegetables. The only time he doesn't eat bread and jam is for breakfast, when he has chocolate cereal, and for tea, when he occasionally has a slice of chocolate cake. He also drinks two pints of semi-skimmed milk a day.

Craig's strange diet started when he was four years old. As a baby he had refused to eat solid food, and rejected everything until his father gave him a sugar sandwich when he was nine months old. He also ate chocolate spread sandwiches, and this, with milk, was his diet until he was four when he asked to try jam, and started an eleven-year obsession.

Craig sometimes craves some variety, but every time he tries something else he feels ill. Doctors believe that his condition may have been caused by choking on solid food when he was a baby. 'They tell me I'll grow out of it', says Craig, 'but I don't know if I'll ever change'. Although Craig's parents eat a normal diet, their family meals are made more difficult by the fact that Craig's sister Amy, 13, is a vegetarian. And every time they go out for a meal together, they have to phone in advance – to check they can bring jam sandwiches for Craig!

Adapted from the British press

a Read the article and mark the sentences T (true), F (false) or DS (doesn't say).

1 Craig doesn't eat any protein.
2 He eats ten jam sandwiches a day.
3 The only other things he eats are chocolate cereal and cake.
4 When he was a baby he didn't like solid food.
5 His obsession with jam sandwiches started when he was eleven.
6 Craig doesn't want to try any other kinds of food.
7 Doctors have done a lot of tests on Craig.
8 They think Craig's diet will change when he gets older.
9 Craig's family eat out about once a month.
10 Craig also has jam sandwiches when his family eat out.

b Guess what the highlighted words and phrases mean. Check with your teacher or a dictionary.

CAN YOU UNDERSTAND THESE PEOPLE?

a 1.18 Listen and circle the correct answer, a, b, or c.

1 What drinks do they get?
 a A coffee, a tea, and two orange juices.
 b A tea and three orange juices.
 c A coffee and three orange juices.
2 Why doesn't the woman want anything to eat?
 a Because she's not hungry.
 b Because she doesn't feel well.
 c Because she's on a diet.
3 What does Robertson do now?
 a He owns a pub.
 b He works in Leeds.
 c He works with young players.
4 Who's coming to lunch?
 a The man's mother-in law and his sister.
 b The man's mother and his sister-in law.
 c The man's mother-in-law and her sister.
5 What are they going to give their granddaughter for her birthday?
 a Money.
 b Clothes.
 c They can't decide.

b 1.19 You will hear a man phoning to book a tennis court. Complete the information on the secretary's form.

Hamworth Sports Centre
Tennis court bookings:

Name: *Mark* 1 _____
Membership number: 2 _____
Day: 3 _____
Time: 4 _____
Court number: 5 _____

CAN YOU SAY THIS IN ENGLISH?

Can you...? Yes (✓)
☐ talk about your diet
☐ describe a sporting event you have been to (where, when, what happened)
☐ describe a member of your family and his / her personality
☐ say how you think families will change in the future

2 A

G present perfect and past simple
V money
P saying numbers

Ka-ching!

1 VOCABULARY & LISTENING money

a **2.1** Listen to a song about money and complete it with these words. What is 'Ka-ching'?

a<u>ffo</u>rd	blow	broke	<u>cr</u>edit card	earn
<u>gree</u>dy	loan	mall	<u>mort</u>gage	spend

b Now look at words 1–10 in the song and match them with their meanings.

A _____ (verb) to give or pay money for something

B _____ (noun) money that a person or a bank lends you

C _____ (verb) to have enough money to buy something

D _____ (noun) a shopping centre (US)

E _____ (adj) having no money (informal)

F _____ (noun) a small plastic card you use to buy things

G _____ (verb) to get money by working

H _____ (adj) wanting more money, etc. than you really need

I _____ (verb) to spend a lot of money on something (informal)

J _____ (noun) the money a bank lends you to buy a house

c Listen again and read the lyrics. What do you think the song is saying?

1 Money always makes people happy.
2 The world has become obsessed with money.
3 The singer would like to have more money.

d ➲ **p.147 Vocabulary Bank** *Money*.

Ka-ching

We live in a ¹_____ little world
that teaches every little boy and girl
to ²_____ as much as they can possibly,
then turn around and spend it foolishly.
We've created us a ³_____ mess,
we ⁴_____ the money that we don't possess.
Our religion is to go and ⁵_____ it all,
so it's shopping every Sunday at the ⁶_____.

Chorus
All we ever want is more,
a lot more than we had before.
So take me to the nearest store.
Can you hear it ring?
It makes you want to sing.
It's such a beautiful thing – Ka-ching!
Lots of diamond rings,
the happiness it brings,
you'll live like a king,
with lots of money and things.

When you're ⁷_____ go and get a ⁸_____.
Take out another ⁹_____ on your home,
consolidate so you can ¹⁰_____
to go and spend some more when you get bored.

Chorus

Ka-ching!

2 GRAMMAR present perfect and past simple

a Shelley and Ben are having an argument about money. Read what Shelley says and complete the dialogue with Ben's answers from the box below. Then try to guess his last answer.

> We've had it for at least three years. Maybe longer.
> It's old.
> No. What is it?
> Why not?
> ~~Yes. I've just bought it.~~
> I can't.

Shelley Is that a new camera?
Ben ¹ *Yes. I've just bought it.*
Shelley What's wrong with our old camera?
Ben ²_____
Shelley Old? How long have we had it? A year?
Ben ³_____
Shelley Three years? I'm sure we bought it last year. Look. We can't afford a new camera.
Ben ⁴_____
Shelley Have you seen this?
Ben ⁵_____
Shelley The gas bill. It arrived this morning. And we haven't paid the phone bill yet. Take it back to the shop and get your money back.
Ben ⁶_____
Shelley Why not?
Ben Because…

b **2.2** Listen and check.

c In pairs, read the dialogue again and underline five examples of the present perfect and two examples of the past simple. Then answer the questions.

Which form of the verb do we use for…?
1 a completed action in the past
2 things which started in the past and are true now
3 recent actions when we don't say exactly when
4 recent actions when we say exactly when

d ➲ **p.132 Grammar Bank 2A.** Read the rules and do the exercises.

3 SPEAKING

In pairs, interview each other with the questionnaire. Ask for more information.

> Have you ever wasted money on something you've never used?

> Yes, I bought an exercise bike.

> Why did you buy it?

The MONEY Questionnaire

"You'll never use it."

Have you ever…?

(waste) money on something you've never used

(sell) anything on the Internet

(lose) a credit card or your wallet

(save) for something for a long time

(win) any money (e.g. in a lottery)

(be) robbed

(lend) money to someone who didn't pay you back

Have you…recently?

(buy) anything on the Internet

(be) to a mall or shopping centre

(buy) anyone a present

(use) a credit card

(take) money out of a cash machine

(borrow) money from someone in your family

4 READING

a Which of these sentences best describes your attitude to money?

  1 All I want is enough money to enjoy life.
  2 Money is very important to me. I'd like to earn as much as possible.
  3 I would be happy to live with less money and fewer possessions.

b You're going to read an article about a woman who lives without money. Why do you think she does it? How do you think she survives? Read the article to find out.

c Read the article and answer the questions.

  1 What was Heidemarie's job?
  2 What possessions does she have now?
  3 How did the experiment start?
  4 Where has she lived since the experiment started?
  5 Does she still work?
  6 What does she do when she needs something?
  7 What is she trying to show with her experiment?
  8 What did she do with the money she earned from her book?

d Match the highlighted phrasal verbs with their definitions. Write the verbs in the infinitive.

  1 _throw away_   put into the rubbish bin
                   e.g. *Please … those sweet papers.*
  2 _____   stop (doing something)
                   e.g. *He wants to … smoking.*
  3 _____   arrive, appear
                   e.g. *I invited 20 people to my party but only 10 will …*
  4 _____   give something to somebody without wanting anything in return
                   e.g. *She decided to … her old clothes to the local hospital.*
  5 _____   start a new company or organization
                   e.g. *My brother is going to … a software company.*
  6 _____   be responsible for somebody or something
                   e.g. *Nurses … people in hospital.*

e In pairs, answer the questions.

  1 Do you agree with Heidemarie that…?
    • all jobs are equally important
    • most people don't like their jobs
    • people judge you according to how much you earn
  2 What do you think of Heidemarie? Would you like to have her as a friend?

My life without money

Heidemarie Schwermer, a 63-year-old German woman, has lived without money for the last ten years, and has written a book about her experiences called *My life without money.*

At the age of 54 Heidemarie gave up her job as a psychotherapist, gave away all her money and her flat and threw away her credit cards. Today, apart from a few clothes (three sweaters, two skirts, two pairs of shoes, and a coat) and a few personal belongings, she doesn't own anything.

It all began as a one-year experiment. In her home city of Dortmund she set up a 'swapping circle' where people swap services without using money, for example, a haircut for a mathematics class. To prove that this could work she decided to give up using money for a year. But when the year ended she continued and has not used money since then.

At first she house-sat for friends who were on holiday. She stayed in their house in return for watering the plants and looking after their animals. At the moment she is staying in a student residence where she can sleep, have a shower, or use a computer in return for cooking for the young people who live there. She also 'works' as a psychotherapist. 'Before I treated very wealthy people but now I help anyone who turns up. Sometimes they give me something in return, but not always.'

Heidemarie says, 'I can live thanks to my contacts. A lot of people who know me understand what I'm doing and want to help me. When I need a bus ticket, for example, or a new tube of toothpaste I think, "Who can I ask? What can I give them in return?" If I want to go to the cinema, I might offer to look after somebody's children for the afternoon.

It is one of the mistakes of our society that most people do something they don't like just to earn money and spend it on things they don't need. Many people judge you according to how much you earn. In my opinion, all jobs are equally important. You may not earn a lot of money but you may be worth a lot as a person. That's my message.'

So what did she do with all the money she earned from the sales of *My life without money*?

'I gave it all away…'

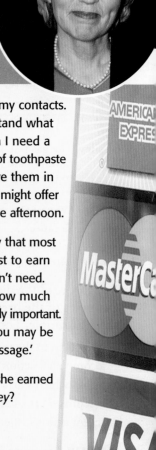

5 VOCABULARY & PRONUNCIATION
saying numbers

a (2.3) Write the numbers. Then listen and repeat. Practise saying them.

Numbers

_____	fifteen
_____	fifty
_____	a hundred
_____	seven hundred and fifty
_____	one thousand five hundred
_____	seven thousand five hundred
_____	seventy-five thousand
_____	seven hundred and fifty thousand
_____	a million
_____	seven and a half million

b (2.4) Complete the numbers. Then listen and check.

Money, percentages, decimals and fractions

£2.50	two _____ fifty
$8.99	eight _____ _____
€3.20	three _____ _____
50%	fifty _____ cent
0.5	nought _____ five
3.9	_____ _____ _____
½	a _____
⅓	a _____
¼	a _____
¾	three _____
6½	six _____ a half

c In pairs, practise saying these numbers.

⅔   0.7   1¾   7.8

30%   £90

100%

430

€600   2,800   9,250

$200,000   3,000,000

6 LISTENING & SPEAKING

SIXTV NEWS OXFORDSHIRE

a (2.5) Listen to a news bulletin. How many different news items are there?

b Listen again and answer the questions with a number.

1 How many people were injured in the crash?

2 How fast was the lorry going?

3 How many workers have walked out of the Peugeot factory?

4 What pay rise do they want?

5 How many more unemployed are there this year?

6 How many are there in total?

7 By how much have house prices increased in the last five years?

8 How much does a three-bedroomed house cost in south-east England?

c Answer the questions with a number, percentage, etc. If you don't know the exact number, use *about* or *approximately*.

1 What's the population of…? your country   your town / city

2 What proportion of people in your country…?
speak good English   have more than two children
have a dog   smoke

3 How much do these things cost?
a cup of coffee   a laptop computer   a small flat in the centre of town
a newspaper   a DVD   a small car

2 B

G present perfect continuous
V strong adjectives: *exhausted, amazed,* etc.
P sentence stress, strong adjectives

Changing your life

1 LISTENING

a Answer the questions in pairs.

1 If you could spend a year working or studying in another country, which country would you choose? Why?
2 What would you like to do there?
3 What problems do you think you might have?

b Read about Karen and describe what you can see in the photos.

c 〔2.6〕 Listen to Karen and answer the questions.

1 Why did she choose Beirut?
2 Why did she want to take a year off?
3 Who is Omayma?
4 Why does Karen say Arabic is a difficult language?
5 How long has Karen been teaching belly dancing?
6 How do her students feel about an English woman teaching them belly dancing?
7 What does she like most about living in Lebanon?

d Compare your answers with a partner. Then listen again to check.

2 GRAMMAR   present perfect continuous with *for* / *since*

a 〔2.7〕 Listen and complete these questions and answers from the interview with Karen.

1 How long have you been _____ here?
2 I've been _____ and _____ since I was little.
3 What have you been _____ here since you arrived?
4 I've been _____ classes with her since October.
5 I've been _____ belly dancing for about six years.

b Look at sentences 1–5 and answer the questions.

1 Are the verbs action or non-action verbs?
2 Do they refer to single actions or continuous / repeated actions?
3 Do they refer to a completed action or one which is still happening?

c ◯ **p.132 Grammar Bank 2B.** Read the rules for present perfect continuous for unfinished actions. Do exercise **a** only.

'My name's Karen and I'm a primary school teacher. A few months ago, I decided to change my life. I took a year off and went to live in Beirut with my husband, Mike, who's an English teacher.'

3 PRONUNCIATION sentence stress

⚠️ An important part of clear communication in English is stressing the words in a sentence which carry the information, and **not** stressing the other ones.

a 🔊 **2.8** **Dictation**. Listen to five sentences. Try to write down the stressed words. Look at the words and try to remember the whole sentence. Then listen again and write the complete sentences.

b 🔊 **2.9** Listen and copy the rhythm.

1 I've been <u>living</u> <u>here</u> for <u>two</u> <u>years</u>.
2 <u>How</u> <u>long</u> have you been <u>learning</u> <u>English</u>?
3 She's been <u>working</u> in <u>Italy</u> since <u>October</u>.
4 <u>How</u> <u>long</u> have you been <u>waiting</u>?
5 It's been <u>raining</u> <u>all</u> <u>night</u>.
6 We've been <u>looking</u> for a <u>flat</u> for <u>ages</u>.

4 SPEAKING

a Look at the circles, and write something in as many as you can.

A sport you **play** regularly (or a kind of exercise you **do** regularly)

Something you are **learning** (to do)

A friend you **know** very well

A magazine / newspaper you **read** regularly

A bar or restaurant you often **go** to

A thing you **have** which is very important for you

A club, organization, gym, etc. you **are** a member of

The make of car you **drive**

The place where you **live**

b Compare circles with a partner. Ask your partner at least three questions about the things they've written. One question must be *How long have you…?*

⚠️ Remember after *How long…?* with **action** verbs, e.g. *play*, use present perfect continuous, with **non-action** verbs, e.g. *know*, use present perfect simple.

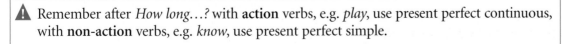

How long have you been playing volleyball?

Since I was about 15.

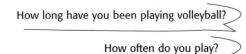

How often do you play?

5 READING

a Can you think of one way that a holiday could change your life for the better?

b You're going to read an article about two people whose lives were changed by a holiday. Work in pairs. A read about Victoria, B about Sally.

c In pairs, take turns to tell each other about the two women. Answer these questions.

What is she doing now?
What was she doing before?
What made her change her life?
How does she feel now?

d Read the text that you didn't read before. Did your partner leave out any important information?

e In pairs, try to guess the meaning of the highlighted words. Then match them with their definitions below.

First text
1 of little importance _____
2 crazy _____
3 a person who looks after animals (e.g. in a zoo) _____
4 animals like large monkeys _____
5 not looked after well _____

Second text
6 the London underground _____
7 very tasty _____
8 asked for (in writing) _____
9 burning brightly _____
10 very small _____

f Whose life do you think has changed the most? Which of the two holidays would you choose?

It was just a holiday, but it changed my life

Holidays can be good for your health. You lie on a beach and relax, and tensions disappear. But sometimes a holiday can change your life completely, which is what happened two years ago to Victoria Smith and Sally Gook.

Victoria Smith, six years ago, was working as a manager at Next, a British chain store. Then she went on holiday to Borneo…

'It was a working holiday,' said Victoria, 'where you could study orang-utans in the wild – I have always been interested in apes, so I thought it would be fun.' The holiday was wonderful, and when Victoria came home she found it very difficult to return to her old life. 'Suddenly the problems in the store just seemed so trivial.' Although everybody told her she was mad, she decided to go back to university and study biology. Four years later she became a chimpanzee keeper.

For the last two years Victoria has been working at Monkey World, a centre in south-west England which looks after apes which have been ill-treated. Many have been rescued from laboratories and circuses all over the world. She works long hours, and the pay isn't very good, but she loves it. 'Apes are like a big family, each with their own personality.'

'I'm really happy now. Since I started working here I feel that I've been doing something important, not just wasting my life.'

'I feel I've been doing something important.'

'Suddenly I knew there was a different life waiting for me.'

Sally Gook wakes up every morning to a deep blue sky and blazing sun. For the last two years she has been living on the tiny Greek island of Lipsi, which is only 16 square kilometres in size and has a population of just 650.

But until a few years ago she lived in London. 'I was working for American Express and I had a good social life and earned a lot of money. But I had to get up very early every morning, often in horrible weather, and get a train and the tube to work.'

Then one day she and a friend decided they needed a relaxing holiday, and they came to Lipsi. 'I loved it – the people, the mountains, the sun, and the delicious food. Suddenly I knew there was a different life waiting for me here.' A few months later she applied for a job at the travel company which had organized her holiday.

Since then she has been living on Lipsi and working as a tourist guide. Her boyfriend, who is Greek, is a farmer. Sally said, 'I've only been back to London once, and I can't imagine ever living there again.'

Adapted from the British press

6 VOCABULARY & PRONUNCIATION strong adjectives

a Write synonyms for the strong adjectives.

Strong adjectives	Normal adjectives
1 The island's **tiny** – only 16 square kilometres.	= very _small_
2 The food in Lipsi was **delicious**.	= very _tasty_
3 Her father's **furious**. She crashed his car.	= very _____
4 I'm **terrified** of flying. I never travel by plane.	= very _____
5 I've been working all day. I'm **exhausted**.	= very _____
6 It's going to be **boiling** tomorrow – about 40°!	= very _____
7 Can I have a sandwich? I'm **starving**.	= very _____
8 The flat's **enormous**. It's got five bedrooms.	= very _____
9 I'm not going to swim. The water's **freezing**.	= very _____
10 Your car's **filthy**. Why don't you wash it?	= very _____
11 That's a **great** idea! Let's do it.	= very _____
12 This book's **awful**. I can't finish it.	= very _____

b Cover **a**. Complete the responses with a strong adjective.

1 Are you hungry?   Yes, I'm _starving_.
2 Was your mother angry?   Yes, she was _____.
3 Is her flat small?   Yes, it's _____.
4 Are you tired?   Yes, I'm _____.
5 Is the floor dirty?   Yes, it's _____.
6 Are you afraid of spiders? Yes, I'm _____ of them.

c (2.10) Listen and check. Are the strong adjectives stressed? Listen again and repeat.

d ⊙ **Communication** *Are you hungry? Yes, I'm starving!* A p.116 B p.119.

7 GRAMMAR present perfect continuous (for recent continuous actions)

a Look at the pictures. How do the people look? What do you think has been happening?

b (2.11) Listen and check. What have they been doing? Complete the sentences.

1 Sharon and Kenny _____.
2 The man _____.
3 The man and woman _____ and _____.

c ⊙ **p.132 Grammar Bank 2B.** Read the rules for present perfect continuous for recent continuous actions. Do exercise **b**.

d Look at the adjectives and imagine that you are *exhausted*, *filthy*, etc. Think of an explanation for each one. Then in pairs, invent a short dialogue using each adjective.

exhausted	filthy	furious
very stressed	very red	

Hi. You look exhausted. What have you been doing?

I've been working in the garden.

G comparatives and superlatives
V transport and travel
P stress in compound nouns

Race to the sun

1 READING

a In pairs, ask and answer the questions.

1 When was the last time you travelled…?
by train   by car   by plane
Where did you go?
How long did your journey take?
Did you have a good journey?

2 In general, which of the three forms
of transport do you prefer? Why?

b Read the introduction to the article, *Race to the sun*. Answer the questions
with *by car*, *by train*, or *by plane*.

Which journey do you think was…?

the quickest _____   the most comfortable _____

the cheapest _____   the most convenient _____

c You're going to read about the first **two** journeys, but the paragraphs
are not in the right order. Find the first paragraph for the plane journey,
and then the other three. Do the same for the train journey. Then compare
with a partner.

The plane   **The train**

1 ___ 2 ___ 3 C 4 G   1 ___ 2 ___ 3 B 4 ___

d Now read about the two journeys again carefully in the right order.
Answer the questions with T (the train) or P (the plane).

On which journey…?

1 did the traveller have to get up earlier ☐
2 could the traveller have something to eat or drink ☐
3 was the traveller more stressed ☐
4 could the traveller see beautiful scenery ☐
5 did the traveller have a meal when he arrived ☐
6 did the traveller arrive earlier than expected ☐

Which journey was…?

7 quicker ☐
8 cheaper ☐
9 more comfortable ☐
10 more convenient ☐

HOW WORDS WORK…

The bus took 45 minutes.

It took me just 30 minutes from home.

How long does it take you to get to school?

Use *take* (+ person) + time (+ *to get to*)… to talk about the duration
of a journey.

Ask and answer the questions in pairs.

How long does it take you to get to work / school?
How long does it take to get from your house to the centre?
a by car   **b** by bus / underground   **c** on foot

[Map showing Stansted, London, Calais, English Channel, Nîmes, Avignon]

Every year thousands of British tourists
travel to the South of France for their
summer holiday. But what is the best way
to get there, by car, train, or plane?

A British newspaper sent three of its
journalists to find out. They had to travel
from their homes in London to Avignon.

All three travellers set off one Saturday
morning in July.

Charles went by train (the Eurostar).

Rosemary flew with a 'cut price' airline.

Martin travelled by car.

A When I got to security I saw that there was an enormous queue. I began to worry that I might miss my flight, because the boarding limit is 40 minutes before take-off. I had to run to gate 48 and I arrived completely out of breath.

B I arrived on time! I picked up my suitcase and followed the Exit signs. It was great not to have to wait ages for my luggage or to worry about getting a bus or taxi to the city centre.

C We boarded. Because there are no seat numbers on these flights, everybody tries to get on as quickly as they can. I sat next to a friendly Frenchman. We took off and soon I was looking down on London. There was no meal, not even coffee, but we landed 10 minutes ahead of schedule.

D At 4.15 a.m. a taxi picked me up and took me 32 miles to Stansted airport. Although it was early morning, there was a lot of traffic and I arrived later than I had planned. I took my luggage to check in and asked for a window seat but the woman said there were no seat numbers.

E At 7.10 a.m. I arrived at Waterloo station by taxi. It took me just 30 minutes from home. I bought the papers and walked to the platform. I got on and found my seat. As soon as we started moving, I went to find the buffet car and had a cup of coffee.

F Just outside the station I looked up and saw the medieval walls of Avignon's historic city centre. It was 2.20* in the afternoon and I was just in time for a late lunch! My ticket cost £65.80, and I gave the journey 8/10 for comfort and 9/10 for convenience.

G I only had to wait twenty minutes for my luggage. Then I walked outside into bright sunshine and waited for the bus to Avignon, about 40 kilometres away. I didn't have to wait long and the bus took 45 minutes. It was only 11.00* and I had the whole day in front of me. My ticket cost £63, and I gave the journey 5/10 for comfort and 5/10 for convenience.

H I looked out of the window. Although we were moving at 340 kilometres an hour, the journey was smooth and relatively quiet. The part where we travelled under the English Channel took just 22 minutes. Soon I was looking at the fields and farmhouses of France. The sun was shining. I closed my eyes and went to sleep.

* France is one hour ahead of the UK.

Adapted from the British press

2 LISTENING

a 🔊 2.12 Listen to Martin talking about his journey from London to Avignon by car. Number the pictures 1–7.

b Listen again. Mark the sentences T (true) or F (false).

1 There's a lot of traffic in London on Saturday mornings.
2 Petrol is more expensive in Britain than in France.
3 There are two ways to cross the English Channel by car.
4 You can't drive through the Channel Tunnel.
5 The journey through the tunnel takes an hour.
6 Drivers must sit in their car when they go through the tunnel.
7 The speed limit on French motorways is 120 km/h.
8 French motorways aren't free.
9 It's 970 kilometres from Calais to Avignon.

c 🔊 2.13 Listen to Martin talking about his journey and fill in the **By car** column in the chart. Now compare the information with your answers in 1a.

London to Avignon	By plane	By train	By car
How long did it take? (from home)	5 hours 45 mins	6 hours 40 mins	
How much did it cost?	£63	£65.80	
Comfort /10	5	8	
Convenience /10	5	9	

d Think of a town / city in your country. How many different ways are there of getting there? Which do you think is the best? Why?

3 GRAMMAR comparatives and superlatives

a Read the sentences. Are the highlighted phrases right or wrong? Put a tick (✔) or a cross (✘), and correct the wrong sentences.

1 What's the quicker way to get to the South of France?

2 Driving is more boring than going by train.

3 Petrol isn't as cheap in Britain than in France.

4 Does the plane cost the same as the train?

5 Going by train is less expensive as flying.

6 It was the more comfortable hotel I've ever stayed in.

7 The worst month to travel through France is August.

8 Do the British drive more carefully than the French?

b ⭕ **p.132 Grammar Bank 2C.** Read the rules and do the exercises.

c With a partner compare the experiences below using the **bold** adjectives.

1 **safe, exciting, healthy**
travelling by motorbike
travelling by car
travelling by bike

2 **enjoyable, dangerous, relaxing**
travelling by yourself
travelling with friends
travelling with your family

3 **difficult, expensive**
learning to drive
learning to ride a bike
learning to ride a horse

4 VOCABULARY transport and travel

a Put the words into the correct column.

buffet car	check in	gate	motorway
platform	rush hour	speed limit	
station	take off		

train	car	plane
___	___	___
___	___	___
___	___	___

b ⭕ **p.148 Vocabulary Bank** *Transport and travel*.

5 PRONUNCIATION & SPEAKING stress in compound nouns

a 🔊 2.14 Listen and repeat the compound nouns. Which word is usually stressed more?

traffic lights	pedestrian area
boarding pass	road works
car park	rush hour
car crash	seat belt
cycle lane	speed camera
parking fine	speed limit
traffic jam	ticket office

b Ask and answer the questions in pairs.

In your town / city...

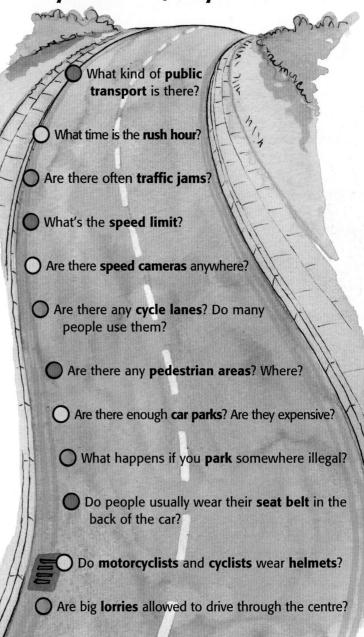

What kind of **public transport** is there?

What time is the **rush hour**?

Are there often **traffic jams**?

What's the **speed limit**?

Are there **speed cameras** anywhere?

Are there any **cycle lanes**? Do many people use them?

Are there any **pedestrian areas**? Where?

Are there enough **car parks**? Are they expensive?

What happens if you **park** somewhere illegal?

Do people usually wear their **seat belt** in the back of the car?

Do **motorcyclists** and **cyclists** wear **helmets**?

Are big **lorries** allowed to drive through the centre?

6 LISTENING & SPEAKING

a Read the beginning of a newspaper article and then talk to a partner:

1 Do you (or your family) ever do any of these things while driving a car?

2 Which three do you think are the most dangerous? Number them 1–3 (1 = the most dangerous).

Which of these things is the most dangerous when you're driving a car?

- making a call on your mobile
- listening to your favourite music
- listening to music you don't know
- opening a packet of crisps or a can of drink
- picking up a specific CD from the passenger seat
- talking to other passengers

A car magazine tested car drivers in a driving simulator. The drivers had to 'drive' in the simulator and at the same time do the things in the list above. The results of the tests were surprising (and worrying).

b **2.15** Now listen to a road safety expert talking about the tests. Number the activities 1–6. Were your top three right?

c Listen again and answer the questions.

1 What should you do when you are driving?

2 Why is opening a packet of crisps or a can so dangerous?

3 What do people often do when they pick up a CD?

4 What gets worse when drivers are talking on the phone?

5 How do people drive when they are listening to their favourite music?

6 What happens if the music is fast and heavy?

7 What's the main problem when drivers talk to other passengers?

8 Why is listening to music you don't know the least dangerous?

d Look at the statements below and decide whether you agree or disagree. Tick (✔) the ones you agree with and put a cross (✘) next to the ones you disagree with. Think about your reasons.

Drivers should not use any kind of phone when they are driving.

The minimum age for riding a motorbike should be 25.

People who drink and drive should lose their licence for life.

The speed limit on motorways should be 100 kilometres an hour.

Cyclists are just as dangerous as car drivers.

Speed cameras do not stop accidents.

People over 70 are more dangerous drivers than young people.

e In groups, give your opinions on each sentence. Do you agree?

REQUESTS AND PERMISSION

a (2.16) Cover the dialogue and listen. Answer the questions.

1 What does Jacques ask Mark to do?
2 What does Mark ask Ben to do?
3 What does Nicole ask Allie?

b Read the dialogue. In pairs, what do you think the missing words are? **Don't write them in yet.**

c Listen again and complete the dialogue.

Jacques	Mark? Would you mind _____ me those concert dates?
Mark	Of _____ not. Ben, are you busy?
Ben	Me? Never.
Mark	_____ you help me? I can't open this document.
Ben	_____.
Mark	Thanks.

....

Allie	Hi, Nicole.
Nicole	Could you sign these, please?
Allie	Sure.
Nicole	Is it _____ if I take tomorrow afternoon off?
Allie	I'm _____, but tomorrow's really difficult.
Nicole	What about Friday afternoon?
Allie	Friday? That's fine. Do you _____ you could _____ me the request by email?
Nicole	Er, yes, of _____.
Allie	Hello? Hi, Mark. Could you hold a moment, Mark? Thank you, Nicole. _____ you come and see me when you have a moment?

d (2.17) Listen and repeat the highlighted phrases. Copy the rhythm.

e Look at the highlighted phrases in the dialogue. Complete the chart.

Request	Response
Would you mind...?	
Permission	

f ⊙ **Communication** *Requests p.119.*

SOCIAL ENGLISH Office gossip

a (2.18) Listen. Who do Mark and Nicole talk about?

b Listen again and mark the sentences T (true) or F (false).

1 Mark hasn't found a flat yet.
2 Mark likes Ben and Jacques.
3 Jacques's wife is a lawyer.
4 Nicole likes the way Allie dresses.
5 She thinks Allie is friendly.
6 Allie orders a soft drink.

c (2.19) Complete the USEFUL PHRASES. Listen and check.

d Listen again and repeat the phrases. How do you say them in your language?

USEFUL PHRASES

Have you started l_____ for an apartment?
I haven't had time y_____.
J_____ a minute.
H_____ do you like (the office)?

Have you h_____ of (Isabelle)?
L_____ me get you (a drink).
Thanks. I'll h_____ a (Diet Coke).

Study Link MultiROM

Nightmare journeys

We asked you to tell us about your nightmare journeys. Jutta from Germany wrote to us about hers...

A nightmare journey I remember was three years ago [1]____ I was going to the airport with my friend. We were going to Mallorca on holiday and we had to be at Dresden airport two hours before the flight.

We leaved home with plenty of time, [2]____ when we got to the motorway there was a huge traffic jam! The traffic wasn't moving at all. We didn't knew what to do. It was too late to go another way, [3]____ we just sat in the car getting more and more stressed. [4]____ ten minutes the traffic started moving slowly. We decided to leave the motorway and try to found another way to the airport, [5]____ I wasn't sure of the way and we got completely lost. We was sure we were going to miss the flight. We finally arrived at the airport just thirty minutes before the plane was going to leave. The woman at the check-in desk said we couldn't to check in our luggage [6]____ it was too late [7]____ we had to run with all our cases to the departure gate.

[8]____ my friend felt over and hurt her leg, we managed to get to the gate in time and [9]____ we caught our flight.

a Read the story once. What happened in the end? Then correct the six grammar mistakes with the verbs (wrong tense or wrong form).

b Read the story again and complete with a connecting word or phrase.

after	although	because	but (x2)	in the end	so (x2)	when

c Look at the list of possible travel problems in the **Useful language** box below. Mark them C if they refer to a car journey and P if they refer to a plane journey.

Useful language: travel problems

the flight was delayed
you broke down
you got lost
you missed your flight

there was a traffic jam
you got a puncture
you forgot your passport
your flight was overbooked

WRITE about a nightmare journey you've had (or invent one).

PLAN what you're going to write using the paragraph summaries below: Use the **Useful language** box and **Vocabulary Bank** *Transport and travel* **p.148** to help you.

Paragraph 1 When was the journey?
Where were you going? Who with? Why?

Paragraph 2 What went wrong? What happened?

Paragraph 3 What happened in the end?

CHECK the story for mistakes (grammar , punctuation , and spelling).

GRAMMAR

a Complete the sentences with one word.

1 **A** Shall we watch the film?

   B No. I've [1]_____ seen it three times.

2 **A** How [2]_____ have you lived here?

   B [3]_____ 2004.

3 **A** [4]_____ you read this novel?

   B No. Is it good?

   A I haven't finished it [5]_____.

b Complete the second sentence so that it means the same as the first.

1 I started work here three years ago.

   I've _____ _____ here for three years.

2 I made some coffee a moment ago.

   I've _____ _____ some coffee.

3 The train is cheaper than the plane.

   The plane is _____ _____ than the train.

4 Women drive more carefully than men.

   Men don't drive as _____ _____ women.

5 None of the other sofas are as comfortable as this one.

   This sofa is _____ _____ comfortable one.

`10`

VOCABULARY

a Word groups. Underline the word that is different. Say why.

1 coin   cheque   bank   note
2 save   waste   mortgage   owe
3 exhausted   terrified   hungry   furious
4 delicious   wonderful   great   awful
5 flight   journey   trip   travel
6 coach   van   helmet   lorry
7 cycle lane   railway station speed limit   traffic jam

b Write words for the definitions.

1 It's an adjective. It means very dirty. **f**_____

2 It's a noun. It's money that you pay to the government. **t**_____

3 It's a noun. It's the time of day when buses and trains are full. **r**_____ **h**_____

4 It's a verb. To give someone money which they must later pay back. **l**_____

5 It's a noun. It's the place in a railway station where you get on / off a train. **p**_____

6 It's a verb. It means to receive money from a relative after their death. **i**_____

7 It's a noun. It's the piece of paper you need to get on a plane. **b**_____ **p**_____ / **c**_____

8 It's an adjective. It means very small. **t**_____

c Complete the sentences with one word.

1 What time did the plane take _____?

2 She took some money _____ of the cash machine.

3 Who paid _____ the meal last night?

4 When can you pay me _____ the money you owe me?

5 Can I pay _____ credit card?

`20`

PRONUNCIATION

a Underline the word with a different sound.

1	afford	board	coach	enormous
2	tiny	pick up	traffic	ticket
3	crash	station	rush	charge
4	coin	cheque	cycle	carriage
5	seat	earn	speed	greedy

b Underline the stressed syllable.

invest   security   luggage   pedestrian   terrified

`10`

CAN YOU UNDERSTAND THIS TEXT?

Why I didn't want to be a millionaire

When Lydia Nash appeared on the TV programme *Who wants to be a millionaire?* and was fortunate enough to win £16,000, she decided to give all the money away. This wouldn't have been surprising if she had been rich or famous, but Lydia is a 19-year-old student.

Lydia gave all the money to a charity which helps orphan children in Thailand and where she had also worked as a volunteer for the previous three years. 'I first visited the orphanage when I was seventeen, and I felt very depressed by what I saw. When I got back to England I felt angry – looking around all I could see were people who were obsessed with money. That convinced me to return to Thailand the following year.'

After she won the money some of her friends at university thought that maybe she had made the wrong decision. 'Some people said I should have saved it for a deposit to buy a house or to pay back my student loan.' Lydia said. 'That really annoyed me. Students seem to live in an unreal world, where they constantly complain about being poor. But there's an enormous difference between our situation and people who have absolutely no money.'

With the help of the money Lydia gave them, the charity has just finished building 'Rainbow House', a new facility that will house 50 young children, where they will live until they are adopted .

If Lydia had won a million pounds and not only £16,000, would she still have given away all the money? She said, 'Before going on the show I thought a lot about what it would be like to have a lot of money and I realized that I wouldn't like it at all. And then, of course, as I had been to the orphanage and had seen all the work that needed to be done, I knew how useful that money could be. It was far more important for the charity than it could ever be for me. I definitely think I got more enjoyment out of giving the money away than if I had kept it for myself.'

Adapted from the British press

a Read the text once. Then read it again and choose a, b, or c.

1 People were surprised that Lydia gave away the money she won because _____.
  a she is young and not very wealthy
  b she already had a lot of money of her own
  c she had won a lot of money

2 Before winning the money, Lydia had been to the orphanage in Thailand _____.
  a once   b twice   c several times

3 Lydia thinks that students today _____.
  a are broke all the time
  b have a lot of money
  c are not as poor as they think

4 The charity has used the money to _____.
  a build a new house
  b adopt more children
  c build a school

5 Lydia _____.
  a wouldn't mind being rich
  b wouldn't like to be rich
  c would like to be a bit richer

b Look at the highlighted words and phrases. Can you guess what they mean?

CAN YOU UNDERSTAND THESE PEOPLE?

a **2.20** Listen and circle the correct answer, a, b, or c.

1 Where did the woman probably lose her credit card?
  a In the petrol station.
  b In the flower shop.
  c In the restaurant.

2 How long has he been working as a teacher?
  a 1½ years   b 2½ years   c 3½ years

3 How can people travel today?
  a By road.   b By rail.   c By air.

4 Which airline are they going to fly with?
  a British Airways   b Anglo Air   c Euroflight

5 Who is working at the moment?
  a Her brother.
  b Her brother's wife.
  c Her brother and his wife.

b **2.21** Listen to a conversation between a bank manager and a client. Complete the sentences with a number.

1 Ms Stephens wants to borrow £_____.

2 The period of loan will be _____ years.

3 The monthly repayments will be £_____.

4 The interest rate is _____ %.

5 The first repayment will be on _____.

CAN YOU SAY THIS IN ENGLISH?

Can you…? Yes (✓)

☐ talk about different things you can do with money
☐ say how long you've been living in this town and learning English
☐ compare travelling by car, train, and plane in your country

3
A

G *must, have to, should* (obligation)
V mobile phones
P sentence stress

Modern manners

1 VOCABULARY & SPEAKING   mobile phones

a Match the word with the country. How do you say 'mobile phone' in your language? Which name do you like best?

1 France	a cell phone
2 Germany	b telefonino
3 Italy	c celular
4 the USA	d movil
5 the UK	e portable
6 Spain	f mobile
7 Argentina	g Handy

b **3.1** Listen and match the sentences with the sounds.

A ☐ He's **dialling** a number.
B ☐ She's **texting** a friend.
C ☐ He's just **hung up**.
D ☐ She's choosing a new **ring tone**.
E ☐ He's **calling back**.
F ☐ She **left a message** on his **voice mail**.
G ☐ The line's **engaged / busy**.

c Use the questionnaire to interview another student (who has a mobile phone). Ask for more information.

Mobile phone questionnaire

What make is your mobile?
How long have you had your mobile?
Are you thinking of getting another one soon?
What ring tone do you have?
Do you ever use it 'hands free'?
What do you use it for (apart from talking)?
Where and when do you normally switch off your mobile?
How often do you text?
Do you use…?
a voice mail   b speed dialling

Have you ever…?

…lost your mobile

…sent a text to the wrong person

…forgotten to turn your phone off (with embarrassing consequences)

2 GRAMMAR *must, have to, should* (obligation)

a In pairs, look at the picture and answer the questions.

1 What's the man doing? Does it annoy you when people do this?
2 Does this happen a lot in your country?
3 What other things do people do with mobiles that annoy you?

b 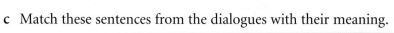 Listen to five people talking about things that annoy them about mobiles. Match the speakers with what they say.

Who…?

A says talking on your mobile can be dangerous ☐
B complains about people who are very impatient to use their mobiles ☐
C complains about people using mobiles on social occasions ☐
D hates having to listen to other people's conversations ☐
E complains about people who interrupt a conversation to answer the phone ☐

c Match these sentences from the dialogues with their meaning.

1 **You shouldn't** answer the phone if you're talking to a shop assistant. ☐
2 **You have to** switch off your mobile when you fly. ☐
3 **You mustn't** use your phone until you get off the plane. ☐
4 **You don't have to** shout – the other person can hear you. ☐
5 **You should** talk really quietly if you are in a public place. ☐

A You don't need to do this. It isn't necessary.
B Don't do this. It isn't allowed / permitted.
C Do this because it's a rule or the law.
D I think it's a bad thing to do this.
E I think it's a good thing to do this.

d ⟳ **p.134 Grammar Bank 3A.** Read the rules and do the exercises.

3 PRONUNCIATION & SPEAKING sentence stress

a 3.3 Listen and repeat the sentences. Copy the rhythm.

1 You mustn't use your phone on a plane.
2 I don't have to go to work tomorrow.
3 We have to do an exam in June.
4 You should switch off your mobile in class.
5 You shouldn't talk loudly on a mobile phone.
6 I must go to the bank this morning.

b Read the definition of manners. Then look at phrases 1–8. Are these laws (or against the law) or just good / bad manners? Mark M (manners) or L (law).

> **manners** [pl noun] a way of behaving that is considered to be polite in a society or culture

Manners or the law?

1 Play noisy games on a mobile phone in public
2 Send text messages when your car is stopped at traffic lights
3 Switch off your mobile phone on a plane
4 Switch off your mobile phone in class
5 Talk loudly on a mobile on public transport
6 Use a hand-held mobile while driving a car
7 Make very personal calls in public
8 Use your mobile at a petrol station

c Compare with a partner. Then make sentences with…

You should / shouldn't …(for manners)
You have to / mustn't …(for the law)

4 READING

a Look at the postcard. What does it say about the English?

b Read *Culture shock* and tick (✔) the sentence which says what the article is about.

☐ The English have very good manners.

☐ The English and Russian idea of good manners is different.

☐ The English are polite but insincere.

☐ The Russians are very rude and unfriendly.

Culture shock

Adapted from the British press

Good manners are always good manners. That's what Miranda Ingram, who is English, thought, until she married Alexander, who is Russian.

When I first met Alexander and he said to me, in Russian, '*Nalei mnye chai* – pour me some tea', I got angry and answered, 'Pour it yourself'. Translated into English, without a '*Could you…?*' and a '*please*', it sounded really rude to me. But in Russian it was fine – you don't have to add any polite words.

However, when I took Alexander home to meet my parents in the UK, I had to give him an intensive course in *pleases* and *thank yous* (which he thought were completely unnecessary), and to teach him to say *sorry* even if someone else stepped on his toe, and to smile, smile, smile.

Another thing that Alexander just couldn't understand was why people said things like, 'Would you mind passing me the salt, please?' He said, 'It's only the salt, for goodness sake! What do you say in English if you want a *real* favour?'

He also watched in amazement when, at a dinner party in England, we swallowed some really disgusting food and I said, 'Mmm…delicious'. In Russia, people are much more direct. The first time Alexander's mother came to our house for dinner in Moscow, she told me that my soup needed more flavouring. Afterwards when we argued about it my husband said, 'Do you prefer your dinner guests to lie?'

Alexander complained that in England he felt 'like the village idiot' because in Russia if you smile all the time people think that you are mad. In fact, this is exactly what my husband's friends thought of me the first time I went to Russia because I smiled at everyone, and translated every '*please*' and '*thank you*' from English into Russian!

At home we now have an agreement. If we're speaking Russian, he can say 'Pour me some tea', and just make a noise like a grunt when I give it to him. But when we're speaking English, he has to add a 'please', a 'thank you', and a smile.

c Read the article again and mark the sentences T (true) or F (false). Correct the wrong sentences.

1 Miranda got angry because her husband asked her to make the tea.
2 Miranda had to teach him to say sorry when something wasn't his fault.
3 Her husband thinks English people are too polite.
4 Alexander wasn't surprised when people said they liked the food at the dinner party.
5 The food was delicious.
6 Miranda didn't mind when her mother-in-law criticized her cooking.
7 Alexander thought his mother was right.
8 In Russia it isn't normal to smile all the time when you speak to someone.
9 His Russian friends thought Miranda was very friendly because she smiled a lot.
10 Alexander never says thank you for his tea when he and Miranda are speaking in Russian.

d Now cover the text. Can you complete the phrases with the missing verbs?

1 _____ on someone's foot or toe (by accident)
2 _____ some wine into a glass or tea into a cup
3 _____ a noise, like a grunt
4 _____ food (so that it goes from your mouth to your stomach)
5 _____ a word from English into Russian

e Are people in your country more like Miranda or Alexander?

5 LISTENING

a **3.4** Listen to four people who have lived in England answering the question 'Are English people *too* polite?' Do they answer yes or no? If yes, what do they think the English should do?

1 László, an English teacher from Hungary   **Yes / No** _____
2 Paula, a businesswoman from Argentina   **Yes / No** _____
3 Melik, an economist from Turkey   **Yes / No** _____
4 Renata, a student from Germany   **Yes / No** _____

b Listen again and answer the questions.

1 Why were László and his friends in London?
2 Did he and his friends think they were going to pass or fail? Why?
3 What happened in the end?
4 What do Latin people think when English people are polite?
5 How does Paula describe Latin people?
6 What does Melik think about the English people he has met in his job?
7 What kind of English people does he say <u>aren't</u> polite?
8 What happened to Renata when she was in London?
9 What did she say to the last person? Why?

6 SPEAKING

Look at the five situations. In groups, discuss…

Do people do these things in your country?
Do you think it's good or bad manners to do these things, or doesn't it matter?

> In my country, we don't kiss people when we meet them for the first time.

Good manners?
Bad manners?
Does it matter?

Greeting people

- kiss people on both cheeks when you meet them for the first time
- call older people by their first names
- use more formal language when speaking to an older person

In a restaurant

- let your children run around and be noisy
- be very affectionate to your partner
- talk on your mobile

Driving

- always stop at a pedestrian crossing
- hoot at someone who's driving slowly
- drive with the window down and your music playing

Men and women – a man's role

- pay for a woman on the first date
- wait for a woman to go through the door first
- make sure a woman gets home safely at night

Visiting people

- take a present if you're invited to dinner at someone's house
- arrive more than 10 minutes late for a lunch or dinner
- smoke in a house where the owners don't smoke

3 B

G *must, may, might, can't* (deduction)
V describing people
P *-eigh, -aigh, -igh*

Judging by appearances

1 READING

a Answer the questions in pairs.

1 How many documents do you have which have your photo on them?
2 Where was your passport or ID card photo taken?
   a in a photo booth   **b** at home
   c at a photo studio
3 Do you think the photo looks like you?
4 Do you like the photo? Why (not)?

b Look at the three people and their passport photos. Do they look like their passport photos?

c Read the first paragraph of the article and answer the questions.

1 Why is our passport photo important?
2 Which nationality are the least happy with their photo?
3 Which are the happiest?
4 Which nationality are the vainest?

d Now read the rest of the article. Who is happy with their photo? Who isn't? Why?

e Look at the highlighted words in the text and choose the correct meaning.

1 a a study
  b a book
2 a feeling uncomfortable
  b feeling happy
3 a journalists
  b famous people
4 a feeling pleased with yourself
  b feeling unhappy with yourself
5 a very beautiful
  b very ugly
6 a without hair
  b with a lot of hair
7 a a kind of document
  b false hair

Do I really look like this?

Our passport (or identity card) photo is the photo we show to the largest number of different people during our lives. But how happy are we with our photo? Do we make an effort to get a good one? According to ¹ research done by the US printer company Lexmark, the answer varies according to nationalities. It seems that the Italians are the most ² embarrassed about their passport photo (21% said they didn't like showing it to other people). On the other hand, 98% of Norwegians said they were happy with their photos. And the French spend most time trying to get the perfect photo (sometimes spending an hour in the photo booth!). We asked three British media ³ celebrities how they felt about their passport photos…

Michael Winner
film director

'I used to be very ⁴ proud of my passport photo,' said Michael Winner. 'For more than forty years I looked like an elegant film director.' But recently Michael renewed his passport and took a new photo in a photo booth. 'Now I look like a drug dealer', he says.

Ruth England
TV holiday show presenter

Ruth England spends her life travelling and showing her passport photo to passport officials around the world. She confessed, 'Once I had a passport photo where I looked really ⁵ hideous and so I deliberately 'lost' my passport and got a new one. For my latest passport, I took several photos and I chose the best one. I quite like it. I've had much worse ones.'

Toby Young
author and journalist

Toby Young said, 'I'm often stopped when I go through passport control because I don't look like my passport photo at all. In my photo I had a lot more hair but now I'm ⁶ bald. No one believes it is me. So, now I have two possibilities: take a ⁷ wig with me every time I travel or get a new passport photo!'

Adapted from the British press

HOW WORDS WORK...

Look at two sentences from the text:

> Once I had a passport photo where I looked really hideous.
> I looked like an elegant film director.

You can use the verbs *look* and *look like* to talk about a person's appearance.

- Use *look* + adjective (or an age).
- Use *look like* + a noun or pronoun.

Complete the sentences with *look* or *look like* in the correct form.

1 This photo doesn't _____ you at all. When was it taken?
2 You _____ very young in this photo. How old were you?
3 Your brother _____ a rugby player. He's enormous.
4 You _____ tired. Why don't you go to bed?

2 VOCABULARY describing people

a ⊙ p.149 **Vocabulary Bank** *Describing people*.

b **3.5** Look at the four men and listen. Which one is the bank robber?

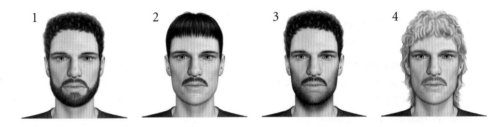

1   2   3   4

3 PRONUNCIATION -eigh, -aigh, -igh

a Look at the pink letters in the words below. Are they pronounced /eɪ/ or /aɪ/? Put the words in the correct column.

| bright | height | high | in his eighties | light brown |
| might | neighbour | overweight | sight | straight | weigh |

🚂 /eɪ/	🚲 /aɪ/

b **3.6** Listen and check.

c How is *-igh* always pronounced? How is *-eigh* usually pronounced? Which word is an exception here?

d **3.7** Practise saying the sentences. Listen and check.

1 She has light brown hair. It's short and straight.
2 He's medium height and slightly overweight.
3 He's in his eighties, but his eyesight's very good.
4 She likes wearing tight straight-leg jeans.

4 GRAMMAR *must, may, might, can't* (deduction)

a Look at the photo of the three women. Who do you think is who? Match texts A–C with the photos.

Judging by appearances

Millionaire's daughter?

Managing director?

Policewoman?

Who do you think is who?

b Read the texts again. In pairs, answer the questions.
1 Which two women feel they are judged because of their appearance? How?
2 Which woman thinks she is judged because of her name? How?

c Look at the highlighted phrases in the texts and answer the questions.
1 Which phrase means *it's impossible*? _____
2 Which phrase means *it's certain*? _____
3 Which phrase means *it's possible*? _____

d ➲ **p.134 Grammar Bank 3B.** Read the rules and do the exercises.

e ➲ **Communication** *Who do you think they are? p.116* Match more people with their jobs.

Laura Day, policewoman, Soho, London

When people first meet me they think I might be a teacher or a hairdresser. When I'm not wearing my uniform, they never believe me that I'm a policewoman. When I tell people what I do, the typical reaction is, 'You can't be a policewoman, you're too small!' I'm only 5 feet 4 inches* tall. People always think that policewomen are big and masculine. Often people only believe me when I show them my police identity card.

* = 1.6 metres

B

Sam Roddick, daughter of Anita Roddick (the millionaire founder of _Body Shop_)

When I introduce myself to people and say my name they often say, 'Oh you must be the _Body Shop_ woman's daughter.' Later they can't remember my name. I'm very proud of my mother but I would never say, 'My mum's Anita Roddick'. I don't know if I am very different from the typical 'rich kid' because I don't know any. My friends never mention my background or money and neither do I.

C

Thea Callan, managing director of _Nails Inc._ (the biggest UK chain of nail bars*)

People often ask me who my boss is. They think, 'She can't be the managing director – she's a woman'. They're expecting to see an older man in a suit. Or when people speak to me on the phone and hear that I am a woman then they think that I must be a 50-year-old woman who wears trouser suits and is very unfeminine. They're very surprised when they see me – I'm not like that at all. In the office I just wear jeans and trainers.

* = salons where you can have manicures and pedicures

5 LISTENING

a In pairs, look at the man in the photo and answer the questions. Use _must, may, might, can't be_. Say why.

1 Where do you think he's from?
England   Sweden   Spain

2 How old do you think he is?
In his 20s   In his 30s   In his 40s

3 What do you think his job is?
priest   musician   accountant

b **3.8** Listen to the first part of a radio interview with him and check your answers. Were you right?

c Listen again and make notes under the headings below. Compare with a partner.

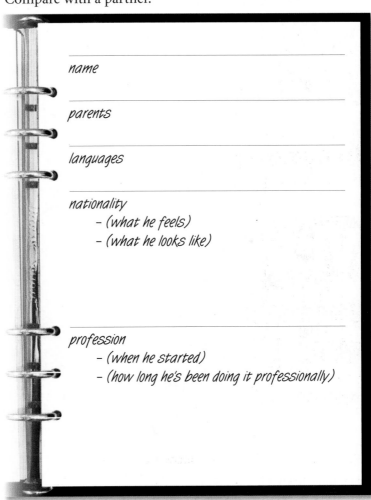

name

parents

languages

nationality
– (what he feels)
– (what he looks like)

profession
– (when he started)
– (how long he's been doing it professionally)

d **3.9** Now listen to the second part of the interview and answer the questions.

1 In which of the two countries is it easier for him to make a living?
2 In what other countries is there a lot of interest in his job?
3 What is the stereotype of someone doing his job?
4 In which of the two countries does he think people judge him by his appearance?

e How important is appearance in your country? Do people in _your_ country judge by appearances?

3 C

G *can, could, be able to* (ability and possibility)
V *-ed / -ing* adjectives
P sentence stress

If at first you don't succeed, ...

1 GRAMMAR *can, could, be able to*

a Look at the title of the lesson, which is the first half of a well-known saying. Look at the different second halves below. Which do you think is the real saying? Which do you think is the best advice?

…ask for advice.   …leave it until tomorrow.
…give up.   …pay someone else to do it for you.
…have a cup of tea.   …try, try again.

b Look at the definition of *be able to*. What other verb is it similar to?

> **be able to do sth** to have the ability, opportunity, time, etc. to do something, e.g. *Will you be able to come to the meeting next week?*

c Read the article about people who have tried (but failed) to learn something. Complete the text with these phrases.

A	I've never been able to say
B	I was able to learn
C	you'll never be able to speak
D	I just wasn't able to do it
E	I hate not being able to communicate
F	I would suddenly be able to do it
G	all my friends are able to do

I'm a failure!   I've never been able to...

...pass my driving test

I started having driving lessons when I was 17. Although I'm normally a quick learner, ¹_____. After 18 months I failed my first test – I was really disappointed. Since then I've taken the test again three times, but I've always failed – usually on reversing or parking. The problem is I get so nervous during the tests that I can't drive properly. It's so embarrassing to admit that I can't learn to do something that ²_____!

Amanda, Brighton

...learn to dance

I've always wanted to be able to dance salsa, and when I was working in Ecuador there were free classes, so I joined. But the art of salsa is to keep your arms still and move your hips, and I just couldn't do it. When I hear music my arms start moving but my hips don't. After about ten hours of classes ³_____ the steps, but I was dancing like a robot! I didn't give up, but soon everyone in the class was dancing and I was just slowly moving from side to side and counting out loud 'one, two, three, four'. I was sure that one day ⁴_____ – but that never happened. I can still remember the first two steps, though, and I still try to dance when I hear a salsa tune, as long as nobody is watching.

Sean, Oxford

YOU IS LOVE OF MY LIVE

...speak a foreign language

I've started learning English at least ten times. I've been to classes, I've had a private teacher, I've used a self-study course, but ⁵_____ anything in English. I even had an English girlfriend once but she learned Spanish before I managed to improve my English, so we always spoke in Spanish. I travel a lot in my job and ⁶_____ – it's so frustrating. I'm thirty-two now and I think if you don't learn a language when you're a child, or go and live in the country, ⁷_____ it well.

*Guillermo, Madrid **

* translated from Spanish

d Look at phrases A–G. What tense or form of *be able to* are they?

e → **p.134 Grammar Bank 3C.** Read the rules and do the exercises.

f → **Communication** *Guess the sentence A p.116 B p.119 .*

2 PRONUNCIATION   sentence stress

a 〔3.10〕 **Dictation.** Listen and write six sentences with *can / can't* or *could / couldn't*.

b 〔3.11〕 Listen and repeat the sentences. Copy the rhythm.

   1 I'd <u>love</u> to be <u>able</u> to <u>ski</u>.

   2 We <u>won't</u> be <u>able</u> to <u>come</u>.

   3 I've <u>never</u> been <u>able</u> to <u>dance</u>.

   4 She <u>hates</u> <u>not</u> being <u>able</u> to <u>drive</u>.

c 〔3.12〕 Listen and make new sentences with the verbs you hear.

   ride a horse

            I'd love to be able to ride a horse.

HOW WORDS WORK...

1 Look at the two uses of *so*. Match them with their uses.

   1 It's **so** frustrating!

   2 The classes were free, **so** I joined.

   ☐ to emphasize an adjective or adverb

   ☐ to connect a cause and a result

2 Look at the sentences below. Is *so* use 1 or use 2?

   A I love Paris – it's so beautiful. ☐

   B The bus didn't come so I walked home. ☐

   C Why does he talk so much? ☐

   D I was so tired that I went to bed at 9.00. ☐

   E I was tired so I went to bed. ☐

3 SPEAKING

Interview your partner with the chart.

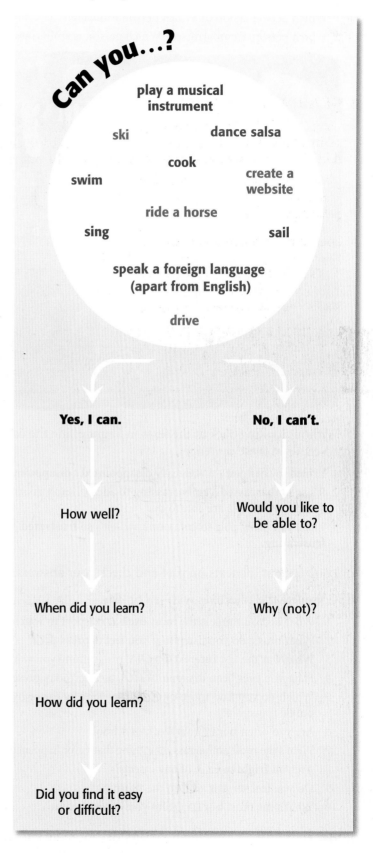

Can you...?

play a musical instrument

ski   dance salsa

cook

swim   create a website

ride a horse

sing   sail

speak a foreign language (apart from English)

drive

Yes, I can.   No, I can't.

How well?   Would you like to be able to?

When did you learn?   Why (not)?

How did you learn?

Did you find it easy or difficult?

4 VOCABULARY -ed / -ing adjectives

a Look at the picture.

1 Which person is bored? Which person is boring?
2 Which person is embarrassed? Which person is embarrassing?

b Without looking back at the texts in 1, underline the correct adjective in these sentences.

1 I failed my first test – I was really **disappointed / disappointing**.
2 It's so **embarrassed / embarrassing** to admit I can't do something that all my friends are able to do.
3 I hate not being able to communicate – it's so **frustrated / frustrating**.

c Look back at the texts on p.44 and check your answers.

d Complete the adjectives with -ed or -ing.

1 What do you think is the most **excit**_ing_ sport to watch?
2 What music do you listen to if you feel **depress**_ed_?
3 What was the last **interest**_ing_ TV programme you watched?
4 Have you ever been **disappoint**_ed_ by a birthday present?
5 Which do you find more **tir**_ing_ travelling by car or by public transport?
6 Are you often **bor**_ed_ at work or school?
7 What's the most **embarrass**_ing_ thing that's ever happened to you?
8 Are you **frighten**_ed_ of any insects?
9 Do you feel very **tir**_ed_ in the morning?
10 What's the most **bor**_ing_ film you've seen recently?

e Ask and answer the questions in pairs. Ask for more information.

5 LISTENING

a You're going to hear a psychologist talking about how to succeed at learning to do something new. Before you listen, match these phrasal verbs with their meanings.

1 I want to **take up** scuba diving.
2 I'm going to **give up** learning Japanese – it's too difficult.
3 If I like this course, I'll **carry on** next year.
  ☐ a stop, abandon
  ☐ b continue
  ☐ c start something new

b **3.13** Read these seven tips. Now listen to the programme. Tick (✔) the five things the psychologist says.

1 ☐ Be realistic about what you choose.
2 ☐ Always take up a new activity at the beginning of the year.
3 ☐ Don't think you'll be bad at all sports just because you're not good at one.
4 ☐ Don't give up an activity before you've given it a good chance.
5 ☐ If you're learning something new, don't think you're going to become the best in the world at it.
6 ☐ Always take up a new activity with a friend.
7 ☐ Learning something new is a good way of meeting people.

c Listen again. What examples does she give for each point you've ticked?

6 READING

a Can you think of anyone you know or a famous person who has been successful in very difficult circumstances?

b Work in pairs. **A** read about Natalie, **B** read about Bethany. Complete the chart.

	Natalie	Bethany
1 How did she lose a limb?		
2 When did she start her sport again?		
3 How did she feel?		
4 What has she achieved since then?		
5 How does she see her future?		

c **A** use the chart to tell **B** about Natalie. **B** complete the chart. Then swap roles.

d Now read the other text. <u>Underline</u> five words / phrases in either text that you want to remember.

e What have the two women got in common? What's different about them?

Never give up

Bethany, the surfer who lost an arm

Bethany Hamilton was the best girl surfer of her age when she lost an arm in a shark attack. She was only thirteen years old and was surfing in Hawaii when a tiger shark attacked her and tore off her left arm. It happened so fast she didn't even scream.

But Bethany was determined to get back on a surf board as soon as possible. As soon as she left hospital, she began practising her surfing exercises on the beach. Everyone was amazed to see her surfing so soon after her accident. Incredibly, she finished 5th at the National Surfing Championships.

'The first time I went back into the sea I was so happy I cried,' she said. 'It was easier than I thought. But obviously it's much more difficult than with both arms, and I have to accept I'll probably never be world champion, which used to be my dream.'

Since then Bethany has signed a contract with Rip Curl, and has written a book about her experiences which has been made into a film. 'I always dream of the sea,' she says. 'When you surf a wave, it's like walking on water, and when you're in the air, it's like flying.'

Natalie, the swimmer who lost a leg

Natalie du Toit, the South African swimmer, was only seventeen when she lost her leg in a road accident. She was going to a training session at the swimming pool on her motorbike when a car hit her. Her leg had to be amputated at the knee. At the time she was one of South Africa's most promising young swimmers. Everybody thought that she would never be able to swim competitively again.

But Natalie was determined to carry on. She went back into the pool only three months after the accident. And just one year later, at the Commonwealth Games in Manchester, she swam 800 metres in 9 minutes 11.38 seconds and qualified for the final – but not for disabled swimmers, for able-bodied ones! Although she didn't win a medal, she still made history.

'I remember how thrilled I was the first time that I swam after recovering from the operation – it felt like my leg was there. It still does,' says Natalie. 'The water is the gift that gives me back my leg. I'm still the same person I was before the accident. I believe everything happens in life for a reason. You can't go back and change anything. Swimming was my life and still is. My dream is to swim faster than I did before the accident.'

7 3.14 SONG ♫ *You can get it if you really want*

HOW TO GET THERE

a **3.15** Cover the dialogue and listen. Where is the flat that Mark is going to see? What's the best way to get there? How is Mark going to get there?

b Read the dialogue. In pairs, what do you think the missing words are? **Don't write them in yet.**

Mark	Where _____ is it? I'm sorry, I didn't catch that. OK. _____ far is it? OK, OK. Merci. Au revoir.
Jacques	Any luck?
Mark	I think I've found an apartment. How do I _____ to Belleville?
Jacques	The easiest _____ is to get the metro at Pyramides. Take Line 14 and _____ at Châtelet.
Mark	OK.
Jacques	Then take Line 11 _____ Mairie des Lilas.
Mark	Where do I _____ off?
Jacques	At Belleville.
Mark	How many _____ is it?
Jacques	Six, I think.
Mark	Oh right, I've found it on the map. How long does it _____ to get there?
Jacques	About half an hour.
Nicole	Have you found a flat?
Mark	Yes, in Belleville this time.
Nicole	When are you going to see it?
Mark	This afternoon.
Nicole	If you can wait till six, I'll _____ you a lift. I live near Belleville so I'm driving that way.
Mark	That's great. Thanks.

c Listen again and complete the dialogue.

d **3.16** Listen and repeat the highlighted phrases. Copy the rhythm.

e In pairs, try to remember the questions for these answers.
1 The easiest way is to get the metro.
2 At Belleville.
3 Six, I think.
4 About half an hour.

f ⬩ **Communication** *How do I get there? A p.117 B p.120.*

SOCIAL ENGLISH What's going on?

a **3.17** Listen. Does Mark decide to rent the flat?

b Listen again and answer the questions.
1 What are the main advantages and disadvantages of the flat?
2 What two lies does Mark tell? Why? Do you think Nicole believes him?

c **3.18** Complete the USEFUL PHRASES. Listen and check.

d Listen again and repeat the phrases. How do you say them in your language?

USEFUL PHRASES

So, what do you t____?	I can't w____ (to see it)!
It's a long w____ from (the station).	Are you on your o____?
It's a p____ (there isn't a lift).	I'll call you b____.
What's it l____?	

Christelle went to Scotland and stayed with Stephanie and David. After she had gone home, she wrote to thank them.

a Look at the list of things she says in her letter. Number them in a logical order 1–7.

A ☐ She suggests the best time to come to Geneva.

B ☐ She thanks them for having her to stay.

C ☐ She talks about what she's been doing recently.

D ☐ She apologizes for not writing before.

E ☐ She mentions two really good experiences in Scotland.

F ☐ She thanks them again and invites them to stay.

G ☐ She talks in general about the nice things that happened in Scotland.

b Now read Christelle's letter and check your answers to **a**.

c Find and correct five punctuation mistakes in the second paragraph.

d Look back at the emails on p.17. What difference is there in style between an informal letter and an email?

Useful language: informal letters / emails

Beginnings

Dear + name (**email**: Dear or Hi)

Sorry for not writing earlier but…

Thank you / Thanks (so much) for (your letter, having me to stay, etc.).

It was great to hear from you…

Endings

That's all for now.

Hope to hear from you soon. / Looking forward to hearing from you.

(Give my) regards / love to…

Best wishes / Love (from)

PS I enclose a photo of the three of us (**email**: I attach…)

Imagine you have some British friends in the UK, and you stayed with them for a week last month.

WRITE a letter to thank them.

PLAN what you're going to say. Use 1–7 above and the **Useful language** box to help you.

CHECK the letter for mistakes (grammar , punctuation , and spelling).

rue de la Tour 9
1207 Genève
Switzerland
10 September

Dear Stephanie and David,

Sorry for not writing earlier but I've been incredibly busy since I got back!

Im writing to thank you for letting me stay with you in august I had a fantastic time. The weather was perfect and I really think my english got better. i hope you think so too!

It was very nice to meet Claire and Emma. There were a lot of memorable days, but I'll never forget the open air concert we went to – it was amazing – or the visit to Edinburgh Castle.

For the last three weeks I've been very busy organizing everything for my next year at university. I have to matriculate for all my subjects and choose the optional ones I want to do. I've also been doing a lot of exercise as I put on three kilos while I was in Glasgow! I've been going swimming every day and playing football with my friends. Talking of football, I was sorry to see that Celtic lost on Saturday. Let's hope they play better next week.

Anyway, that's all for now. Thanks again for everything. Don't forget my invitation to come to Geneva – my family would love to meet you. Spring would be a great time as it's warm and not too crowded.

Give my love to Claire and Emma.

Best wishes

Christelle

PS I enclose a photo I took of the girls in Edinburgh.

GRAMMAR

Complete the second sentence with **two words** so that it means the same as the first. Contracted forms, e.g. *isn't*, count as one word.

I really think it's important for you to learn to drive.

You really *must learn* to drive.

1 Why don't you join a tennis club? It would be good for you.

I think you _____ _____ a tennis club.

2 I'm sure she's not American. She hasn't got an American accent.

She _____ _____ American, she hasn't got an American accent.

3 I can't go out tonight.

I won't _____ _____ to go out tonight.

4 It's prohibited to take photos there.

You _____ _____ photos there.

5 I'm not sure if she'll like her present.

She _____ _____ like her present.

6 Wearing a uniform is not obligatory.

You _____ _____ to wear a uniform.

7 The lights are on so I'm sure he's at home.

The lights are on so he _____ _____ at home.

8 I think perhaps this is their house.

This _____ _____ their house.

9 Paying in advance is obligatory at this school.

You _____ _____ pay in advance at this school.

10 Drinking a lot of coffee isn't a good idea.

You _____ _____ a lot of coffee.

`10`

VOCABULARY

a Complete the description.

My cousin Ann is very attractive. She's in her ¹m_____-twenties – 24 or 25 I think. She's blonde, with shoulder-²l_____ hair. It's completely ³s_____, not curly at all. Her ⁴f_____ is very long and gets in her eyes. She's very short-sighted but she ⁵w_____ contact lenses.

b Complete with an adjective from the **bold** verb.

1 Are you _____ in sport? **interest**
2 I was very _____ when I failed the exam. **depress**
3 This book is really _____. I can't finish it. **bore**
4 I completely forgot his name. It was so _____! **embarrass**
5 I felt very _____ because I just couldn't do it. **frustrate**

c Complete with one word.

1 Please switch _____ your mobile. You can't use it here.
2 I'm afraid John's out. Can you call _____ later?
3 I can't believe it! He hung _____ in the middle of our conversation!
4 She looks _____ her mother. They both have big eyes.
5 He's _____ his late forties.

`15`

PRONUNCIATION

a Underline the word with a different sound.

1		dial	might	fifties	frightened
2		weight	height	straight	engaged
3		curly	bored	short	tall
4		grey	ugly	glasses	fringe
5		check	moustache	switch	choose

b Underline the stressed syllable.

disappointed   embarrassing   interested   mobile   overweight

`10`

CAN YOU UNDERSTAND THIS TEXT?

The best day of my life

This week's contributor is the thriller writer Minette Walters.

One of the best days of my life was when my agent phoned to say that my first novel, *The Ice House*, had been accepted by a publisher. I'd finished the book 18 months earlier, and I didn't think it was ever going to be published. It was one morning in the autumn of 1990 when the phone call came. I was 39, and a friend of mine turned up, sat down at my kitchen table and burst into tears because she was having problems with her marriage. I was doing my best to try to console her when the phone rang. So there I was, listening to the best news of my life, while my friend was crying over the worst news of her life. My agent said, 'Aren't you pleased? Why aren't you more excited?' I said, 'I am…but I'll tell you later'. I put the phone down and tried to be sympathetic to my friend. But at 11 o'clock I couldn't stand it any longer so I said, 'Stay there. I have to go out for ten minutes'. I came back with a bottle of champagne. 'You and I are going to drink some champagne,' I said, and told her my good news. She was a much happier lady when she left! I can't remember how many publishers had turned down my book, because my agent didn't tell me. I don't know how many copies it's sold now – a couple of million I should think, because it's published in 36 countries. But I have absolutely no sympathy for those publishers who rejected my book. I was deeply hurt at the time, but now I'm laughing!

Adapted from the British press

a Read the article and choose a, b, or c.

1 In 1990 Minette Walters was _____ about the chances of her first novel being published.
   a quite optimistic   b quite pessimistic   c quite worried

2 When her agent first phoned, Minette felt that she _____ celebrate the news.
   a shouldn't   b had to   c could

3 Her agent couldn't understand _____ .
   a why she was crying   b what she was saying
   c her reaction

4 In the end Minette's good news made her friend _____ .
   a feel better   b feel worse   c leave early

5 Now that she is very successful, she _____ the publishers who rejected her.
   a feels positive towards   b feels negative towards
   c understands

b Look at the highlighted words and phrases. Can you guess what they mean?

CAN YOU UNDERSTAND THESE PEOPLE?

a **3.19** Listen and circle the correct answer, a, b, or c.

1 Where's the girl's mobile?
   a In the café.   b In her pocket.   c In her bag.

2 How late are their friends?
   a Less than 15 minutes.   b 15 minutes.
   c More than 15 minutes.

3 Who looks good in their passport photo?
   a The woman.   b The man.   c Neither of them.

4 The girl's new boyfriend is…
   a tall and with long dark hair.
   b tall with short dark hair.
   c short with short dark hair.

5 How many times has the woman failed her driving test?
   a One.   b Two.   c Three.

b **3.20** Listen and complete the form with the missing information.

Anglo language school

Name: [1]_____
Surname: [2]_____
Nationality: [3]_____
Student wants to study [4]_____ level.
Student has been to [5]_____ .

CAN YOU SAY THIS IN ENGLISH?

Can you…? Yes (✓)

☐ talk about bad mobile phone manners, and what you think people should do

☐ describe yourself and other people

☐ talk about something you've tried to learn but weren't able to and why

4
A

G first conditional and future time clauses + *when, until,* etc.
V education
P /ʌ/ or /juː/?

Back to school, aged 35

1 VOCABULARY education

a Answer the questions in pairs.

> 1 When did the Second World War end?
> 2 What is the capital of Colombia?
> 3 Who wrote *Hamlet*?
> 4 How many kilobytes are there in a megabyte?
> 5 Who invented the theory of relativity?
> 6 What's 5 × 18 ÷ 4?
> 7 How many legs does an insect have?
> 8 What is water made of?

b Match the questions with these school subjects.

chemistry ☐
geography ☐
history ☐
information technology ☐
literature ☐
maths ☐
physics ☐
biology ☐

c ➡ **p.150 Vocabulary Bank** *Education.*

2 PRONUNCIATION & SPEAKING /ʌ/ or /juː/?

⚠ The letter *u* between consonants or at the beginning of a word is usually pronounced /ʌ/ or /juː/.

a Put the words in the correct column.

| computer | lunch | nun | pupil | result |
| student | study | subject | uniform | university |

⬆	/juː/

b **4.1** Listen and check. Practise saying the words. Why do we say *a university* but *an umbrella*?

c **4.2** Practise saying these sentences. Listen and check.

1 What subject did you study at university?
2 Do pupils at your school wear a uniform?
3 Most students have lunch in the canteen.
4 I usually get good results in my music exams.

d Interview your partner using the questionnaire. Ask for more information.

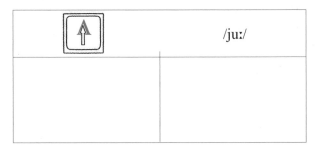

Your education

What kind of secondary school / you go to?

/ you like it?

How many pupils / there in each class?

How much homework / you have?

/ you have to wear a uniform?

/ discipline very strict?

/ pupils behave well?

Which subjects / you good and bad at?

Which / your best and worst subject?

So school these days is easy? Think again.

People and politicians complain that school is getting easier. Damian Whitworth, a 35-year-old journalist, decided to see for himself. He spent a week as a pupil at a British secondary school, Brentwood County High School. It's a large state school and has about 1,800 pupils, girls and boys, aged between 11 and 18.

3 READING

a Look at the photo above. What's unusual about one of the pupils?

b Read the introduction. Why did Damian Whitworth go back to school? What kind of school did he go to?

c Read Damian's diary for one of the days he spent back at school. Does he think school is easier or harder now?

d Read the text again and put the phrases A–H in the correct places.

A A crowd of pupils are watching.

B However, the pupils are totally involved.

C He's friendly with the pupils but not *too* friendly.

D When I was the same age as these children I had never used a computer.

E It's a magical moment and the most effective class I have seen.

F ~~'Are you really in our class?'~~

G One boy says he has chips every day.

H Phones that ring in class are confiscated until the end of the week.

e In pairs, look at the highlighted words and phrases. Try to guess what they mean from the context. Then check with your dictionary or the teacher.

f In pairs, look at each heading (**French**, **Maths**, etc.) and say if what happens is the same, similar, or different from the secondary school you went to (or go to). Say why.

French

My first lesson is French. I am in a class of thirteen year olds. Outside the classroom some girls start interrogating me. [1] *Are you really in our class?* 'How old are you?' 'How old do you think I am?' I reply.
'Well… you're not 13!'
First we have a listening test which I find difficult. I get 14 out of 20. Not bad. Then we make revision lists on the computer. [2]_____. Now every pupil has one.

Maths

As we wait outside the maths classroom a teacher tells me to do up the top button of my shirt. The maths teacher uses an interactive whiteboard which has graphics and video, but the pupils don't look very interested in the lesson. A mobile rings and the owner hurries to switch it off. [3]_____

History

Mr Fishleigh is the history teacher. He doesn't have any problems controlling the noise level (other teachers do). [4]_____. He talks to them as if they were adults and gets their attention in return.

Lunch

In the canteen we can choose between traditional and fast food. Burger and chips is the most popular meal. [5]_____

Information and communication technology

We are designing spreadsheets for mobile phone sales and I cannot imagine a more boring lesson. [6]_____.

Most children have Internet access at home and the school has a website where parents can see what homework their children have and when they have to give it in.

Religious education

The teacher introduces us to meditation. We sit cross-legged on our desks and try to fill our minds with blackness and think positively about people who we have been thinking negatively about. For 15 minutes the children sit, eyes closed, in total silence. When they leave the class they are slightly dazed :
'Incredible!'
'Amazing!'
'We should do this in maths!'

[7]_____

The bell goes. End of school for the day.

As we leave there is a fight at the school gates. [8]_____ 'If anyone hits anyone, I'll call the police,' says a teacher.

So has school got easier?

It's difficult to say if lessons are harder or easier since I was a child because teaching methods have changed so much. All I can say is that during my working life I have had many tiring experiences. Being back at school for a week was as tiring as any of them. Being a pupil today is very, very hard work.

4 GRAMMAR first conditional and future time clauses

a In pairs, answer the questions.

1 When was the last time you did an exam? Did you pass or fail?
2 What's the next exam you are going to do? How do you feel about it?
3 How do you usually feel before you do an exam?
4 What do you usually do the night before an exam?
5 Have you ever failed an important exam you thought you had passed (or vice versa)?

b Charlotte and Viktor are waiting for their exam results.
4.3 Listen to Charlotte and answer questions 1–5. **4.4** Then do the same for Viktor.

Charlotte has just taken her A-levels.

Viktor has just taken the FCE exam.

1 Do you think you have passed?
2 When and how will you get the results of the exam?
3 How will you celebrate if you get good results?
4 What will you do if you get good results?
5 What will you do if you fail, or if you don't get the results you need?

c **4.5** Listen and complete the sentences.

1 They won't give me a place **unless**
_____ .
2 **As soon as** _____ , I'll take the letter upstairs and open it.
3 I don't want to plan any celebrations **until**
_____ .
4 **If** I don't get into Cambridge, _____ .
5 **When** I_____ , the grades will be on the notice board.

d ◯ **p.136 Grammar Bank 4A.** Read the rules and do the exercises.

e Choose **five** sentence beginnings from the list below and make true sentences about yourself. Then tell your partner.

I won't stop studying English until I…	I'll have a big party if…
I'd like to retire when…	I'll always live here unless…
I'll leave home as soon as…	I'll have more free time when…
I'll be really annoyed if…	I'll have something to eat as soon as…
I don't want to have children before…	I won't get married until…

f **4.6** Listen to Charlotte and Viktor. Did they pass or fail? What grade did they get? What are they going to do?

5 LISTENING

a Look at this extract from a TV guide and the photo and answer the questions.

8.00 That'll Teach 'Em

Final part of the six-part series following a group of modern 16-year-old school children in a 1950s boarding school. This week: Exams!

1 What do you think the idea of the programme was?

2 Which of these things do you think pupils hated the most?

the food	wearing a uniform
not being able to watch TV	going for cross-country runs
not being able to use mobiles	having cold showers
having a lot of homework	

3 What do you think the discipline was like? How do you think the children were punished for behaving badly?

4 Do you think the pupils did well or badly when they took 1950s exams?

b **4.7** Listen to a TV critic talking about the programme *That'll Teach 'Em*. Check your answers to **a**. Were you surprised?

c Listen again and mark the sentences T (true) or F (false).

1 16 children took part in the experiment.
2 They didn't have to sleep at the school.
3 The uniforms were not very comfortable.
4 They had to stay inside the school grounds all the time.
5 The children weren't allowed to talk during the classes.
6 They really missed being able to use computers and calculators.
7 They thought the classes were boring.
8 Exams today are easier than in the 1950s.
9 The children failed because they weren't intelligent enough.
10 Most of the children enjoyed the experiment.

d Do you think school exams in your country are easier than they used to be?

6 SPEAKING

a In groups, each choose one different topic from the list below. Decide if you agree or disagree, and write down at least three reasons.

Private schools are usually better than state schools.

All schools should let children wear whatever they want at school.

Cooking and housework should be taught at all schools.

Physical education should be optional.

Girls study better without boys in the class.

School summer holidays should be shorter.

Boys study better in a mixed class.

b Explain to the rest of your group what you think about your topic. The others in the group should listen and say if they agree or disagree with you and why.

Useful language

First of all… My first point is that…

Secondly… Another important point is that…

Finally…

4 B

G second conditional
V houses
P sentence stress

In an ideal world...

Getting personal

Our weekly questionnaire. This week we ask the actress and model Isabella Rossellini and dancer Joaquín Cortés...

1 If you could live in another period of time for its fashion, when would you choose and why?

2 If you could come back in another life, who (or what) would you like to be?

3 If you could change one part of your body, what would it be?

4 What would you wear if you were invited on a date by someone you really liked?

5 What would you eat for your last meal and who (dead or alive) would you share it with?

Adapted from the British press

1 GRAMMAR second conditional

a Look at the two photos on p.56 and describe the people. Do you know anything about them?

b Read the questions in *Getting personal* and match two answers with each question. Try to guess which answers are Isabella Rossellini's and which are Joaquín Cortés's.

A ☐ *A fly on the wall, so I could watch people.*

B ☐ *Either the thirties, for its elegance, or the seventies, for its hippy clothes and great music.*

C ☐ *Jeans and a shirt.*

D ☐ *My back. I would like 13 new vertebrae.*

E ☐ *With a fabulous woman. I wouldn't really care about the food.*

F ☐ *I'd change everything.*

G ☐ *Some super comfortable French pyjamas that everyone thinks are clothes.*

H ☐ *A bird.*

I ☐ *I would have a pasta supper with my dog, Macaroni. It's what she has wanted her whole life.*

J ☐ *I'd choose today or any time after the end of the corset.*

c Look at *Getting personal* again, and answer these questions.
1 In questions 1–4, what tense is the verb in the *if* clause?
2 What tense is the other verb?
3 How is question 5 different?
4 Do the questions refer to real or imaginary situations?

d ⊙ **p.136 Grammar Bank 4B.** Read the rules and do the exercises.

e ⊙ **Communication** *What would you do if…? A p.117 B p.120.*

2 PRONUNCIATION & SPEAKING sentence stress

a Match the sentence halves.

1 I <u>wouldn't wear</u> that <u>hat</u> ☐ A if she <u>practised more</u>.

2 If you <u>did</u> more <u>exercise</u>, ☐ B I'm <u>sure</u> she'd <u>understand</u> you.

3 If it <u>wasn't</u> so <u>expensive</u>, ☐ C if I could <u>find</u> the <u>right person</u>.

4 I'd get <u>married tomorrow</u> ☐ D you'd <u>feel much better</u>.

5 She'd <u>play better</u> ☐ E I'd <u>buy</u> it.

6 If you <u>talked</u> to her, ☐ F if <u>I</u> were <u>you</u>.

b 🔊 **4.8** Listen and check.

c Listen again and repeat. <u>Copy</u> the <u>rhythm</u>. Then cover A–F and try to remember the sentences.

d Choose three of the sentence beginnings below and complete them in a way which is true for you. Tell a partner and say why.

If I won a 'dream holiday' in a competition, I'd go…

If I could choose any car I liked, I'd have a…

If I could be very good at a sport, I'd choose…

If I could choose my ideal job, I'd…

If I had more time, I'd learn…

If I could buy a house in another country, I'd buy…

3 VOCABULARY houses

a Look at the cover of *Ideal Home* magazine. Which room is it? How many things in the room can you name?

b ◯ p.151 Vocabulary Bank *Houses*.

c In pairs, ask and answer the questions.

Where do you live?

What do you like about the area where you live?

What don't you like?

What do you like about your house / flat?

What would you change?

4 LISTENING & SPEAKING

a ⬭ **4.9** Listen to four people describing their 'dream house'. Match the speakers 1–4 with the pictures.

b Listen again and match the people with what they say.

Which speaker…?
- ☐ would not like to have other people living nearby
- ☐ would like to live somewhere that was partly old and partly modern
- ☐ would not spend much time inside their dream house
- ☐ doesn't think they will ever get their dream house

c Think for a few minutes about what your dream house would be like and make notes. Use **Vocabulary Bank** *Houses* to help you.

Where would it be?
What kind of house or flat would it be?
What special features would it have?

d In groups, describe your houses. Whose do you like best?

5 READING

a Have you ever visited the house where a famous person was born or lived? Where was it? What do you especially remember about it?

b Read the article about Casa Azul. Which part of the house are these things connected to? Why are they mentioned?

   two giant statues

    Leon Trotsky

     a yellow floor

    a monkey and a parrot

   a pair of shoes

    a cupboard with a glass door

     July 7 1910

    1929–1954

c Match the highlighted words with their meaning.

1 _____ a piece of furniture with cupboards at the bottom and shelves above, to hold cups and plates, etc.

2 _____ material which you can see through

3 _____ the door, gate, or opening where you go into a place

4 _____ a room where paintings are hung

5 _____ the floor above where you are

6 _____ with a lot of fresh air inside

7 _____ wooden or metal covers which are fixed outside windows

8 _____ an area, usually behind a house, where people can sit and eat outside

d What did you find out about Frida Kahlo and her life? Would you like to visit her house?

6 ⬭ **4.10** SONG ♫ *Our house*

Houses you'll never forget
Casa Azul (The Blue House)

On the corner of Londres and Allende Street in Coyoacán, an old residential area of Mexico City, there is a house with bright blue walls, tall windows and green shutters, surrounded by trees. It is one of the most extraordinary places in Mexico, the home of the surrealist painter Frida Kahlo, who died in 1954, aged only 47.

The entrance is guarded by two giant statues nearly seven metres tall. As you walk past them, you enter a garden with tropical plants and fountains. When you go inside the house the first room is the spacious and airy living room. Here Frida and her husband, the painter Diego Rivera, entertained their famous friends, including the millionaire Nelson Rockefeller, the composer George Gershwin, and the political leader Leon Trotsky. Now the room is a gallery where some of Frida's paintings can be seen.

The first thing you notice when you go into the kitchen is the floor – painted bright yellow to stop insects from coming in. There is a long yellow table where Frida and Diego often had lunch parties, and a yellow dresser holding traditional green and brown Mexican dishes. Here, their guests often found themselves in the company of Frida's pets, Fulang Chang, a beloved monkey, or Bonito the parrot, who used to perform tricks at the table in return for butter!

Everywhere in the house you can feel the spirit of Frida and Diego. Upstairs Frida's palette and brushes are still on the worktable in her studio, as if she had just put them down. In Diego's bedroom you can see his stetson hat and a huge pair of shoes – he had enormous feet. In another bedroom there is a cupboard with a glass door, which contains one of the colourful Mexican dresses which Frida loved wearing.

Above the cupboard, in Spanish, are painted these words: 'Frida Kahlo was born here on July 7 1910'. In fact, she was born three years earlier (July 6th 1907) but she changed her birth date to the year of the Mexican Revolution. On the walls of the patio is another inscription 'Frida and Diego lived in this house from 1929–1954'. Again, this is not entirely true. She and her husband lived in separate houses for five years during that period, and they divorced in 1939, though they remarried a year later. The house, like Frida's life, is full of contradictions.

4C

G *usually* and *used to*
V friendship
P /s/ or /z/?

Still friends?

1 VOCABULARY & SPEAKING friendship

a Complete the text with the phrases below.

> argue   close friend   colleague   get on very well
> have a lot in common   keep in touch   known
> lost touch   met

I have a *close friend* called Irene. I've [1]_____ her for about 15 years now. We [2]_____ at work – she was a [3]_____ of mine at the company where I used to work, and we used to have our coffee breaks at the same time.

We [4]_____ although we don't [5]_____ – we have quite different interests. We don't work together any more, and when I changed jobs we [6]_____ for a couple of years. But now we [7]_____ regularly. We phone each other once a week, and we see each other about twice a month. We don't often [8]_____, only sometimes about films as we have completely different tastes!

b Think of a close friend of yours. In pairs, ask and answer the questions.

How long have you known him / her?
  Where did you meet?
    Why do you get on well?
    What do you have in common?
Do you ever argue? What about?
  How often do you see each other?
    How do you keep in touch the rest of the time?
    Have you ever lost touch? Why? When?
Do you think you'll stay friends?

2 GRAMMAR *usually* and *used to*

a Have you ever tried to get in touch with an old friend? Why? Did you succeed?

b Read about the *Friends Reunited* website and answer the questions.

1 What's it for?
2 How do you use it?

> *Friends Reunited* is a website which helps you to find old friends and lets you read what people you've lost touch with are doing now.
>
>
>
> ### How does it work?
> New visitors find their old schools or workplaces, which are usually listed on the web page, and then add their names to the list of people already registered. They can also post photos and information about what they are doing now. When they want to contact another member, *Friends Reunited* forwards the message. Communication takes place without revealing personal email addresses or contact details until members decide they want to do so.

c Now read about two people who registered on the website. Who did they want to meet? Why?

d Complete the texts with the sentences below.

> he used to go to   I used to know   I used to live
> used to come   we used to go out

e Look at the two texts again. When do we use *used to*? How do you make negatives and questions?

f ○ p.136 Grammar Bank 4C. Read the rules and do the exercises.

Friends Reunited?

Carol, 52, from Cornwall

When I was 15 I fell in love with a boy called Robert. I was at school, a girls' convent, and he was in his first year at university. [1]_____ in secret because my parents didn't like him at all – Robert was a long-haired hippy who played the guitar. But after a year I broke up with him because my parents were making my life impossible. Robert was very angry, and we completely lost touch. But I always wondered what had happened to him, and when I heard about *Friends Reunited* I decided to try to get in touch again. I'm divorced now, and I thought 'you never know…'. I remembered the name of the school that [2]_____ and I went to their web page on *Friends Reunited* and there was his name! I sent him an email and two days later I got a reply…

Alex, 24, from Manchester

[3]_____ in Manchester but when I was eighteen my family moved south to London. Two years ago I had a really bad motorbike accident. I was in a coma for two weeks and in hospital for six months. I completely lost my memory, not just of the crash itself but also of my past. While I was in hospital, my family [4]_____ every day and play me my favourite music and show me photos. Little by little I began to remember who I was and who my family were. But I still couldn't remember anything about the rest of my life. Then my sister had the idea of contacting *Friends Reunited*. Through them she contacted people [5]_____ in Manchester when I was at school. She arranged a reunion in a pub near Piccadilly Station and I travelled to Manchester in search of my past.

3 LISTENING

a **4.11** Read the text about Carol again. Now listen to her talking about what happened next. Was the meeting a success?

b Listen again and answer questions 1–5.
1 Why was Carol surprised at Robert's choice of job?
2 What happened when she got to the restaurant?
3 What do Carol and Robert look like now?
4 What did Carol realize as soon as she saw Robert?
5 How had Robert changed?

c **4.12** Read the text about Alex again. Now listen to him talking about what happened next. Was the meeting a success?

d Listen again and answer questions 6–10.
6 Did he recognize any of the people?
7 How did he feel?
8 What did they talk to him about?
9 What did he remember when he saw the photos?
10 Who is Anna? What does he think of her now?

4 PRONUNCIATION & SPEAKING /s/ or /z/?

a **4.13** Listen to the sentences. Is the se in the verbs pronounced /s/ or /z/? Write s or z in the box. Which pronunciation is more common?
1 I used to live in London. ☐
2 I used my credit card to pay. ☐
3 Excuse me. Can you help me? ☐
4 You need to practise your pronunciation. ☐
5 We won't win, we'll lose. ☐
6 They advertise on TV. ☐
7 They promised to keep in touch. ☐
8 Could you close the window? ☐

b Now practise saying the sentences.

c In pairs, tell each other about three of the following. Give as much information as you can.

A machine you used to use a lot but don't any more

A friend you used to have but who you've lost touch with

A teacher at school you used to hate

A sport you used to play but don't any more

A singer you used to listen to a lot and who you still like

A food or drink you didn't use to like but like now

An actor you used to like a lot but don't any more

5 READING

a How often do you see your really good friends? Would you like to see them more often? Do you spend much time with people you don't really like?

b Now read the magazine article. What does 'edit your friends' mean?

Do you need to 'edit your friends'?

Is your mobile phone directory full of phone numbers of people you don't really want to talk to? Do you go out with people from work or university more often than with your <u>real</u> friends? Do you say yes to invitations because you think you should, not because you want to? If you answered yes to at least two of these questions, then perhaps it's time to 'edit your friends'?

Nowadays people tend to spend a lot of time socializing with colleagues at work or classmates at university. The result is that we don't have enough time to see our real, close friends. As our lives get busier it becomes more important to spend the little free time we have with people we really want to see, people we love and who really love us.

Who are the friends you need to edit? A few years ago I read a book about how to get rid of unnecessary possessions.

It said you should ask yourself about each thing you have: Is it useful? Do I really like it? Do I feel better every time I look at it? If the answer is no to any one of those questions, you should throw it away. Maybe we should ask similar questions about our friends.

What kind of friends will you probably need to edit? Sometimes it's an old friend. Somebody who you used to have a lot in common with, but who, when you meet now, you have very little or nothing to say to. Or it might be a new friend who you get on quite well with, but who is taking up too much of your time. Next time one of these people calls you and suggests a meeting, think, 'Do I <u>really</u> want to see this person?' and if the answer is no, say no, and make an excuse. That way you'll have more time to spend with your real friends.

Adapted from the British press

c Now read the article again. Choose the best summary of each paragraph, a, b, or c.

1 People need to 'edit' their friends if…
   a they have moved to a different area.
   b all their friends are people from work or school.
   c they are spending a lot of time with people who are not real friends.

2 People today are often very busy, so…
   a they should see their friends less.
   b they should think carefully about how they spend their free time.
   c they should try to make friends with people from work / school.

3 The writer says that…
   a we should ask ourselves who our real friends are.
   b most of our friends are unnecessary.
   c we shouldn't treat friends as possessions.

4 The kind of friends we probably need to 'edit' are…
   a old friends who don't talk very much.
   b new friends who talk too much.
   c friends that you don't really want to see any more.

d Read the article again. <u>Underline</u> five new words or phrases you want to learn.

e Do you agree with the article? Do you need to 'edit your friends'?

HOW WORDS WORK...

1 Look at these expressions with *get* which have appeared in this lesson. Match them with their meanings A–G.

1 ...a book about how to get rid of unnecessary objects ☐   A make contact with somebody

2 ...a new friend who you get on with quite well ☐   B be friendly with

3 ...I sort of relaxed and felt I was getting to know them again ☐   C become

4 ...I got to the pub late ☐   D know somebody (or something) little by little

5 ...I decided to try to get in touch ☐   E receive

6 ...and two days later I got a reply ☐   F throw away

7 ...I got really excited ☐   G arrive at / in

2 Complete the questions with *get* or an expression with *get*. Ask and answer the questions in pairs.

1 Who do you _____ best in your family?

2 Does it take you long to _____ new people?

3 Do you _____ more emails from friends than work-related ones?

4 How do you normally _____ with your friends (by text, phone, etc.)?

5 How often do you _____ things (e.g. clothes) that you don't use any more?

6 LISTENING & SPEAKING

a **4.14** Read sentences A–F below. Now listen to three people talking. Which sentences are they talking about? Write 1, 2, or 3 next to the sentence.

A Men keep their friends longer than women.

B It's more difficult to keep in touch with friends than it used to be.

C It's impossible to stay 'good friends' with an ex-partner.

D You should never criticize your friend's partner.

E You should never lend money to a friend.

F You can only have two or three close friends.

b Listen again. Do they agree or disagree with the statements? What are their reasons? What examples do they give?

c Now look at the sentences and tick (✔)the ones you agree with and cross (✘) the ones you don't agree with. Think about your reasons.

d In groups, compare opinions. Try to give real examples from your own experience or of people you know. Use the phrases below to help you.

"Sorry, Frank, but I can no longer go on with this charade. Not only am I not your best friend, I'm not even sure I like you at all."

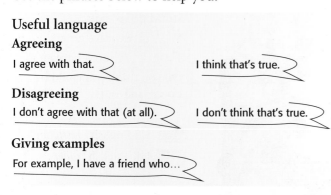

Useful language

Agreeing

I agree with that.   I think that's true.

Disagreeing

I don't agree with that (at all).   I don't think that's true.

Giving examples

For example, I have a friend who...

MAKING SUGGESTIONS

a **4.15** Cover the dialogue and listen. What's the problem? Where do Mark and Allie decide to take Scarlett?

b Read the dialogue. In pairs, what do you think the missing words are? **Don't write them in yet.**

Allie	I got a message this morning. It's from Jacques. (*Allie plays the message.*)
Allie	You've met Scarlett Scarpino, haven't you, Ben?
Ben	The punk princess? Yeah, I met her in London last year.
Allie	What's she like?
Ben	Let's say she's a bit … difficult.
Allie	What are we going to _____ with her?
Mark	Why _____ you show her around Paris?
Allie	I have a _____ idea. Why don't *you* show her around Paris?
Mark	What, me? I'm new here!
Allie	You can't leave me to do this on my own.
Mark	OK, why _____ we take her to Notre Dame? I mean, it's her first time in Paris, isn't it?
Ben	I don't think churches are really her thing.
Mark	How _____ taking her on a boat trip?
Allie	Brilliant!
Mark	And then we could go up the Eiffel Tower.
Allie	_____ a good idea. I'm sure she'll love the view.
Ben	And she might fall off!
Mark	Thanks for your help, Ben. _____ we have lunch after that?
Allie	_____ go somewhere really nice. Do you have any recommendations, Ben?
Ben	_____ about La Renaissance? It's Jacques's favourite.
Allie	That sounds perfect. Er, Ben, do you want to come too?
Ben	Sorry, Allie. I'm really busy. But I'm sure you'll have an unforgettable meal.

c Listen again and complete the dialogue.

d **4.16** Listen and repeat the highlighted phrases.

e Look at the highlighted phrases again. Then cover the dialogue. Try to remember the missing words for making suggestions.

Making suggestions

_____ _____ _____ take her to Notre Dame?

_____ _____ taking her on a boat trip?

_____ _____ have lunch after that?

_____ go somewhere really nice.

_____ _____ La Renaissance?

f Imagine you are going to go out with the other students next Saturday. In small groups, ask and answer the questions.

1 What time and where shall we meet?
2 Where shall we have dinner?
3 What shall we do after dinner?

SOCIAL ENGLISH   An unforgettable meal

a **4.17** Listen. What does Scarlett have for lunch?

b Listen again and mark the sentences T (true) or F (false).

1 Scarlett isn't hungry.
2 She doesn't eat meat or fish.
3 She's allergic to seafood.
4 She didn't enjoy the boat trip.
5 They went up the Eiffel Tower.
6 Allie doesn't like Scarlett.
7 Mark guesses what Scarlett would like to eat.

c **4.18** Complete the USEFUL PHRASES. Listen and check.

d Listen again and repeat the phrases. How do you say them in your language?

USEFUL PHRASES

What w_____ you like?

Aren't you h_____?

(The seafood) l_____ good.

I'm a_____ to (mushrooms, strawberries, nuts…)

S_____ we leave now?

No, h_____ on. I have an idea.

Do you think you could p_____ do me a favour?

🇺🇸	US English	*restroom*
🇬🇧	UK English	*toilet*

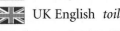
Study Link MultiROM

Four-bedroom house, Alberta, Canada

Would you like to stay in this beautiful house in the heart of the Canadian Rocky Mountains?

It's a spacious house with four bedrooms, a living room, a large kitchen, two bathrooms, and a store room. There are breathtaking views of the mountains from all the windows. It has a large balcony, which is ideal for eating outside in the summer. The house has wooden floors, a jacuzzi, cable television, and Internet.

It's a quiet, safe neighbourhood and the neighbours are very warm and friendly. The house is walking distance from stores and restaurants in the local town and a short drive from areas with excellent skiing and hiking. In the area around the house you can see amazing wildlife such as bears, wolves, deer, and mountain goats.

This house is perfect for families or two couples. It's a no-smoking house and, sorry, no pets.

Two-bedroom apartment, Manhattan, New York City

Rent this _nice_ two-bedroom apartment. It's perfectly situated between 43rd Street and 8th Avenue, five minutes from Time Square and most of the theatres, and a fifteen-minute walk from Central Park.

superb

It's a _nice_ 150-square-metre apartment on the 19th floor of a new building. It has two bedrooms, a _nice_ living room with a huge balcony, a kitchen/dining room and two bathrooms. The flat has very big windows, so during the day it's very light and at night you have a _nice_ view of downtown Manhattan, especially on the 4th of July when you can see all the fireworks!

The neighbourhood is colourful, and it's _nice_ for people who like eating out or going to the theatre and clubs. There's a subway station on the street and it's a ten-minute walk to Grand Central train station. JFK airport is less than half an hour away by taxi.

This apartment is _nice_ for couples. Sorry, no children or pets and definitely no smoking.

a Read the two adverts from a website. Which one would you prefer to rent for a two-week holiday? Why?

b Read about the house in Canada again. Highlight any adjectives which help to 'sell' the house.

c Now read about the New York apartment again. Improve the description by replacing the word _nice_ with one of the adjectives below. Often there is more than one possibility.

| breathtaking | ideal | magnificent | perfect | spacious | ~~superb~~ |

Useful language: describing location

It's | perfectly situated…
| walking distance from…
| a (fifteen-minute) walk from…
| a short drive from…

The neighbourhood is (safe, friendly, etc.)
It's a (beautiful) area…

WRITE a description of your house / flat (real or imaginary) for a website.

PLAN what you're going to write. Use the **Useful language** box and **Vocabulary Bank** _Houses_ **p.151** to help you.

Paragraph 1   A brief introduction. What kind of house / flat is it? Where is it exactly?
Paragraph 2   Describe the house / flat. What rooms does it have? Does it have any special characteristics?
Paragraph 3   Describe the neighbourhood. How far is it from places of interest, public transport, etc.?
Paragraph 4   Say who the house / flat is suitable for. Are there any restrictions?

CHECK the description for mistakes (grammar , punctuation , and spelling).

GRAMMAR

a Complete the sentences with the right form of the verb in brackets.

1 If I don't pass the exam, I _____ it again in January. (do)
2 You'd sleep better if you _____ less coffee. (drink)
3 Don't buy it unless you _____ sure you like it. (be)
4 If I could change a part of my body, I _____ my nose. (change)
5 As soon as he _____, we can have dinner. (arrive)

b Choose a, b, or c.

1 Where _____ if you took the job in London?
  a will you live   b did you live
  c would you live
2 I used _____ with that boy over there.
  a going out   b to go out   c go out
3 I _____ enjoy flying but now I love it.
  a not used to   b didn't used to
  c didn't use to
4 In the summer I _____ to the country.
  a usually go   b use to go
  c usually to go
5 _____ to wear glasses?
  a She used   b Does she use
  c Did she use

| 10 |

VOCABULARY

a Word groups. Underline the word that is different. Say why.

1 cottage   village   flat   detached house
2 sink   dishwasher   fridge   shower
3 secondary   uniform   boarding   state
4 cheat   pass   exam   fail
5 classmate   friendship   colleague   close friend

b Complete the sentences.

1 Maths, physics, and geography are **s**_____.
2 A school year is often divided into three **t**_____.
3 A school where you have to pay is a **p**_____ school.
4 A senior university teacher is a **p**_____.
5 The area outside the central part of a city is called the **s**_____.
6 Smoke comes through the **c**_____.
7 The part which covers the top of a house is the **r**_____.
8 The 'door' of a garden is the **g**_____.

c Fill each gap with one word.

1 They often argue _____ politics.
2 Do you keep _____ touch _____ old school friends?
3 They live _____ the suburbs.
4 Do you get _____ well with the people in the office?
5 My son is _____ university.
6 We don't have very much _____ common.

| 20 |

PRONUNCIATION

a Underline the word with a different sound.

1	⬆	touch	study	student	subject
2	/juː/	punish	music	argue	university
3	☎	close	cosy	country	stone
4	🐱	flat	cottage	balcony	maths
5	⏰	block	copy	modern	homework

b Underline the stressed syllable.

| uniform | exam | secondary | residential | colleague |

| 10 |

We don't need no education... or do we?

The children who sang on *Another Brick in the Wall* by the British group Pink Floyd have changed their tune since 1979. 25 years later, they are trying to take the group to court because of unpaid royalties.

The song, which was a number 1 in the UK and abroad, was an attack on school and education and it had the famous chorus, 'We don't need no education, we don't need no thought control… teacher, leave those kids alone!' The chorus was sung by thirteen schoolchildren from Islington Green School in London, who were taken to the Britannia Row record studios to sing on the recording by their music teacher. They never met the group and were not paid for their work. When the head of the school heard the song with its anti-school lyrics, she banned the children from receiving any publicity or from appearing on TV.

Peter Rowan, a royalty expert from Edinburgh, has spent two years trying to find the children, now adults, and he intends to help them make a legal claim for royalties. Mr Rowan said, 'They probably won't get more than a few hundred pounds each, but this is about recognition. They deserve to have their work recognized even if it has taken 25 years.'

Ian Abbott, 40, was one of the children who sang on the record. He said, 'Now I don't agree that "We don't need no education." Education is so important. I really regret that I didn't study more at school. I would like to go to university now and get a degree. But work gets in the way when you get older. Sometimes I say to my nieces, "You must study harder," and they say, "But why? Look at what you sang on that song."'

Mirabai Narayan, another one of the children, now works as a teacher herself. She said, 'I sometimes wonder if the song influenced my career. My job now is to help kids with learning difficulties.'

Adapted from the British press

CAN YOU UNDERSTAND THIS TEXT?

a Read the article and mark the sentences T (true), F (false), or DS (doesn't say).

1 *Another Brick in the Wall* was also successful outside the UK.
2 The children got a little money for singing on the record.
3 The music teacher was a friend of the group Pink Floyd.
4 The head of the school wasn't happy about the song.
5 Peter Rowan was one of the thirteen children.
6 He thinks the children will get a lot of money.
7 Ian Abbott is sorry that he didn't work harder at school.
8 He doesn't have any children of his own.
9 Mirabai Narayan is sure the song made her become a teacher.

b Look at the highlighted words and phrases. Can you guess what they mean?

CAN YOU UNDERSTAND THESE PEOPLE?

a **4.19** Listen and circle the correct answer, a, b, or c.

1 What problem does the teacher want to discuss?
   a A girl copied from Sean.   b Sean cheated in an exam.
   c Sean is lazy.
2 The woman in the pub is…
   a slim with blonde hair.   b tall and dark.
   c short and fat.
3 Which house are they going to buy?
   a The cottage.   b The detached house.
   c They haven't decided.
4 When did Dennis leave school?
   a 1967   b 1971   c 1978
5 When are they going to have lunch?
   a Thursday 2.00   b Thursday 1.00   c Tuesday 1.00

b **4.20** Listen to a conversation between two men talking about a 'flat share' and complete the missing information.

Flat share

1 _____ Bradley Road.
Rent: £2 _____ a month + 3 _____ bills
Room free from 4 _____
5 _____ permit costs £10 a month

CAN YOU SAY THIS IN ENGLISH?

Can you…? Yes (✓)

☐ talk about a school you used to go to (or go to now)
☐ describe your ideal house
☐ talk about a close friend (where and when you met, how often you meet, etc.)

G quantifiers
V noun formation
P -ough and -augh

Slow down, you move too fast

1 GRAMMAR quantifiers

a Answer the questions and compare with a partner.

How much time (approximately) do you spend on a **weekday**...?

- sleeping
- having meals (breakfast, lunch, etc.)
- working (or studying)
- cooking
- doing housework or shopping
- relaxing, doing sport, or seeing friends

b Read the article *Are you happy with your work–life balance?* Which situation is most typical in your country?

c Read the texts again and <u>underline</u> the correct phrases.

d ➲ **p.138 Grammar Bank 5A.** Read the rules and do the exercises.

e Talk in small groups about the things below. Are you happy with your work–life balance?

How much time do you have...?
for yourself
to do exercise
to see friends
to be with your family

How much...do you have?
work
school / university work
English homework
energy

Dan, project manager, software company, Boston, USA

1 I'm not happy with my work–life balance at all. I work at least 50 or 60 hours a week so I don't have ¹*any time* / *no time* at all for myself or to see my children. I communicate with my wife by leaving messages on the fridge. We hardly ever see each other because we work different hours and I never have time to see my friends or keep fit. Also, I eat very badly because my lunch 'hour' (about 10 minutes!) isn't ²*enough long* / *long enough* for me to have a proper meal. OK, I earn ³*a lot of* / *a lot* money but I don't have ⁴*enough time* / *time enough*. Is it worth it?

Amélie, lawyer, Paris, France

2 I didn't use to have ⁵*much time / many time* for anything because I was working ⁶*too much / too many* hours – 45 or more a week. But then here in France the government decided that people should only work 35 hours a week. Nowadays I have ⁷*plenty of / plenty* time for myself. I play tennis two evenings a week, and I finish work at lunchtime on Friday, so I can have long weekends. I am much happier. I think when you have time to enjoy your personal life, you work much better.

Nayuha, store assistant, Tokyo, Japan

3 Yes, I am happy with it because I've chosen a lifestyle that I like and that gives me ⁸*quite a lot of / quite* free time. But my father, on the other hand, works more than 70 hours a week for a car company, which I think is madness. ⁹*Lots of / Much* Japanese people do the same. There's an expression in Japanese, karoshi, which means 'dying because you work ¹⁰*too hard / too much hard*.' A lot of people in Japan get ill or die because they work ¹¹*too / too much*. I think my generation is different. We don't want our lives to be ruled by work. I work ¹²*a few / a little* hours a day in a store – that gives me enough money to live. I spend the rest of my time seeing my friends and playing baseball.

2 PRONUNCIATION -ough and -augh

⚠ Be careful with the letters *ough* and *augh*. They can be pronounced in different ways.

a Write the words in the list in the correct column.

although   bought   brought   caught   daughter
enough   laugh   thought   through   tough

b **5.1** Listen and check. Which is the most common sound? Which three words finish with the sound /f/?

c **5.2** Practise saying the sentences. Then listen and check.
1 I bought some steak but it was very tough.
2 Although it was dark, we walked through the tunnel.
3 I thought I'd brought enough money with me.
4 I laughed when my daughter caught the ball.

3 LISTENING

a **5.3** You are going to hear an expert telling us five ways in which we can slow down in our daily lives. Listen once and complete **Tips** 1–5 with two words.

Tips	Why?
1 Eat breakfast _____ _____.	
2 Forget the _____. Do _____ instead.	
3 Go for a _____ _____.	
4 Spend 10 minutes each day _____ _____.	
5 Have a _____, not a _____.	

b Listen again and write down any other information you can in the **Why?** column. Compare with a partner.

c Which do you think are the best two tips? Do you already do any of them?

5A 69

4 READING & VOCABULARY

a Read the leaflet and match the verbs with their meanings.

We promise to...	
increase	teachers' salaries
reduce	unemployment
promote	national products abroad
encourage	people to do more sport
protect	wildlife
ban	smoking in streets and parks

1 _____ influence somebody in a positive way, e.g. *I … my children to do sport.*

2 _____ to make something bigger, e.g. *The boss is going to … my salary.*

3 _____ to say something is not allowed, often by law, e.g. *We want to … smoking everywhere.*

4 _____ to help something to happen or develop, e.g. *The meeting helped to … better relations.*

5 _____ to make something smaller, e.g. *… the noise, the number of cars.*

6 _____ to defend somebody or something, or keep them safe, e.g. *We need to … these birds as they are becoming extinct.*

b Read the introduction to the article. What is the 'counter-revolution'?

c Work in pairs, **A** and **B**.

A read **Do you eat** 'Slow Food'? and find out the answers to these questions.

1 Who started the Slow Food movement? Why?
2 What did he think was wrong with today's world?
3 What are the aims of the Slow Food movement?
4 How big is the Slow Food movement now?

B read **Would you like to live in a** 'Slow City'? and find out the answers to these questions.

1 How did the Slow City movement start?
2 What are the aims of the Slow City movement?
3 Where has it spread to?
4 What do the people of Aylsham in the UK think about living in a Slow City?

d Cover the article. **A** tell **B** about the Slow Food movement. **B** tell **A** about the Slow City movement.

e Do you think these movements are a good idea?

Slow down, you move too fast

The clock rules our lives. The more we try to save time, the less time we seem to have. In every area of our lives we are doing things faster. And many of us live in towns and cities which are getting noisier and more stressful as each day passes.

But now a worldwide movement, whose aim is to slow life down, has started a counter-revolution. Its supporters are people who believe that a happier and healthier way of life is possible...

Slow Food®   Do you eat 'Slow Food'?

The Slow Food movement was founded the day that an Italian journalist, Carlo Petrini, saw that McDonald's had opened a restaurant in Piazza di Spagna, the beautiful square in Rome. He thought it was tragic that many people today live too quickly to sit down for a proper meal and only eat mass-produced fast food. He decided that he had to try to do something about it and so he started the Slow Food movement. Although he didn't succeed in banning McDonald's from Piazza di Spagna, Slow Food has become a global organization and now has more than 80,000 members in 100 countries.

'We believe,' says Fiona Richmond of Slow Food UK, 'that people should take time to enjoy food.'

Slow Food also encourages people to eat local and regional food, to use local shops and markets, to eat out in small family restaurants, and to cook with traditional recipes. Says Richmond, 'There is nothing more satisfying than relaxing around a lively table in the company of family and friends. The pleasure of eating quality food should be celebrated.'

Would you like to live in a 'Slow City'?

The idea of 'Cittaslow' or 'Slow Cities' was inspired by the Slow Food movement and it was started by the mayor of the small Italian town of Greve in Chianti. The aim of Slow Cities is to make our towns places where people enjoy living and working, and where they value and protect the things that make the town different. Towns which want to become a Slow City have to reduce traffic and noise, increase the number of green areas, plant trees, build pedestrian zones, and promote local businesses and traditions.

Many other small towns in Italy have joined the movement and it has spread to other countries all over the world, from the UK to Japan and Australia. Aylsham in the UK recently became a Slow City, and most people are delighted.

'Slow Cities are about having a community life in the town, so people don't come home from work, shut their doors and that's it,' said a local resident. 'It is not "slow" as in "stupid". It is "slow" as in the opposite of "frantic" and "stressful". It is about quality of life.'

But not everybody in Aylsham is happy. For teenagers, who have to go 25 km to Norwich, the nearest city, to buy trainers or CDs, living in a Slow City is not very attractive. 'It's all right here,' says Lewis Cook, 16. 'But if you want excitement, you have to go to Norwich. We need more things here for young people.'

Adapted from the British press

5 VOCABULARY   noun formation

> ⚠ Nouns are often formed:
> from verbs, by adding -*ment*, -*ion*, -*ation*, and -*al*
> from adjectives by adding -*ness* or -*ity*

a Form nouns from the verbs and adjectives below and write them in the chart.

discuss	govern	happy	mad	move	organize
possible	propose	react	relax	similar	survive

-ment	-ation	-ion

-al	-ness	-ity

b 🔊 **5.4** Listen and check. Underline the stressed syllable in each word. Which ending has a stressed syllable?

6 SPEAKING

a Imagine that your town is thinking of becoming a 'Slow City' and is planning to do the following things:

- Ban all fast food restaurants.
- Promote small family restaurants.
- Ban cars from the city centre.
- Create more pedestrian zones.
- Create more green areas and plant more trees.
- Reduce the speed limit in the town to 30 km/h.
- Use speed bumps and police cameras to control speed.
- Move all big supermarkets outside the city.
- Encourage local shops and ban multinational chain stores.
- Ban loud music in bars and clubs.

Tick (✔) the ones you agree with and cross (✘) the ones you disagree with. Think of reasons.

b Work in groups. Have a 'meeting' to discuss each proposal and then vote for or against it.

Useful language

I'm for / against (banning...)

I think / I don't think it would be a good idea (to create...)

The problem with (reducing...) is that...

I don't think that would work.

That would really make a difference.

c Compare with other groups. Which proposals are the most popular?

G articles: *a / an*, *the*, no article
V verbs and adjectives + prepositions
P sentence stress, *the*, /θ/ or /ð/?

Same planet, different worlds

1 GRAMMAR articles: *a / an*, *the*, no article

a Read the text and complete it with *a / an*, *the*, or – (= no article).
Do you agree with the text?

Five things you don't usually hear a woman say to a man

1 'No thanks. I don't like _____ chocolate.'
2 'I know it's our anniversary _____ next Saturday, but let's not go out. Let's stay in and watch _____ Cup Final on TV.'
3 'I want to buy _____ new car – I really like _____ new BMW. It's got fuel injection and does 180 kilometres _____ hour.'
4 'I'm glad you like _____ beer. I love _____ men with _____ fat stomachs – I find them very attractive.'
5 'Don't worry, I wasn't expecting _____ present. I don't like _____ presents anyway.'

b ⊃ **p.138 Grammar Bank 5B.** Read the rules and do the exercises.

c Read the text and complete it with *a / an*, *the*, or – (= no article).
Do you agree with the text?

Five things you don't usually hear a man say to a woman

1 'I see Brad Pitt has _____ new film out. Would you like to go to _____ cinema tonight and see it?'
2 'I'm completely lost so I'll stop and ask _____ woman over there for directions.'
3 'I thought _____ sheets needed changing so I put them in _____ washing machine.'
4 'I think _____ red dress suits you, but take your time. There are lots of other shops we can try.'
5 'I really admire the way you can go to _____ work, run _____ house, and bring up _____ children so well!'

2 PRONUNCIATION sentence stress, *the*, /θ/ or /ð/?

a **5.5** **Dictation.** Listen and write six sentences. Practise saying them with the correct rhythm. Are articles normally stressed?

b **5.6** Listen and repeat the phrases. When is *the* pronounced /ðə/? How is it pronounced in the other phrases?

the shop	the address	the owner	the sun	the engineer	the world

> ⚠ Remember *th* can be 🗣 e.g. *the*, or 🗣 e.g. *think*.

c **5.7** Listen and circle *th* when it is pronounced /ð/. Then repeat the sentences.

1 That man over there is very wealthy.
2 June is the sixth month of the year.
3 There are three things you have to remember.
4 I threw it away the other day.
5 We have maths in the third term.
6 The athletics track is through that gate.

3 READING & SPEAKING

a In pairs, look at the list of subjects below. Who do you think talks about them more, men or women? Write **M** or **W**.

sport ___ work ___ clothes ___ health ___
family ___ films ___ politics ___ cars ___
their house ___ the opposite sex ___

b Read the first paragraph of *A gossip with the girls?* Does the writer agree with you? Who talks about most topics?

A gossip with the girls?

Women are experts at gossiping, and they always talk about trivial things, or at least that's what men have always thought. However, some new research suggests that when women talk to women, their conversations are far from frivolous, and cover many more topics (up to 40 subjects) than when men talk to other men. Women's conversations range from health to their houses, from politics to fashion, from films to family, from education to relationship problems. Football is notably absent. Men tend to have a more limited range of subjects, the most popular being work, sport, jokes, cars, and women.

According to Professor Petra Boynton, a psychologist at University College London, who interviewed over 1000 women, women also tend to move quickly from one subject to another in conversation, whereas men usually stick to one subject for longer periods of time.

At work, this difference can be an advantage for men, where they can put other matters aside and concentrate fully on the topic being discussed. On the other hand, it also means that they sometimes find it hard to concentrate when several things have to be discussed at the same time in a meeting.

Professor Boynton also says that men and women chat for different reasons. In social situations, women use conversation to solve problems and reduce stress while men chat with each other to have a laugh or to swap opinions.

c Now read the whole article. What does the writer say? Choose a, b, or c.

1 When women talk to each other they generally talk about _____.
   a unimportant things
   b very serious things
   c many different things
2 Men _____ as women.
   a don't talk as much
   b don't talk about as many things
   c don't work as much
3 In conversation women _____ than men.
   a talk more quickly
   b change the subject more often
   c talk more about work
4 At work, if there is a meeting which focuses on one subject, _____.
   a men will probably concentrate better than women
   b women will probably concentrate better than men
   c men and women will both concentrate well
5 One of the reasons why women talk to each other is _____.
   a to relax
   b to exchange ideas
   c to tell jokes

d Now prove that the article is wrong! Work in pairs or small groups.

If you're a woman, try to talk for two minutes about:
football   cars   computers

If you're a man, try to talk for two minutes about:
fashion   shopping   losing weight / dieting

HOW WORDS WORK...

1 Look at the highlighted words and phrases in *A gossip with the girls?* Which one(s) do we use...?
   1 to compare and contrast two facts or opinions *whereas*
   2 to introduce an opposite point of view _____ _____
   3 to introduce some extra information _____
   4 to explain who says or believes something _____

2 Complete the sentences with one of the words or phrases. Sometimes there are two possibilities.
   1 My sister plays tennis and she _____ goes swimming once a week.
   2 Travelling by yourself can be fun. _____, it is often more dangerous.
   3 _____ doctors, we shouldn't drink too much coffee.
   4 Dogs are very affectionate, _____ cats are more independent.
   5 New technology makes our lives easier. _____, it can be difficult to learn to use.

4 LISTENING

a Have you ever been to a spa or health farm? If yes, did you enjoy it? If no, would you like to go? Why (not)?

b Read the introduction to the article. Why did the journalists go to the spa?
Which treatment do you think a) Joanna and b) Stephen will like best?

Spas – women love them. Can men enjoy them too?

The Sunday Times decided to find out. They sent two journalists, Joanna Duckworth and Stephen Bleach, to spend a day at a health spa, which offers thermal baths, saunas and steam rooms, an outdoor swimming pool, and of course a wide variety of massages and treatments.

These are some of the treatments they had:

Banana, papaya and strawberry body polish – a treatment which will smooth and hydrate your skin, with a head massage – 40 minutes.

Kanebo Kai Zen facial – a deep intensive cleansing, with face and neck massage – 1hr 40 minutes.

Elemis foot treatment – a foot bath, pedicure and foot massage – 55 minutes.

c Listen to the two journalists talking after the first treatment and write the information in the chart. Listen again to check. Repeat for the second and third treatments.

	Stephen		Joanna	
	marks out of 10	reasons	marks out of 10	reasons
1 **The body polish** 5.8				
2 **The facial** 5.9				
3 **The foot treatment** 5.10				

d 5.11 Listen to five extracts from the recording. Try to write down the missing word. How do you think you spell it? What do you think it means?

1 It was hot and _____ and incredibly uncomfortable.
2 The head massage was _____!
3 My face feels different – much _____.
4 I just use _____ and water.
5 I love the colour they painted my_____.

e Which of the treatments would *you* choose to have?

5 SPEAKING

Look at *A man thing or a woman thing?* Talk in small groups. In your country who does these things more, men or women? Why do you think this is?

Useful language

Generally speaking / In general, I think women go to spas more than men…

I think it's more common for men to watch football…

I think women tend to read novels more than men…

⚠ Remember not to use an article when you generalize, e.g. I think men… NOT ~~the men~~

A man thing or a woman thing?

- Going shopping
- Going to health spas
- Going to the gym
- Going to the cinema
- Reading novels
- Going to sports events
- Doing housework
- Learning languages
- Going to bars and pubs
- Playing games (e.g. cards, chess)

6 VOCABULARY verbs and adjectives + prepositions

Men think that women always **talk about** trivial things.
In fact, they cover more topics than when men **talk to** men.

a Complete the **prepositions** column.

Verbs	Prepositions
1 Do you often **talk** ___ a friend ___ your problems?	___ ___
2 Do you often **think** ___ the future?	___
3 Do you often have to **wait** ___ a bus or train?	___
4 Do you **agree** ___ your friends about politics?	___
5 What dish or dishes do you usually **ask** ___ in a restaurant?	___
6 Have you ever **borrowed** money ___ your family?	___
7 Do you often **write** emails ___ English-speaking people?	___
8 How often do you **listen** ___ classical music?	___
9 Do you think a man should **pay** ___ dinner on a first date?	___
10 Do you know anyone who **works** ___ a multinational company?	___
11 Do you know anyone who **works** ___ a DJ?	___
12 Are you going to **apply** ___ a job soon?	___

Adjectives	Prepositions
13 Are you **good** ___ sport?	___
14 Are you **bad** ___ remembering birthdays?	___
15 Are men's hobbies very **different** ___ women's hobbies?	___
16 Are you **afraid** ___ any insects?	___
17 Are you **interested** ___ fashion?	___
18 Are you **worried** ___ anything at the moment?	___

b Cover the prepositions column. Work in pairs. A ask B the first question. B ask A the second question. Continue with the rest of the questions.

Then swap roles.

7 ⬤5.12 SONG ♫ *Sk8er Boi*

5C

G gerunds and infinitives
V work
P word stress

Job swap

1 VOCABULARY work

a Look at the picture story and match a sentence with each picture.

A But he was happy because he had a good **salary** and a company car. ☐
B He **applied for** a job with a food **company**, and sent in his **CV**. ☐
C He **was sacked**. Jake was unemployed again… ☐
D After six months he **got promoted**. ☐
E Jake was **unemployed** and was looking for **a job**. ☐
F He had to work very hard and **do overtime**. ☐
G But then he had an argument with his **boss**. ☐
H He **had an interview**, and he **got the job**. ☐

b Cover the sentences and look at the pictures. Tell the story from memory.

c ➡ **p.152 Vocabulary Bank** *Work.*

2 PRONUNCIATION & SPEAKING
word stress

a Underline the stressed syllable in each word. Use the phonetics to help you.

1 apply /əˈplaɪ/
2 contract /ˈkɒntrækt/
3 employee /ɪmplɔɪˈiː/
4 experience /ɪkˈspɪəriəns/
5 overtime /ˈəʊvətaɪm/
6 permanent /ˈpɜːmənənt/
7 qualifications /kwɒlɪfɪˈkeɪʃnz/
8 resign /rɪˈzaɪn/
9 retire /rɪˈtaɪə/
10 temporary /ˈtemprəri/

b **5.13** Listen and check. Practise saying the words.

c Talk to a partner.

Do you know anybody who…

• is applying for a job? What kind of job?
• has just retired? How old is he / she?
• has been promoted recently? What to?
• does a lot of overtime? Why?
• was sacked from his / her job? Why?
• is self-employed? What does he / she do?
• is doing a temporary job? What?
• has a part-time job? What hours does he / she work?

3 GRAMMAR gerunds and infinitives

a Complete sentences 1–16 in the questionnaire. Put the verbs in the gerund, e.g. *working*, or the infinitive + *to*, e.g. *to work*.

b Read the sentences and tick (✔) **only** the ones that you **strongly** agree with. Compare your answers with another student.

c Now see in which group(s) you have most ticks. Read the paragraphs on the right to find out which jobs would suit you. Would you like to do any of them?

d Look at the sentences in the questionnaire. Complete the rules with **the gerund** or **infinitive** + *to*.

1 After some verbs,
   e.g. *enjoy, don't mind* use… _____
2 After some verbs,
   e.g. *want, would like* use… _____
3 After adjectives, use… _____
4 After prepositions, use… _____
5 As the subject of
   a phrase or sentence, use… _____

e ◗ **p.138 Grammar Bank 5C.** Read the rules and do the exercises.

The right job for you
– match your personality to the job

1 I am good at _listening_ to people.	listen
2 I enjoy _____ people with their problems.	help
3 I don't mind _____ a very large salary.	not earn
4 I'd like _____ as part of a team.	work

If you have most ticks in 1–4, the best job for you would be in the 'caring professions'. If you are good at science, you could think of medicine, for example a doctor or nurse. Alternatively, teaching or social work are areas which would suit your personality.

5 I am good at _____ quick decisions.	make
6 _____ risks doesn't stress me.	take
7 I don't find it difficult _____ by myself.	work
8 I'm not afraid of _____ large amounts of money.	manage

If you have most ticks in 5–8, you should consider a job in the world of business, for example sales or marketing. Other possibilities include accountancy or working in the stock market.

9 I am good at _____ myself.	express
10 I always try _____ my instincts.	follow
11 It's important for me _____ creative.	be
12 I enjoy _____.	improvise

If you have most ticks in 9–12, you need a creative job. Depending on your specific talents you might enjoy a job in the world of music, art, or literature. Areas that would suit you include publishing, journalism, graphic design, fashion, or the music industry.

13 _____ complex calculations is not difficult for me.	do
14 I enjoy _____ logical problems.	solve
15 I find it easy _____ theoretical principles.	understand
16 I am able _____ space and distance.	calculate

If you have most ticks in 13–16, you have an analytical mind. A job in computer science or engineering would suit you. You also have good spatial sense which would make architecture and related jobs another possibility.

f Choose **five** of the topics below and tell your partner about them.

- somewhere you'd **like to go to** this weekend
- somebody you find **difficult to talk to**
- something you found **easy to learn**
- something you **prefer doing** by yourself
- something you've **decided to do** soon
- something you **enjoy doing** on Sunday mornings
- something you **regret buying**
- something you often **forget to do**
- something you're **afraid of doing**
- a job **you'd love to be able to do** (but think you couldn't)

4 READING

a Read the title of the article. What kind of personality do you think you need to be a good political reporter?

b Read the text and put these headings in the right place.

The challenge   The contestant
The teachers   The training
~~The programme~~

c In pairs, find the following words in the text:

1 A person who takes part in a competition
   contestant

2 A person who writes about the news in a newspaper or speaks about it on TV
   _____

3 A person who decides how criminals should be punished or who decides the result or winner of a competition
   _____

4 A person who works in the media (newspapers, magazines, TV, or radio)
   _____

5 A person who is a Member of Parliament (abbreviation)
   _____

6 A person whose job is concerned with politics _____

d ◗ **Communication** *Test your memory A p.117 B p.120.* Who can remember most about the programme?

e Do you think Jessica will pass the test? Why (not)?

From librarian to political reporter... In a month!

How Jessica went from working in a local library to interviewing politicians on TV in just 28 days

1 _The programme_
The Pretenders is a very successful and popular TV series. In each programme there is a contestant who has just four weeks to learn to do a completely new job. At the end of the month the contestant has to do a 'test', where he or she has to do the new job together with three other real professionals. A panel of three judges has to decide which of the four people is pretending to be a professional. Sometimes they spot who is pretending, but sometimes they don't!

2_____
Jessica Winters is a 26-year-old librarian who lives in Southampton with her parents. She studied English Literature at the University of Bath before getting a job in her local library. She didn't know it, but two of her friends sent her name to the TV company to take part in *The Pretenders*. 'When someone from the programme phoned me, I thought it was a joke', said Jessica. 'First of all I said no, but they asked me to think about it. In the end my friends and family persuaded me to say yes.'

3_____
Jessica had four weeks to turn from a quiet, shy, librarian into a confident TV reporter. At the end of the month she had to do her final test. This was a live TV interview with the Minister of Education. She had to try to make the judges think that she really was a professional reporter.

4_____
An experienced political journalist, Adam Bowles, and ex-MP Sally Lynch had the job of transforming Jessica. When they first met her, they were not very optimistic. 'Jessica needs to be a lot tougher. She's much too sweet and shy,' said Adam. 'Politicians will eat her alive.' They had just 28 days to teach her to be a reporter...

5_____
Jessica had to spend the month in London. She was completely isolated from her family and friends – she could only talk to them on the phone. The training was very hard work. She had to learn how to interview people, how to look more confident, how to speak clearly. She also had to learn about the world of politics. 'I'm feeling really nervous,' said Jessica. 'I'm terrified of the idea of being on TV. Also I've never been interested in politics – I don't know anything about it – I didn't even vote in the last elections.'

5 LISTENING

You're going to hear Jessica and her teacher Adam talking about how she did in her four weeks on *The Pretenders*. Listen to each week and answer the questions in pairs.

Week 1 5.14

1 What did Adam and Sally think of Jessica?

2 According to Adam, what two problems did Jessica have?

3 What three things did Jessica have to do this week?

4 How did she feel at the end of the week?

Week 2 5.15

5 How did Jessica change her image?

6 What did she learn to do this week?

7 What did she have to do at 10 Downing Street?

8 Was she successful? Why (not)?

Week 3 5.16

9 What did Adam think about Jessica?

10 What did she have to do this week?

11 What mistake did she make?

12 What did Adam say that Jessica needed to do?

Week 4 5.17

13 What was Jessica's final test? How did she feel about it?

14 Did the interview go well for Jessica? Why (not)?

15 Did the judges realize that Jessica wasn't a professional reporter?

16 Would Jessica like to become a reporter? Why (not)?

6 SPEAKING

Talk to a partner. Imagine you were asked to appear on the programme. Look at the list of jobs that other contestants trained to do. Which ones would / wouldn't you like to learn to do? Why?

football coach   dog trainer   rock singer   mechanic   TV director   stuntman   chef   DJ   car salesman

Useful language

I wouldn't like…   I wouldn't mind…   I think I'd enjoy…   I think I'd be (quite) good at…   I'd be terrible at…

GIVING OPINIONS

a **5.18** Cover the dialogue. Listen to Allie, Mark, and Jacques discussing promotion for Scarlett's CD. Who has the best idea? What is it?

b Read the dialogue. In pairs, what do you think the missing words are? **Don't write them in yet.**

Allie	That was a great concert last night, Scarlett.
Scarlett	Thanks.
Allie	As we know, Scarlett's got a new CD coming out soon. So let's have a look at the best way we can promote it in France.
Mark	OK, well I think Scarlett _____ visit the major music stores. In my _____, that's the best way to meet her fans.
Allie	I'm not so _____. What do you _____, Jacques?
Jacques	Actually, I don't _____ with Mark. Scarlett isn't commercial in that way.
Allie	Scarlett? Scarlett?
Scarlett	I agree _____ Jacques. I don't have a commercial image. It isn't my style.
Mark	OK, but Scarlett needs more publicity. What about a series of TV and radio interviews? _____ you agree?
Allie	Yes, but that's what everybody does. What we want is something different.
Jacques	_____, I think Scarlett should tour clubs and summer festivals. She can DJ, play her favourite music, play the new CD, and meet her fans, too.
Allie	Yes, _____! That's a much better idea. Mark?
Mark	OK, why not?
Allie	Scarlett?
Scarlett	I think that's a _____ idea. Thank you, Jacques.

c Listen again and complete the dialogue.

d **5.19** Listen and repeat the highlighted phrases. Copy the rhythm.

e Look at the highlighted phrases in the dialogue. Put them in the right column in the chart.

Asking people what they think	Saying what *you* think	Agreeing / Disagreeing
What do you think?	*I think…*	*I'm not so sure.*

f ○ **Communication** *What do you think? A p.117 B p.120.* In small groups, give your opinion.

SOCIAL ENGLISH   Why is she smiling?

a **5.20** Listen. Who do they see in the Louvre?

b Listen again and answer the questions.

1 Has Mark been to the Louvre before?
2 Why isn't he very happy?
3 What does Allie say about the meeting?
4 What two theories about the Mona Lisa does Allie mention?
5 What's Mark's theory?
6 Why do they leave in a hurry?

USEFUL PHRASES

What's the m_____?

It's not a big d_____.

You're k_____.

Now I don't know much a_____ (art)…

That's really un_____!

Don't t_____ round!

Let's g_____ out of here.

c **5.21** Complete the USEFUL PHRASES. Listen and check.

d Listen again and repeat the phrases. How do you say them in your language?

Study Link MultiROM

a Look at the job advertisement. Which job could <u>you</u> apply for?

b Complete the CV (Curriculum Vitae) with a heading from the list.

Additional information   Career history   Computer skills
Education   Languages   ~~Personal information~~

c Read the covering letter. Circle the more formal phrase in each pair.

The Olympic Committee is looking for dedicated, enthusiastic, and energetic people to work in different areas for the forthcoming Olympic Games. There are vacancies in the following areas:

• Administration   • Translation and language services
• Hospitality and catering   • Medical support

All applicants must be appropriately qualified and a good level of English is essential. Send your CV and a covering letter (in English) to:
Job applications: The Olympic Committee, PO Box 2456

Mehmet Bolat

[1]*Personal information*

Address	Alper Apt. Daire 3 Turgut Özal Caddesi Seyhan, Adana
Telephone	home: 0090 322 6587688 mobile: 0090 535 9428190
Nationality	Turkish
Marital status	Single
Date of birth	12th September 1982
Email	bolatmehmet@superonline.com.tr

[2] _____

2006–   Junior physiotherapist at Rehabilitation Centre, Balcal̇ University Hospital, Adana
I work mainly with patients who need rehabilitation after an operation. In my free time, I also work as a physiotherapist for a local basketball team.

[3] _____

2001–2005   Degree in physiotherapy, University of Gaziantep
1997–2001   Atatürk High School, Adana

[4] _____

English (CEF level B2). I have a good level of written and spoken English.
I have been studying English at a private language school for the last three years.
German (fluent). My mother is German.

[5] _____

Windows XP

[6] _____

Full driving licence
Member of the university basketball team

Alper Apt. Daire 3
Turgut Özal Caddesi
Seyhan, Adana
30th April

Olympic Committee
PO Box 2456

Dear Sir / Madam,

[1]*I am writing / I'm writing* to apply for a job with the medical support staff in the forthcoming Olympic Games.

I am a qualified physiotherapist and [2]*I've been working / I have been working* at a Rehabilitation Centre here since January 2006. I have a good level of English, and [3]*my German is great / I speak German fluently.*

[4]*I enclose / I'm sending you* my CV as requested.

[5]*Hope to hear from you soon. / I look forward to hearing from you.*

[6]*Best wishes / Yours faithfully*

Mehmet Bolat

Mehmet Bolat

d Complete the **Useful language** box with *Yours sincerely* and *Yours faithfully*.

Useful language: a formal letter

Formal letters	Start	Finish
You don't know the person's name	Dear Sir / Madam	_____
You know the person's surname	Dear Mr / Ms / Mrs García	_____

Layout / style
• Put your address in the top right-hand corner with the date underneath.
• Put the name and address of the person you are writing to on the left.
• Don't use contractions.
• Write your full name under your signature.
• Put *I look forward to hearing from you* if you would like a reply.

WRITE your CV and a covering letter to apply for a job in the Olympics.

PLAN what you're going to write. Use the **Useful language** box and **Vocabulary Bank** *Work* **p.152** to help you.

CHECK the letter for mistakes (grammar , punctuation , and spelling).

GRAMMAR

a Choose a, b, or c.

1 I'm not very good at _____ sport.
   a the   b a   c –

2 He always gets _____ late on Fridays.
   a to home   b to the home   c home

3 There are _____ people in this class.
   a too many   b too much   c too

4 _____ is one of the best forms of exercise.
   a Swim   b Swimming   c Swiming

5 I bought a laptop _____ when I'm travelling.
   a for use   b for to use   c to use

b Complete the second sentence with **two words** so that it means the same as the first.

I really think it's important for you to learn to drive.
You _must_ _learn_ to drive.

1 When they left they didn't lock the door.
They left _____ _____ the door.

2 There aren't very many trees in our street.
There are only _____ _____ trees in our street.

3 It takes him a long time to get up in the morning.
He spends a long time _____ _____ in the morning.

4 Renting a flat is very difficult here.
It's very difficult _____ _____ a flat here.

5 This house is too small for us.
This house isn't _____ _____ for us.

| | 10 |

VOCABULARY

a Complete with a noun from the **bold** word.

1 I think the _____ will lose the next election.   **govern**
2 What was his _____? Was he angry?   **react**
3 My _____ depends on you.   **happy**
4 They said on the radio that there's a _____ of snow tonight.   **possible**
5 You don't need any special _____ to do this job.   **qualify**

b Complete with a preposition.

1 I've applied _____ a job with British Airways.
2 Don't worry _____ anything!
3 I really don't agree _____ you.
4 Are you good _____ science?
5 Are you still _____ university or have you finished?
6 She works _____ a flight attendant.

c Complete the missing words.

1 I have to do a lot of o_____ in my new job. Sometimes I don't finish until 9 p.m.
2 Could I have a day o_____ next Friday? It's my cousin's wedding.
3 He argued with his boss and he was s_____. Now he's unemployed.
4 If you work hard, you may get p_____ to manager.
5 She has a good job and gets a very big s_____.
6 It's a temporary job. I only have a six-month c_____.
7 I'm going to a_____ for a job in a bookshop. I hope I get it!
8 I'm s_____-e_____. I work at home as a translator.
9 If he doesn't like his job, he'll r_____ after the first six months.

| | 20 |

PRONUNCIATION

a <u>Underline</u> the word with a different sound.

1	↑	enough	company	much	movement
2	🚲	afraid	retire	overtime	apply
3	e	many	temporary	regret	prefer
4	🐦	work	short	permanent	earn
5	🐍	resign	boss	salary	works

b <u>Underline</u> the stressed syllable.

| employee | unemployed | responsible | temporary | experience |

| | 10 |

CAN YOU UNDERSTAND THIS TEXT?

The secret to a long and happy life is... being lazy!

Joggers who get up early and run through the park, executives who try to work off stress with a game of squash, and people who do bodybuilding may all be shortening their lives. According to Peter Axt, a German researcher and ex-marathon runner, laziness is good for you.

'No top sportsman,' says Axt, 'has lived to a very advanced age.' Among the examples of athletes who have died young, he mentions Jim Fixx, the author of *The Complete Book of Running*, and the man who almost single-handedly launched the American fitness revolution. He died at the age of 52. As Axt says, 'Better not to start'.

With his daughter Michaela, a doctor, he has written a book called *The Joy of Laziness*. It says that there are three keys to long life: to play less sport, to reduce stress, and to eat less food. He gives the example of an Italian village with an unusually high number of centenarians which seems to owe its communal good health to following the Axt principles. No one runs, siestas stretch through the afternoon from 1p.m. to 4 p.m., and the main activity seems to be sitting in the shade or gossiping.

The Axts' ideas are based on research which argues that animals have only a limited amount of energy. Those who use up energy quickly live for a shorter time than those who conserve energy. So an executive who wants to compensate for a stressful day by going to the gym is in fact multiplying his problems.

However, Peter Axt believes that *light* exercise is beneficial. 'I jog gently for 20 minutes three or four times a week,' he said, 'but I have no time for men over 50 who insist on running several kilometres a day.'

a Read the article and mark the sentences T (true), F (false), or DS (doesn't say).

1 Peter Axt regularly runs marathons.
2 He says that people who do too much sport will probably die younger.
3 Jim Fixx got Americans to do more sport.
4 *The Joy of Laziness* is a bestseller.
5 The book says that the only important thing to help you live longer is to do less sport.
6 In the Italian village people are very healthy but not very active.
7 The book's ideas are based on five years' research.
8 He thinks that if you've had a very tiring day at work then you shouldn't do physical exercise.
9 Axt doesn't have time to run several kilometres a day.

b Look at the highlighted words and phrases. Can you guess what they mean?

CAN YOU UNDERSTAND THESE PEOPLE?

a **5.22** Listen and circle the correct answer, a, b, or c.

1 How many bookshops are there in the town?
   a None   b One   c Two
2 Where are the women going to have lunch?
   a Roberto's   b Trattoria Marco
   c Garibaldi's
3 Who's going to choose the film?
   a The man.   b The woman.
   c The man and the woman.
4 The man has…
   a qualifications but no experience.
   b experience but no qualifications.
   c experience and qualifications.
5 The girl thinks she wants to…
   a do research.   b be a doctor.
   c be a biologist.

b **5.23** You will hear a man and a woman talking about buying a car. Mark the sentences T (True) or F (False).

1 The woman says she prefers the Volvo.
2 The man thinks the Golf is too small.
3 The woman damaged their car when she was trying to park.
4 The Volvo is cheaper than the Golf.
5 In the end, the man and the woman can't decide what to buy.

CAN YOU SAY THIS IN ENGLISH?

Can you...? Yes (✓)

☐ talk about your town and its facilities
☐ talk about your work–life balance
☐ say what men and women usually talk about
☐ talk about a member of your family's job, and about the job you have or would like to have

6A

G reported speech: statements, questions, and commands
V shopping
P consonant sounds: /g/, /dʒ/, /k/, /ʃ/, /tʃ/

Love in the supermarket

1 GRAMMAR reported speech: statements and questions

a Read the short story and look at the pictures. In pairs, guess the last word.

Love in the supermarket

They met next to the washing powder. By the cereals, they told each other their life stories. When they were choosing vegetables, he told her that he was falling in love with her. In front of the frozen food, he asked her if she would marry him and she said yes. But at the chocolates, they had their first argument. When they were queuing to pay, they decided that it was all _____.

b Now complete the speech bubbles with A–K.

A Will you marry me?

B I'll see you around. Bye.

C Yes, I will.

D I work in advertising.

E I don't think you're really my type.

F ~~Do you need any help?~~

G Do you know how many calories there are in a bar of chocolate?

H Thanks. My name's Olga.

I I'm a student. What do you do?

J Olga, I'm falling in love with you.

K Are you saying I'm fat?

c (6.1) Listen and check.

d Write the sentence and question below in reported speech. Then look at the short story to check your answer.

'I'm falling in love with you.'

He told her (that) _____ .

'Will you marry me?'

He asked her if _____ .

e ○ **p.140 Grammar Bank 6A.** Read the rules for reported speech: statements and questions, and do exercise **a** only.

f Look at pictures 1–6. Tell the story in reported speech.

He asked her if she needed any help…

Do you need any help?

2 VOCABULARY shopping

a In pairs, say if you think these are the same or different and why.

1 a supermarket and a market
2 a chemist and a pharmacy
3 a shopping centre and a department store
4 a shopping centre and a shopping mall
5 a library and a bookshop

b What are the last three shops you have been to? What kind of shops are they? What did you buy?

c ⟳ **p.153 Vocabulary Bank** *Shopping.*

3 PRONUNCIATION consonant sounds: /g/, /dʒ/, /k/, /ʃ/, /tʃ/

a 🔊 6.2 Listen and cross out the word with a different sound.

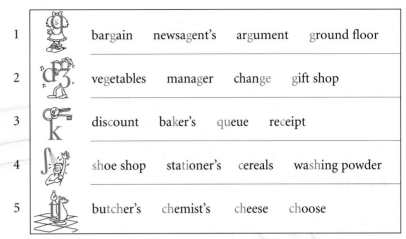

1	bargain	newsagent's	argument	ground floor
2	vegetables	manager	change	gift shop
3	discount	baker's	queue	receipt
4	shoe shop	stationer's	cereals	washing powder
5	butcher's	chemist's	cheese	choose

b 🔊 6.3 Listen and repeat the sentences. Practise saying them.

1 You can't get cheese at a chemist's!
2 I had an argument with the manager of the gift shop.
3 I had to queue for ages at the baker's.
4 Could you give me the receipt for the shoes, please?
5 My new green jacket was a bargain.

c ⟳ **p.159 Sound Bank.** Look at the typical spellings for these sounds.

4 SPEAKING

Interview another student with the questionnaire. Ask for more information.

The shopping
QUESTIONNAIRE

Shops

- What kind of small shops are there near where you live?
- What kind of shops do you most like going to?
- What are your favourite shops for…?
  a clothes   c books and music
  b shoes   d presents
- Do you ever shop in…?
  a street markets
  b supermarkets
  c shopping centres

Shopping

- How often do you go shopping?
- Do you prefer shopping by yourself or with somebody?
- What do you enjoy buying?
- What do you hate buying?
- Do you like shopping in the sales? What do you usually buy?
- Where do you go if you want to find a bargain?
- Do you ever shop online? What for?

5 READING

Making a complaint – is it worth it?

IF YOU WANT MY ADVICE... BUY A NEW ONE.

A ☐ As the machine was no longer under guarantee, Mr Thomas called a local repairer. He charged him £45 to look at it and then told him that he would need to spend £650 plus VAT for a new part. Then he took the laptop to a well-known computer retailer – and they told him to buy a new one!

B ☐ Another customer's experience shows that it's worth complaining to the top people of a company if the local company staff are unhelpful.

C ☐ 'Four days later, someone called me to say the DVD recorder was waiting for me and I could collect 10 recordable DVD discs to compensate for my wasted time,' he says. 'And when I collected them I was treated like royalty.'

D ☐ Mark Oakley from Norfolk wanted to buy a recordable DVD player. At his local branch of *Argos*, a shop which sells electrical goods, they told him that they didn't have the one he wanted in stock, but that they were expecting a delivery 'soon'. However, when he went back, it still hadn't arrived.

E ☐1 Is it really worth complaining when goods or services are not satisfactory? According to a new report from the consumer magazine *Which?*, it certainly is. As they point out, the old saying 'if you don't ask, you don't get' is true for many situations, but particularly so when it comes to compensation. Take the case of Mike Thomas from Cornwall. He bought a Toshiba laptop computer, but just three years later he found that it was getting slower and slower.

F ☐ He returned twice more over the following weeks but each time they told him to come back in a week. He started phoning and trying to reserve the machine instead. But after several weeks of phoning unsuccessfully, Mr Oakley lost patience and wrote to the managing director of *Argos*.

G ☐ However, Mr Thomas still felt that his computer should not be out of date after just three years. He decided to write a letter of complaint to Toshiba. A short time later, the company collected the laptop, diagnosed a software problem, repaired it, and returned it with a new battery, all without charge. 'I'd call that outstanding service,' said Mr Thomas.

Adapted from the British press

a If you have a problem with something you've bought, or with the service in a shop, do you usually complain? Who to? If not, why not?

b Read the article about complaining and number the paragraphs in order 1–7.

c Read the article again in the right order and complete the chart.

	Mr Thomas	Mr Oakley
1 What did he complain about?		
2 What was the problem?		
3 How did he try to solve it?		
4 Why wasn't he successful?		
5 Who did he write to?		
6 What happened as a result?		

d Match the highlighted words or phrases with their meanings.

1 _____ a shop or office which is part of a larger organization
2 _____ employees
3 _____ things that are for sale
4 _____ available in the shop
5 _____ things that other people do for you, e.g. repair your TV
6 _____ money or things you give somebody because you have treated them badly
7 _____ a written promise from a company that it will repair something if it breaks in a certain period of time

e Now read the last part of the article. Complete the tips with a phrase from below. Which two tips do you think are the most important?

| Be reasonable | Keep a record | Don't lose your temper |
| Act quickly | Always go to the top | |

Top tips for complaining

1 _____ when there's a problem and give the company a chance to sort it out.

2 _____ , and ask to speak to the manager. He / She is the one who can compensate you.

3 _____ – note the date, time, and name of the person you've spoken to, and what was agreed.

4 _____ . Getting angry won't help at all.

5 _____ – if a company apologizes and makes a genuine effort to compensate you, be prepared to meet it halfway.

6 GRAMMAR reported speech: commands

a Look at the sentences below from the article. What do you think were the exact words the shop assistants used?

> 1 They told him to buy a new one.
> 2 They told him to come back in a week.

b Look at pictures 1–4. Complete the sentences with a positive or negative infinitive (e.g. *to be* or *not to be*).

1 She asked the shop assistant _____ her a refund.

2 He told the people at the next table _____ so much noise.

3 She asked the receptionist _____ her room.

4 He told the taxi driver _____ so fast.

c ➡ **p.140 Grammar Bank 6A.** Read the rules for reported speech: commands and do exercise **b**.

7 LISTENING & SPEAKING

a **6.4** Listen to part of a radio consumer programme where people are talking about bad service, and answer the questions.

The taxi

1 Why did the man get annoyed?
2 What did he ask the taxi driver to do?
3 What happened in the end?

The hotel

4 What problems were there with the woman's room?
5 What happened when she told the receptionist?
6 What did she tell him to do? Did he do it?

The restaurant

7 Why did the man ask the waitress to change his ravioli?
8 Why wasn't he happy with the bill?
9 What happened in the end?

b Talk to a partner.

1 Who's best at complaining in your family? Why?
2 Can you remember a time when you (or someone in your family) complained…?

   to a taxi driver
   to a hotel receptionist
   to a waiter
   to someone else

Why did you complain? What did you ask the person to do? What happened?

c ➡ **Communication** *I want to speak to the manager A p.118 B p.121.* Roleplay complaining in a shop and a restaurant.

6 B

G passive: *be* + past participle
V cinema
P sentence stress

See the film...get on a plane

1 READING

a Have you ever seen a film which made you want to go to the place where the film was made?

b Read the article and try to complete each text with the name of the film and the country where it was made. Use the photos to help you.

Famous films that moved us (literally!)

Sometimes when you see a film, the sense of place is so strong that it makes you think 'I have to go there one day'. Here are three films, from three different decades, that have made thousands of people pack their cases and catch a plane. There's travel information too, in case you want to go there yourself...

1

The film is set in the 1990s on a small tropical island. It is based on a best-selling book by the young author Alex Garland and it was directed by the British director, Danny Boyle. It's about a young traveller (played by Leonardo DiCaprio) who finds a group of young people living on a beautiful, uninhabited island. But paradise soon turns into a nightmare...

Where was it filmed?
The film was shot on the beautiful island of Phi Phi Leh in   , which is now visited by more than a million tourists every year. Most of the hotels were destroyed in 2004 by the tsunami but they have now been rebuilt.

How do I get there?
Fly to Phuket International airport and travel to the island by boat or small plane.

2

This film was nominated for 11 Oscars and it won seven. It's about a Danish writer (Meryl Streep) who goes to Africa to help her husband run a coffee plantation. To her surprise, she finds herself falling in love with the country, the people, and a mysterious white hunter (Robert Redford). The film was based on an autobiographical novel by the Danish writer, Isak Dinesen, and was directed by the American director Sydney Pollack.

Where was it filmed?
The story is set in   in 1914 and was shot on location in the Masai Mara National Park. Apart from the actors, the 'stars' of the film are the breathtaking scenery and the exotic wildlife, which look so wonderful on the big screen. The film also had an unforgettable soundtrack guaranteed to move even the most unromantic.

The film won the Oscar for Best Picture and the following year tourism replaced agriculture as the country's top industry.

How do I get there?
Fly to Nairobi and then drive to the Masai Mara National Reserve where the cast and film crew lived during filming. Then take a three-day safari to see giraffes, elephants, lions, and much more.

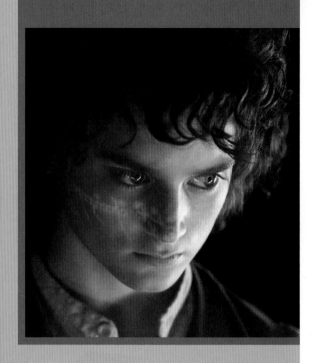

3 _____

This trilogy of films won a total of 17 Oscars, including Best Picture and Best Director.

They are based on the books written by JRR Tolkien. They tell the story of a hobbit, Frodo Baggins, who has to try and destroy a magic ring in order to defeat the evil forces of the Dark Lord Sauron. He is helped on his journey by a group of friends.

Where was it filmed?

The story is set in an imaginary land called Middle Earth. All three films were filmed in _____, which was chosen because of its magnificent and dramatic scenery. The director of the film, Peter Jackson, was born there. The success of the films has attracted thousands of tourists to the country, and last year it was voted the most popular holiday destination by UK travellers.

How do I get there?

You can either fly to Auckland or Wellington, the capital city (where you will be greeted by a huge sign saying 'Welcome to Middle Earth'). From there you can travel to visit all the fantastic film locations, including the battlefields. There are guided tours by road or helicopter.

c Read the article again and answer the questions.

Which film(s)…?

1 had three parts
2 were based on a book
3 was set at the beginning of the 20th century
4 was set in a place where later there was a natural disaster
5 was filmed in a wildlife park
6 didn't win an Oscar
7 was a romantic film
8 was directed by a man born in the country where the film was made

d Answer the questions.

Have you seen any of these films? Did you like it / them?
Which of the three places would you most like to visit?

2 GRAMMAR   passive: *be* + past participle

a Read about *The Beach* again. Underline an example of the present passive, the past passive, and the present perfect passive. How do you form the passive?

b Look at the active sentences in the chart below and underline the verbs. What tense are they? In pairs, complete the chart with passive verbs.

Active	Passive
Films inspire people to travel.	People _are inspired_ to travel by films.
Sydney Pollack directed *Out of Africa*.	*Out of Africa* _was directed_ by Sydney Pollack.
They're making the film on location.	The film _____ on location.
They will release the film next year.	The film _____ next year.
Thousands of fans have visited the country.	The country _____ by thousands of fans.

c ➡ **p.140 Grammar Bank 6B.** Read the rules and do the exercises.

3 PRONUNCIATION   sentence stress

a **6.5** **Dictation.** Listen and write six passive sentences.

b Listen again. Underline the stressed words.

c Listen and repeat the sentences. Copy the rhythm.

4 VOCABULARY cinema

a Try to remember words or phrases from **READING** on p.88 and 89 which mean…

1 the music from a film.   the **s**_____
2 the person who makes a film.   the **d**_____
3 all the actors in a film.   the **c**_____
4 all the people who make a film.   the **f**_____ **c**_____
5 (filmed) in the real place, not in a studio.   **o**_____ **l**_____
6 the part of a cinema or TV where the image appears.   the **s**_____

b Look at **READING** (text 2) again and check your answers.

c ⭕ **p.154 Vocabulary Bank** *Cinema.*

5 SPEAKING

a Read the questionnaire and think about your answers.

b In pairs, interview each other. Do you have similar tastes?

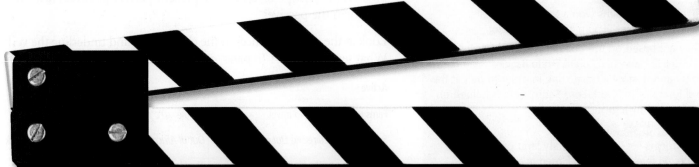

The cinema questionnaire

1 Can you think of a film which…?
made you laugh a lot
made you cry
sent you to sleep
made you feel good
you've seen several times
made you buy the soundtrack

3 Think of a really good film you've seen this year:
Where was it set? When?
Who was in it? Who was it directed by?
Did it have a good plot?
What was the soundtrack like?

2 Do you prefer…?
seeing films on TV or DVD, or in the cinema
seeing foreign films dubbed or with subtitles
films from your country or American films

4 Have you ever…?
met a film actor or director
used a video camera
appeared in any kind of film
seen a film being made

To Dagmara, You have been the most valuable help to me and this film and I am eternally grateful.

Your friend,
Steven Spielberg

a Look at the photograph. In pairs, answer the questions.

1 Who do you think the man and woman are?
2 Where do you think they are?
3 What film do you think was being made?
4 What do you think is happening?

b **6.6** Listen to the first part of an interview with Dagmara and check your answers to **a**.

c Listen again and answer these questions.

1 Where does Dagmara live?
2 What was she doing before the shooting of the film started?
3 Was that her real job?
4 Where did she meet Spielberg?
5 What did she have to do there? Why?
6 How well did she do it?
7 What happened afterwards?

d **6.7** Now listen to the second part of the interview and then make notes under the headings below.

> **What she had to do during the film**
> *go to the film set every day, translate*
>
> **The most difficult thing about the job**
>
> **The worst moment**
>
> **What it was like to work with Spielberg**
>
> **Her opinion of the film**
>
> **How she feels when she watches the film**

e Compare with a partner. Then listen again and complete your notes.

G relative clauses: defining and non-defining
V what people do
P word stress

I need a hero

1 GRAMMAR relative clauses

a In pairs, do the quiz. Choose a, b, or c. Compare with another pair and then check with your teacher.

What do you know about...

1 He was born in…
a Cuba   b Colombia   c Argentina

2 His first name was…
a Alejandro   b Ernesto   c Eduardo

3 At university he studied…
a law   b politics   c medicine

4 He helped…**in the Cuban Revolution.**
a Fidel Castro   b Eva Perón   c Emiliano Zapata

5 He was captured and shot in…
a Chile   b Bolivia   c Venezuela

6 When he died he was in his late…
a twenties   b thirties   c forties

7 He died in…
a 1960   b 1967   c 1973

b Look at the photos and cover the texts. Guess what the connection is between each of the things, people, or places and Che Guevara.

c Now read texts A–E and check.

d Cover the texts. Complete the sentences with **who, whose, which,** or **where.**

1 The film, _____ theme song won an Oscar, is based on the motorbike journey _____ Che made with Alberto across South America.

2 It was the poverty _____ he saw on this trip _____ made him decide that revolution was the only answer to South America's problems.

3 Gael García Bernal is the actor _____ played Che.

4 Rosario is the town in Argentina _____ Ernesto 'Che' Guevara was born.

5 The photo, _____ was taken in 1960, is probably one of the best-known photos in the world.

6 The people _____ wear Che T-shirts tend to be people _____ don't conform.

e Compare your sentences 1 and 2 with text **A.** Find three differences.

f ○ **p.140 Grammar Bank 6C.** Read the rules and do the exercises.

g Cover the text and look at the photos. Can you remember the connections with Che?

Che Guevara?

a Norton 500cc motorbike

Alberto Korda

Aleidita

Gael García Bernal

Rosario

A This is the motorbike that was used in the film *The Motorcycle Diaries*. It is a 1939 Norton 500cc, which is the same model as the motorbike that belonged to Che's friend Alberto. The film, whose theme song won an Oscar, is based on the motorbike journey Che made with Alberto across South America. Che was from a rich family in Argentina and it was the poverty he saw on this trip that made him decide that revolution was the only answer to South America's problems.

B **Gael García Bernal** is the actor who played Che in the film *The Motorcycle Diaries*. He is from Guadalajara in Mexico, and has also starred in *And your mother too* and Pedro Almodovar's *Bad Education*.

C **Rosario** is the town in Argentina where Ernesto 'Che' Guevara was born on 14th May 1928. He was the first of five children, and his parents, Ernesto and Celia, were political radicals. From the age of two the young Che suffered from asthma, but his father told him that learning to live with his illness would make him a stronger person.

D **Alberto Korda** was the photographer whose photo now appears on T-shirts and posters all over the world. The photo, which was taken in 1960, is probably one of the best-known photos in the world – but Korda never received a penny in royalties. However, five years ago he took the people who had made money from the photo to court, and won £30,000, which he gave to the Cuban health service.

E **Aleidita**, daughter of Che and his second wife Aleida, was his favourite child. She says that she doesn't think that Che would mind that his photo has been so commercialized. 'Look at the people who wear Che T-shirts,' she says. 'They tend to be people who don't conform, who are wondering if they can be better human beings. My father would have liked that.'

2 LISTENING & SPEAKING

a **6.8** Listen to a competition on a radio programme. With a partner, try to write down the eight heroes and icons.

b ● **Communication** *Relatives quiz A p.118 B p.121.* Make questions to ask a partner.

3 READING

a In pairs, look at the photos 1–5 and match them with the names below. Do you know what they are famous for?

Aung San Suu-Kyi ☐   Bernard Kouchner ☐
Bono ☐   Queen Rania of Jordan ☐
Thierry Henry ☐

b Now read the article and complete it with the five names.

c Read the article again and answer the questions.

1 Who was asked for some help which he / she couldn't give?
2 Who is trying to fight disease? How?
3 Who had to choose between his / her job and family? What did he / she choose?
4 Who used to be a politician? Why was he / she unusual?
5 Who used their celebrity status to raise money? What are they trying to change?

d Read the article again. Find the nouns from these verbs and adjectives.

1 found (vb)   *foundation*
2 modern (adj)   _____
3 hungry (adj)   _____
4 poor (adj)   _____
5 choose (vb)   _____
6 operate (vb)   _____
7 sell (vb)   _____

e In pairs, look at the photos and say why these people are heroes.

Heroes and icons of our time

Time magazine has chosen a list of people called the *Time 100*. These are people who, the magazine believes, have an enormous impact on today's world and who inspire millions of people. The category *Heroes and Icons* includes a whole variety of people from a queen to a footballer, from politicians to a multi-millionaire rock star.

A _____, one of the world's greatest footballers, has used his hero status on the pitch to fight racism in football. After he saw black players from the England team being insulted by spectators in an international match, he started the campaign 'Stand up, Speak out'. He has raised nearly $16 million for anti-racism groups through the sales of black and white bracelets.

'You probably can't change the racists,' he says, 'but you can make the silent majority stand up and speak out against them. That way we will make them feel less comfortable. In a few years' time I want to be able to watch a football match and not hear a single racist insult.'

B _____ is helping her husband to 'try to reconcile tradition with modernity' in their country. But outside her country, along with the Bill & Melinda Gates Foundation and others, she is working to try to make sure that all children everywhere get vaccinated. As she reminds us, there are more than 30 million children a year who get no vaccinations during their first year of life, so up to 10% of them will die.

C _____, one of the world's biggest rock stars, is also Africa's biggest defender. When he and his wife Ali first went to Africa, they worked in a refugee camp for a month. On the day they were leaving, a man approached him carrying a baby. 'This is my son,' the man said. 'Please take him with you when you leave. If you do, he will live. Otherwise he will die.' He couldn't take the child, but since then he has been working tirelessly to raise money to free Africa from hunger and poverty.

D _____ is the moral leader of Burma. She has been under house arrest since 1989 for opposing the military rulers and fighting for human rights. U2 wrote the song *Walk On* to honour this amazing woman, who put her country before everything, including her family. She had to make an unbearable choice: either to be with her husband and sons in England but never be allowed back to Burma, or to stay in Burma, but not to see her sons grow up and not to be with her husband when he died. She stayed, and to this day continues to fight.

E _____ first came to the public eye when he helped to save many of the boat people who escaped Vietnam. He carried sacks of rice himself, even though he was a French government minister, in 'Operation Restore Hope' in Somalia. Nelson Mandela once said to him, 'Thank you for helping in matters which aren't your problem.' He co-founded *Médecins sans Frontières* (Doctors without borders), which was awarded the 1999 Nobel Peace Prize, and later *Médecins du Monde*.

5

4 VOCABULARY & PRONUNCIATION   what people do, word stress

⚠ Most words which tell us what people do end in *-er*, *-or*, *-ian*, or *-ist*, e.g. Aung San Suu-Kyi is the moral **leader** of Burma.

a Add an ending and put the words in the correct column.

~~act~~   compose   conduct   cycle   design   direct   football   guitar   invent   ~~lead~~   music   paint   photograph   ~~politics~~   ~~physics~~   present   science   sculpt   violin

-er	-or	-ian	-ist
leader	actor	politician	physicist

b ◖**6.9**◗ Listen and underline the stressed syllable. Practise saying the words.

5 SPEAKING

a Think of a person you admire (alive or dead) for three of the categories below.

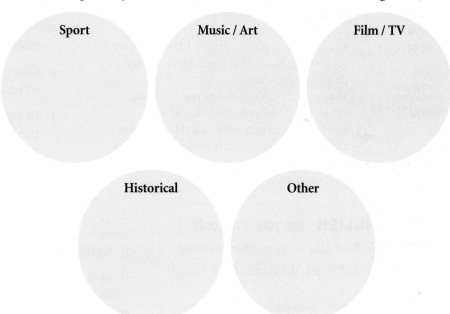

Sport   Music / Art   Film / TV

Historical   Other

b In groups, talk about your people. Explain who they are, what they have done, and why you admire them.

6 ◖**6.10**◗ SONG ♬ *Holding out for a hero*

GIVING AND REACTING TO NEWS

a **6.11** Cover the dialogue and listen. What's Ben's news? Who is more surprised, Jacques or Nicole?

b Read the dialogue. In pairs, what do you think the missing words are? **Don't write them in yet.**

Ben	Hi.
Nicole / Jacques	Hi. / Hello.
Nicole	Did you have a nice weekend?
Ben	Oh yeah. You'll never _____ who I saw on Saturday.
Nicole	Who?
Ben	Allie…and Mark. In the Louvre…together.
Nicole	_____?
Jacques	You're _____.
Ben	It was definitely them. And they looked really close. I think they were holding hands.
Jacques	No! I don't _____ it.
Ben	It's true, I'm _____ you! And I think they saw me because they turned and left really quickly.
Jacques	Are you _____?
Nicole	You know, I'm not surprised. I think they've been seeing each other since Mark arrived. Or maybe even before.
Jacques	That's _____. What makes you say that?
Nicole	When I went to look at Mark's new apartment, I'm sure Allie called him on his mobile. And I've seen her looking at him in a certain way…
Ben	Hey, quiet everyone. It's Mark.

c Listen again and complete the dialogue.

d **6.12** Listen and repeat the highlighted phrases. Copy the rhythm.

e Cover the dialogue. Try to remember five ways of reacting to news with surprise or interest.

f In pairs, invent some news about a famous person to tell other students. Take turns to tell your news. React with surprise / interest.

You'll never guess what's happened! What?

SOCIAL ENGLISH For your eyes only

a **6.13** How does Allie reply to Mark's email?

b Listen again and mark the sentences T (true) or F (false).

1 Jacques had a busy weekend.
2 Mark invites Ben and Jacques to his flat for a meal on Saturday.
3 Mark says he went to the Louvre with a friend.
4 Ben says he saw Mark at the Louvre.
5 Everybody gets the same email from Allie.

USEFUL PHRASES

You must come r_____ for a meal one evening.
That w_____ be very nice.
So didn't you go out at a_____?
I felt l_____ (getting a bit of culture).
That's f_____. I went to the Louvre on Saturday, too.
I didn't see you e_____.

c **6.14** Complete the USEFUL PHRASES. Listen and check.

d Listen again and repeat the phrases. How do you say them in your language?

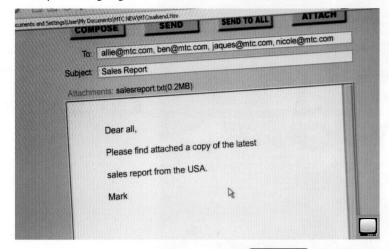

Study Link MultiROM

'Must-have' DVDs: *Cinema Paradiso: 1989*

Tim Hudson reviews a DVD which every film lover should own.

1 *Cinema Paradiso* was directed [1] _by___ Giuseppe Tornatore. It stars Philippe Noiret as Alfredo, and Salvatore Cascio, who plays the part of the boy. The film won an Oscar in 1989 [2]_____ Best Foreign Language film.

2 The film is set in an Italian village in the 1940s and 50s. It was filmed on location in Sicily.

3 The film is [3]_____ a little boy called Salvatore who ends up becoming a famous film director. [4]_____ the beginning of the film, he goes [5]_____ to his village for the first time in thirty years, for the funeral of an old friend, Alfredo. The rest of the film is a 'flashback' about his childhood. [6]_____ his village there is only one cinema, called Cinema Paradiso. Salvatore is crazy [7]_____ films so he spends all his time there. He becomes friends with Alfredo, the man who shows the films, and later he works [8]_____ his assistant. But when he is a teenager he leaves the village and goes [9]_____ work in Rome, and [10]_____ the end he becomes a famous director. He never sees Alfredo again.

4 I strongly recommend *Cinema Paradiso*. It makes you laugh and cry, it has a memorable soundtrack, and it is a moving tribute to the magic of the early days of cinema.

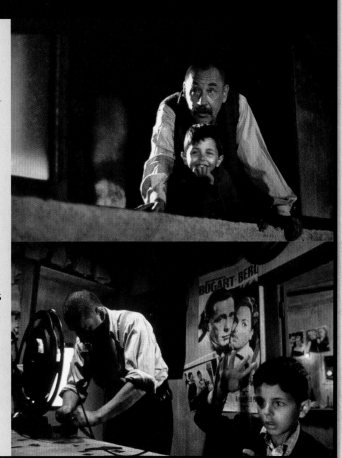

a Look at the title and the photos. Have you seen the film? Would you like to see it?

b Read the film review. Number the paragraph summaries below in order, 1–4.

> **Paragraph** ☐
> The plot
>
> **Paragraph** ☐
> The name of the film, the director, the stars, and any prizes it won
>
> **Paragraph** ☐
> Why you recommend this film
>
> **Paragraph** ☐
> Where and when it was set

c Read the review again and complete it with the missing words.

---
about (x2)   at   as   back   ~by~   in (x2)   for   to

d Look at the third paragraph again. What tense do we usually use to tell the story of a film or book?

Useful language: describing a film
It was directed / written by…
It is set in…
It is based on the book…
It's about…
It stars…
My favourite scene is…

> **WRITE** a film review about a film you would recommend people to buy on DVD.
>
> **PLAN** what you're going to write in the four paragraphs. Use the **Useful language** box and **Vocabulary Bank** *Cinema* **p.154** to help you.
>
> **CHECK** the review for mistakes (grammar , punctuation , and spelling).

GRAMMAR

Complete the second sentence with **two words** so that it means the same as the first.

1 'Do you want to have dinner?' he asked.
   James asked me if _____ _____ to have dinner.
2 'I'll pay,' she said.
   Jacqueline said that _____ _____ pay.
3 'Where am I?' the man asked.
   The man asked me where _____ _____ .

4 'Can you open the window, please?'
   My mother asked me _____ _____ the window.
5 'Don't talk!'
   The teacher told the students _____ _____ talk.
6 They made the film in a studio.
   The film _____ _____ in a studio.
7 They're building a new school.
   A new school is _____ _____ .
8 An American company has bought our company.
   Our company has _____ _____ by an American company.
9 That man's son goes to my school.
   That's the man _____ _____ goes to my school.
10 This is a machine. It cuts paper.
   This is a machine _____ _____ paper.

`10`

VOCABULARY

a Underline the word that is different. Say why.

1 baker's   shoe shop   shop window   newsagent's
2 buy   sales   sell   pay
3 cast   extras   special effects actors
4 horror film   thriller   sequel   comedy
5 dubbed   filmed   directed   plot

b Write words for the definitions.

1 A shop where you can buy meat. **b**_____
2 The piece of paper you are given when you buy something. **r**_____
3 To stand in a line, e.g. in a shop. to **q**_____
4 A basket on wheels that people use at supermarkets. **t**_____
5 The words of a film translated on the screen. **s**_____
6 The music from a film. **s**_____
7 The people who watch a film in a cinema. **a**_____
8 Something you buy more cheaply than usual. **b**_____

c Complete with one word.

1 Can I try _____ these trousers, please?
2 Did you buy your car _____ credit?
3 People always complain _____ high prices.
4 If it's broken, take it _____ to the shop.
5 The film is based _____ a book.
6 *Schindler's List* was directed _____ Spielberg.
7 *Les Misérables* was set _____ 18th century Paris.

`20`

PRONUNCIATION

a Underline the word with a different sound.

1		sell	special	sales	centre
2		cast	market	manager	star
3		baker's	scene	discount	queue
4		director	manager	complain	window
5		chemist's	chain store	butcher's	changing room

b Underline the stressed syllable.

subtitles	complain	receipt	soundtrack	customer

`10`

CAN YOU UNDERSTAND THIS TEXT?

Designer brands aren't for me!

Although I follow fashion, I hate the phrase 'must-have'. If I read that Ugg boots or Prada sunglasses are the latest 'must-haves', my immediate reaction is to think, 'Why must I have them?' Why should I fall for the designer's manipulative tactics, which are only intended to increase his bank balance at the expense of mine?

Designer brands, in general, are for people who are too insecure to trust their own tastes. These people decide that everything at Prada must be 'cool', so if you shop there, you can't go wrong. I find it much more satisfying to pop into one of the cheap chain stores on the High Street and buy a copy of the designer's clothes for a tenth of the price. OK, you have to use your skill to find the one garment in three that looks great. But it's worth it! It's like finding a piece of gold in a river. The find gives you immense satisfaction.

Which is why, according to a survey done by a British bank, young people with money are abandoning the designer shops and buying their clothes in chain stores, second-hand shops, and in markets. This is the best news I've heard all week. It means that young people have the confidence to trust their judgement. They are prepared to take risks to look individual and not mass-produced.

That has always been my shopping philosophy. The exorbitant prices in designer shops leave me open-mouthed. Even if I had the money, I would think of all the other things I could spend it on!

Adapted from the British press

LOUIS VUITTON
Salvatore Ferragamo
GIANFRANCO FERRE
LIU·JO
BOSS
CELINE
PRADA
VECUA

a Read the text and choose a, b, or c.

1 The writer thinks…
 a fashion is ridiculous.
 b Prada sunglasses are 'must-haves'.
 c designers just want to make a lot of money.

2 She thinks people who buy designer brands…
 a are 'cool.'
 b don't have good taste.
 c are frightened of making a mistake.

3 She thinks…
 a it's easy to find great, cheap clothes.
 b you feel good if you find good, cheap clothes.
 c the clothes in high street stores are better than designer clothes.

4 According to the bank survey, rich young people…
 a now want to look different from each other.
 b don't have as much money to spend as they used to.
 c are now buying more designer clothes.

5 The writer…
 a thinks the price of designer clothes is fair.
 b thinks there are better things to spend her money on.
 c would like to have the money to buy designer clothes.

b Look at the highlighted phrases. Try to guess their meaning. Check with your teacher or your dictionary.

CAN YOU UNDERSTAND THESE PEOPLE?

a (6.15) Listen and circle the correct answer, a, b, or c.

1 What was the problem with the woman's steak?
 a It wasn't cooked enough.   b It was cold.   c It was badly cooked.

2 What didn't the man like about the film?
 a The acting.   b The music.   c The plot.

3 How much did the sweater cost?
 a £25   b £67   c £77

4 How did the man feel after he saw the film?
 a Disappointed.   b Nervous.   c Excited.

5 What did Brunel do?
 a He was an architect.   b He was an engineer.   c He was a boxer.

b (6.16) Listen to a guide showing tourists around Westminster Abbey in London. Complete the sentences with one word.

Charles Dickens was born on February 7th [1] _____.
As a child he worked in a [2] _____.
In 1858 Dickens and his wife [3] _____.
His last novel was called *Our Mutual* [4] _____.
He died at the age of [5] _____.

CAN YOU SAY THIS IN ENGLISH?

Can you…? Yes (✓)

☐ talk about a time you complained in a shop or restaurant
☐ describe a film
☐ talk about a person who you admire

7 A

G third conditional
V making adjectives and adverbs
P sentence stress

Can we make our own luck?

1 READING & LISTENING

a Read the article **Bad luck?** In pairs, decide what you think happened next.

b **7.1** Now listen to what happened. Were you right?

c Listen again and check. Then in pairs, write two sentences to explain how the story ended.

d **7.2** Now do the same for **Good luck?**

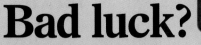

Bad luck?
I missed you!

Ian Johnson, a 27-year-old builder, went to work in Australia for a year, leaving behind his girlfriend, Amy. Ian and Amy missed each other a lot and after being six months apart Ian planned a surprise. Without telling Amy he caught a plane back to England to see her. After a 24-hour flight via Singapore and a 17,600-kilometre journey he finally arrived at her house in Yorkshire in the north of England, carrying flowers, champagne, and an engagement ring. He rang the doorbell, but nobody answered. He had a key to her house so he opened the door and went in. The house was empty. Ian thought Amy had gone out for the evening and sat down to wait for her to come back. Tired after his long journey, he fell asleep. When he woke up, his phone was ringing...

Good luck?
Is there a doctor on the plane?

Mrs Dorothy Fletcher was travelling with her daughter and her daughter's fiancé on a flight from London to Florida. Her daughter was going to be married there the following week. When they changed planes in Philadelphia they had to rush between terminals to catch the connecting flight and Mrs Fletcher, aged 67, began to feel ill.

'I didn't say anything to my daughter because I didn't want to worry her or miss the wedding,' said Mrs Fletcher. But when the plane took off from Philadelphia she suddenly got a terrible pain in her chest, back, and arm – she was having a heart attack. The cabin crew put out a desperate call to the passengers: 'If there is a doctor on the plane, could you please press your call bell...'

Adapted from the British press

2 GRAMMAR third conditional

a Complete the two sentences from the listening in 1c.

> **1 Ian**
> If one of us had _____ at home, we _____ have met.
>
> **2 Mrs Fletcher**
> If those doctors _____ been on the plane, I would _____ died.

b 〔7.3〕 Listen and check.

c Look at sentences 1 and 2 above and answer the questions.

1 Did Ian or Amy stay at home? Did they meet?

2 Were the doctors on the plane? Did Mrs Fletcher die?

3 Do sentences 1 and 2 refer to something that happened or something that didn't happen?

d ○ **p.142 Grammar Bank 7A.** Read the rules and do the exercises.

3 PRONUNCIATION sentence stress

a 〔7.4〕 Listen and repeat the sentences. Copy the rhythm.

1 If you'd <u>told</u> me <u>earlier</u>, I would have <u>gone too</u>.
2 If the <u>weather</u> had been <u>better</u>, we would have <u>stayed longer</u>.
3 If I <u>hadn't stopped</u> for <u>petrol</u>, I would have <u>arrived before</u> he <u>left</u>.
4 We would have been <u>late</u> if we <u>hadn't taken</u> a <u>taxi</u>.
5 She <u>wouldn't</u> have <u>come</u> if she'd <u>known</u> he was <u>here</u>.
6 It would have been <u>cheaper</u> if we'd <u>booked last month</u>.

b ○ **Communication** *Guess the conditional A p.118 B p.121.*

4 SPEAKING

a Read the questionnaire and mark your answers.

b Compare your answers with a partner. Give more information if you can.

c Now look at what your scores mean. Do you agree with the results?

How lucky are you?

Read the following statements and write a number 1–3 in the box

3 = This is usually true about me.
2 = This is sometimes true about me.
1 = This is hardly ever true about me.

1 I enjoy talking to people I haven't met before. ☐
2 I don't worry or feel anxious about life. ☐
3 I enjoy trying new food and drink. ☐
4 I listen to my instinct. ☐
5 When I need to calm down I just go to a quiet place. ☐
6 I try to learn from my mistakes. ☐
7 I try to get what I want from life. ☐
8 I expect people I meet to be pleasant, friendly, and helpful. ☐
9 I'm an optimist. I look on the bright side of life. ☐
10 When things are bad I think things will get better soon. ☐
11 I don't think about bad luck I have had in the past. ☐
12 I expect good things to happen to me in the future. ☐

Your score

12–18 You are naturally unlucky and you don't attract good luck. You need a more positive and more adventurous attitude to life.

19–27 You are quite lucky but you could be luckier. Look back at situations where you were lucky or unlucky and analyze why. Try to learn from the past.

28–36 You are probably someone who is lucky. But you could become even luckier. Don't be afraid of taking risks, as they will probably end up being positive for you.

5 READING

a Look at the title of the article. What do *you* think?

b Read the article. Match exercises A–D to paragraphs 1–4.

Can we make our own luck?

Some people seem to be born lucky – they meet their perfect partners, achieve their ambitions, and live happy lives.

The British psychologist Dr Richard Wiseman has done a lot of research to discover why some people are luckier than others. After interviewing hundreds of people with the questionnaire on p.101 he has concluded that people who *think* they are lucky achieve more success and happiness than those who don't. Without realizing it, they are creating good fortune in their lives.

Using Dr Wiseman's techniques you too can understand, control, and increase your own good fortune.

1 Lucky people make the most of their opportunities
Be open to new experiences and vary your routine. For example, get off the bus a stop earlier than usual. You may see something interesting or new, or bump into an old friend.
Exercise ☐

2 Lucky people trust their instinct
When you are trying to decide what to do, first make an effort to relax. Then when your mind is clear, listen to what it is telling you and act on it.
Exercise ☐

3 Lucky people expect to be lucky
Convince yourself that your future will be bright and lucky. Set realistic but high goals. If you fail, don't give up, and be open to the idea of trying a different way to achieve your goals.
Exercise ☐

4 Lucky people use bad luck to their advantage
If something bad happens, imagine how things could have been worse. You will then realize that things aren't so bad after all. Compare your situation with other people who are in an even worse situation. Take a long view of things – even if things seem bad now, expect them to get better in the end. Learn from your past mistakes and think of new ways of solving your problems.
Exercise ☐

EXERCISES

A Make a list of your goals. They must be specific, not vague, e.g. 'I want to spend more time with my partner', not 'I want to be happy'. Now make a second list of all the advantages you would get if you achieved your goals, and the disadvantages. Compare the advantages with the disadvantages and you will see which goals are worth trying to achieve.

B Make a list of six new experiences you'd like to try. These could be simple, like eating at a new restaurant, or long term, for example learning a new language. Number the experiences 1–6. Then throw a dice and whatever experience is chosen, go out and do it.

C When you experience bad luck, first cry or scream for 30 minutes. Then put your bad luck behind you. Do something to make the situation better, e.g. ask friends for advice and focus on a solution to the problem.

D If you are trying to decide between two options, write one of them down in the form of a letter. For example, if you are unhappy about a relationship, write to your partner explaining that it's all over. Read the letter. Would you really like to send it, or is something telling you that it doesn't *feel* right? If so, don't do it.

c Read just the article again (not the EXERCISES). Cover the text and from memory complete the expressions below with a verb or phrase. Then look at the text again and check your answers.

1	**s**_____ to be	= give the impression of being
2	**a**_____ their ambitions	= make their ambitions come true
3	**v**_____ your routine	= change your routine, make it different
4	**b**_____ **i**_____ an old friend	= meet an old friend by chance
5	**m**_____ an **e**_____ to relax	= try hard to relax
6	**c**_____ yourself that your future will be bright	= make yourself believe that your future will be bright
7	**r**_____ that things aren't so bad	= understand that things aren't so bad

d Read EXERCISES A–D on p.102 again. Which one do you think is the best for making you luckier?

EXERCISES A–D on p.102

HOW WORDS WORK...

When you are trying to decide what to do, first make an effort to relax. Then when your mind is clear, listen to what it is telling you.

We often use *what* as a relative pronoun. It means the thing (or things) which.

Complete the sentences with *what* or *which*.

1 Can you speak a bit louder? I can't hear _____ you're saying.
2 **A** What's this?
  B It's a machine _____ makes ice cream.
3 This is the song _____ won the MTV award.
4 Everybody was very surprised by _____ she said.
5 We went to the restaurant _____ Ann recommended.
6 I didn't get _____ I wanted for my birthday!

6 VOCABULARY making adjectives and adverbs

> **Lucky** people use bad **luck** to their advantage.

a Look at the adjectives and adverbs that can be made from the noun *luck* in the chart below. Then in pairs complete the chart.

noun	⊞ adjective	⊟ adjective	⊞ adverb	⊟ adverb
luck	lucky	unlucky	luckily	unluckily
fortune	fortunate	unfortunate	_____	_____
comfort	_____	_____	_____	_____
patience	_____	_____	_____	_____
care	_____	_____	_____	_____

b Underline the stressed syllable in the three two-syllable nouns. How does that help you to stress the adjectives and adverbs correctly? Practise saying them.

c Complete the sentences with the right form of the **bold** noun.

1 The beach was beautiful but _____ it rained every day. **FORTUNE**
2 If the beds had been more _____, we would have slept better. **COMFORT**
3 You would have got better marks if you hadn't done the exam so _____. **CARE**
4 We were really _____. We missed the flight by just five minutes. **LUCK**
5 Don't be so _____. The programme will start in a minute. **PATIENCE**
6 I fell off my bicycle last week, but _____ I wasn't badly hurt. **LUCK**
7 There was a huge queue to pay, but we waited _____. **PATIENCE**
8 If you had been more _____, you wouldn't have had an accident. **CARE**
9 It was freezing cold but _____ we'd all brought jackets. **FORTUNE**
10 Are you sitting _____? Then I'll begin the story. **COMFORT**

7 🔊 7.5 SONG ♫ *Ironic*

B

G question tags, indirect questions
V compound nouns
P intonation in question tags

Murder mysteries

1 READING & LISTENING

a Read *Jack the Ripper – case closed?* and answer these questions.

1 Where and when did the murders take place?
2 How did 'Jack the Ripper' get his name?
3 How many murders were there?
4 How long did the murders go on for?
5 Who do the suspects include?
6 What does Patricia Cornwell usually do?
7 How did she try to solve the mystery?

Jack the Ripper – case closed?

One of the great unsolved murder mysteries of all time is that of 'Jack the Ripper'.

In the autumn of 1888 a brutal murderer walked the dark, foggy streets of London, terrorizing the inhabitants of the city. The victims were all women and the police seemed powerless to stop the murders. Panic and fear among Londoners was increased by a letter sent by the murderer to Scotland Yard. In the letter he made fun of the police's attempts to catch him and promised to kill again. It finished, 'Yours truly, Jack the Ripper'. This was the first of many letters sent to the police. The murders continued – seven in total. But in November, they suddenly stopped, three months after they had first begun.

Jack the Ripper was never caught and for more than a century historians, writers, policemen, and detectives have tried to discover and prove his identity. Hundreds of articles and books have been written and many films made about the murders. But the question 'Who was Jack the Ripper?' has remained unanswered. There have been plenty of suspects, including a doctor, a businessman, a painter, and even a member of the royal family.

Three years ago the American crime writer Patricia Cornwell left aside her fictional detective, Kay Scarpetta, and tried to solve the real-life murder mystery of Jack the Ripper. After spending a considerable amount of time and money on her investigation, and analyzing DNA samples, Cornwell thinks she has proved who Jack the Ripper really was…

Johnny Depp hunts Jack the Ripper in the film *From Hell*

b 🔊 **7.6** Now listen to the first part of an interview with Ken Morton, an expert on Jack the Ripper. Complete the information about the suspects. Tick (✔) the person who Patricia Cornwell says is Jack the Ripper.

Prince Albert,
Queen Victoria's _____

_____ Maybrick,
a cotton merchant

Walter Sickert,
an _____

c 🔊 **7.7** Listen to the second part of the interview and mark the sentences T (true) or F (false). Correct the false sentences.

1 Cornwell's evidence is mainly scientific.
2 She took DNA samples from a letter written by Sickert.
3 Art lovers were angry with Cornwell.
4 Sickert was probably abroad at the time of the murders.
5 Maybrick confessed to the murders in a letter.
6 Ken Morton thinks that Prince Albert was a serial killer.
7 He doesn't want to say who he thinks the murderer is.
8 He doesn't think the mystery will be solved soon.

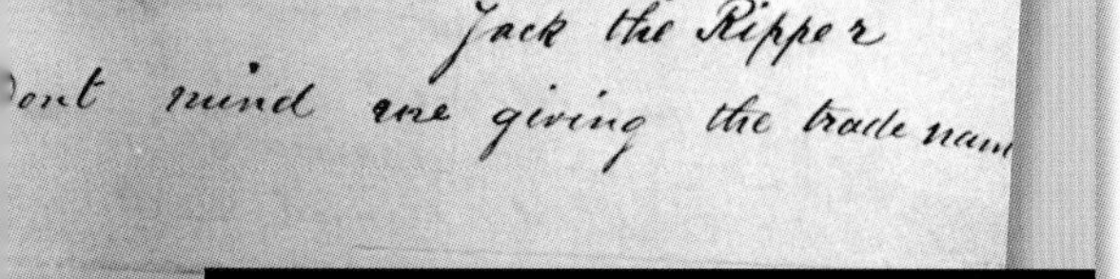

[handwritten letter extract]

> ...lice officers just for jolly wouldn't
> ...on. Keep this letter back till I
> ...o a bit more work then give
> ...t out straight. My knife's so nice
> ...nd sharp I want to get to work
> ...ight away if I get a chance.
> ...ood luck!
>   yours truly
>   Jack the Ripper
> ...ont mind me giving the trade name

Extract from one of Jack the Ripper's letters

2 GRAMMAR question tags

a 🔊 **7.8** Listen to four questions the interviewer asked Ken Morton and complete them with the missing words.

1 You were a detective with Scotland Yard, _____ _____?
2 It's incredible, _____ _____?
3 But you don't think she's right, _____ _____?
4 There's been another recent theory, _____ _____?

b Now look at questions 1–4. Does the interviewer think she knows how the inspector is going to answer?

c ➲ **p.142 Grammar Bank 7B** and read the rules for questions tags. Do exercise **a** only.

3 PRONUNCIATION & SPEAKING intonation in question tags

a 🔊 **7.9** Listen and complete the dialogue between a policeman and a suspect.

P Your surname's Jones, _____?
S Yes, it is.
P And you're 27, _____?
S Yes, that's right.
P You weren't at home last night at 8.00, _____?
S No, I wasn't. I was at the pub.
P But you don't have any witnesses, _____?
S Yes, I do. My brother was with me.
P Your brother wasn't with you, _____?
S How do you know?
P Because he was at the police station. We arrested him last night.

b 🔊 **7.10** Listen and repeat. Copy the rhythm and intonation.

c ➲ **Communication** *Just checking A p.118 B p.121.* Roleplay a police interview.

4 GRAMMAR   indirect questions

a Do you like reading detective stories or watching detective films / TV series? Who are your favourite detectives?

b 🔘 **7.11**   Listen to and read an extract from a Donna Leon detective novel. Which questions does Inspector Brunetti ask? <u>Underline</u> them.

c How do Inspector Brunetti and Signora Trevisan behave during the interview? Do you think Signora Trevisan killed her husband?

Carlo Trevisan, an important international lawyer is found dead in the carriage of an intercity train at Santa Lucia. Brunetti goes to interview his wife, Signora Trevisan.

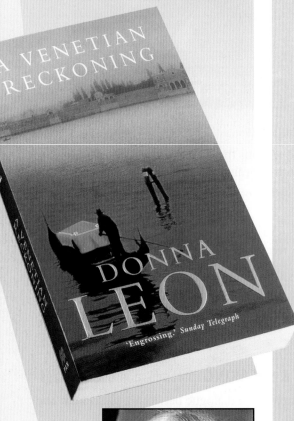

Donna Leon is an American crime writer whose detective novels are all set in Venice. Her detective is Inspector Brunetti.

'I'd like to ask you some questions about your personal life, signora.'

'Our personal life?' she repeated, as though she had never heard of such a thing.

When he didn't answer this, she nodded, signalling him to begin.

'Could you tell me how long you and your husband were married?'

'Nineteen years.'

'How many children do you have, signora?'

'Two. Claudio is seventeen and Francesca is fifteen'.

'Are they in school in Venice, signora?'

She looked up at him sharply when he asked this.

'Why do you want to know that?'

'My own daughter, Chiara, is fourteen, so perhaps they know each other,' he answered, and smiled to show what an innocent question it had been.

'Claudio is in school in Switzerland, but Francesca is here. With us. I mean,' she corrected, rubbing a hand across her forehead, 'with me.'

'Would you say yours was a happy marriage, signora?'

'Yes,' she answered immediately, far faster than Brunetti would have answered the same question, though he would have given the same response. She did not, however, elaborate.

'Could you tell me if your husband had any particularly close friends or business associates?'

She looked up at this question, then as quickly down again at her hands. 'Our closest friends are the Nogares, Mirto and Graziella. He's an architect who lives in Campo Sant'Angelo. They're Francesca's godparents. I don't know about business associates: you'll have to ask Ubaldo'.

'Other friends, signora?'

'Why do you need to know all this?' she said, voice rising sharply.

'I'd like to learn more about your husband, signora.'

'Why?' The question leaped from her, almost as if beyond her volition.

'Until I understand what sort of man he was, I can't understand why this has happened.'

'A robbery?' she asked, voice just short of sarcasm.

'It wasn't robbery. Whoever killed him intended to do it.'

102

From *A Venetian Reckoning* by Donna Leon

d Look at four questions from the book extract. How are 1 and 3 different from 2 and 4?

1 Could you tell me how long you and your husband were married?

2 How many children do you have, signora?

3 Could you tell me if your husband had any particularly close friends or business associates?

4 Why do you need to know all this?

e ⟳ **p.142 Grammar Bank 7B.** Read the rules for indirect questions, and do exercise **b**.

f ⟨7.12⟩ Listen to six direct questions and turn them into indirect ones.

1 Could you tell me _____?

2 Do you know if _____?

3 Could you tell me _____?

4 Can you tell me if _____?

5 Can you tell me _____?

6 Do you know if _____?

g Imagine you are interviewing somebody in the street. Ask your partner these questions. Begin *Can / Could you tell me…* Then swap roles.

What's your name?
Where do you live?
What do you do?
Do you have a TV?
How much TV do you watch a week?

5 VOCABULARY compound nouns

a Make compound nouns using a word from each box.

detective	mystery
murder	film
horror	novel
crime	writer
police	station
police	inspector

b ⟨7.13⟩ Compare in pairs. Then listen and check. Which word is stressed in compound nouns?

c In pairs, try to answer all the questions in two minutes with a compound noun from Files 1–6.

Compound noun race

1 **What do you use to pay for things you buy on the Internet?**

2 **Where do you catch a train?**

3 **What does Steven Spielberg do?**

4 **What do you call the time of day when trains and buses are full?**

5 **What should you put on when you get into a car?**

6 **What do you call a big shop that sells everything?**

7 **Where do you play tennis?**

8 **What do you need before you can get on a plane?**

9 **What's the opposite of a private school?**

10 **Where do you buy petrol?**

11 **What do you call the noise a phone makes?**

12 **What do you call a long line of cars that can't move?**

7C

G phrasal verbs
V television, phrasal verbs
P revision of sounds, linking

Switch it off

1 VOCABULARY & SPEAKING television

a Look at the **bold** words in the TV survey below. What do they mean? How do you pronounce them?

b In pairs, ask and answer the questions.

Your TV habits

How many TVs are there in your house? Where are they?

Do you know anybody who doesn't have a TV?

How many **channels** do you have?

Do you have **satellite** or **cable TV**?

Which channels do you watch the most?

Do you watch any foreign channels? Which one(s)?

How much TV do you watch during the week / at weekends?

Who watches most / least TV in your family?

What kind of TV programmes do you like? What kind do you hate? Write L (like), H (hate), or DM (don't mind) in the boxes.

☐ **quiz shows**   ☐ **cartoons**
☐ **reality shows**   ☐ **documentaries**
☐ **comedy shows**   ☐ **drama series**
☐ **chat shows**   ☐ **films**
☐ **soap operas**   ☐ **sports programmes**
☐ **the news**

Do you think there are too many **adverts** on TV in your country?

Do you think TV programmes in your country are getting better or worse? Why?

2 GRAMMAR phrasal verbs

a How many phrasal verbs can you think of connected with television?

b Read the three stories on p.109 and complete them with phrasal verbs A–H.

> A look out
> B sold out
> C picked up
> D switch off
> E looking forward to
> F turn off
> G find out
> H passed away

c Read the texts again, then cover them and look at the pictures. In pairs, tell the stories from memory.

d Now look at how *look forward to* and *turn off* appear in a dictionary. How does the dictionary show you if the verb and the particle (e.g. *off*, *on*, etc.) can be separated or not?

> **look forward to sth** to wait with pleasure for something to happen
>
> **turn sth off** to stop the flow of electricity, water, etc. by moving a switch, tap, etc.

e ○ **p.142 Grammar Bank 7C.** Read the rules and do the exercises.

TV-B-Gone

An American, Mitch Altman, went to a restaurant with some friends. He was ¹_____ some lively conversation. But instead of talking, his friends spent the whole time watching a TV in the corner. Mitch wished he could ²_____ it _____, and this suddenly gave him the idea for a new gadget. He invented TV-B-Gone, a remote control which allows you to ³_____ any TV within 17 metres of where you are. When the gadgets were first marketed on the Internet, they ⁴_____ after the first two days.

Dead or alive?

The BBC were planning to make a programme about the Bob Marley hit song *No Woman No Cry*. A researcher from BBC3 contacted the Bob Marley Foundation to ⁵_____ if they could interview him over the summer. The researcher added that filming was scheduled for June, July, and August but 'our schedule is flexible'. Unfortunately, Marley's schedule is not: he died in 1981. A friend of the Marley family told the *Daily Mirror*: 'We didn't think there was anyone on the planet who didn't realize Bob ⁶_____ years ago.' A BBC spokesman admitted: 'We're very embarrassed.'

Can I speak to Bob Marley, please?

BOB MARLEY FOUNDATION

Furious football fan forgiven

Two people were nearly killed when a Romanian football fan threw his TV out of the window. Ghita Axinte said he was so angry with the national side when they lost their World Cup qualifier against the Czech Republic 1-0 that he ⁷_____ the TV _____ and threw it out of the window.

Radu Demergiu, his neighbour, was discussing the match on the balcony below with his brother. Suddenly his brother shouted, '⁸_____!' and the TV set crashed onto the balcony, almost hitting the two of them. But Radu is not going to take any action against his neighbour. 'At first I was angry with him, he could have killed us. But when he told me he had been watching the football, I completely understood. We had also been watching it and I was furious with the Romanian team too.'

3 PRONUNCIATION revision of sounds, linking

a Look at the pink letters in each sentence. What's the sound? Write the sound word and symbol.

	Sound word	Symbol
1 We can't go. They've sold out.	_phone_	əʊ
2 I'd like to find out about train times.	___	___
3 I'm looking forward to August.	___	___
4 I was talking to my mother but we were cut off.	___	___
5 In future, remember to switch off the kitchen lights.	___	___
6 Philip's not old enough to look after a five-year-old.	___	___
7 We put on our seat belts before the flight took off.	___	___
8 They don't get on with each other.	___	___

b ○ **p.157 Sound Bank**. Check your answers.

c ⬭ **7.14** Listen and repeat sentences 1–8.

d ⬭ **7.15** You're going to hear some phrases where three words are linked together. Listen and write down the missing words.

1 There's a towel on the floor. ___ ___ ___ .
2 I hate this music. ___ ___ ___ .
3 Your jacket's on the chair. ___ ___ ___ .
4 You don't need a coat. ___ ___ ___ .
5 I can't hear the TV. ___ ___ ___ .
6 Coffee is bad for you. ___ ___ ___ .

4 VOCABULARY & SPEAKING

a ○ **p.155 Vocabulary Bank** *Phrasal verbs.*

b Choose and tick (✓) six questions to ask your partner.

1 Is there anything you're trying to **give up** at the moment?

2 How do you feel when a plane **takes off**?

3 Are you going to **carry on** studying English next year?

4 What are you most **looking forward to** at the moment?

5 Have you ever tried to go to a concert but it was **sold out**?

6 Where and when do you **switch off** your mobile?

7 Have you ever **thrown away** something really important by mistake?

8 Do you like **looking after** small children?

9 How often do you **go away** for the weekend?

10 Would you like to **set up** your own business?

11 Are people in your country trying to **slow down** and work less?

c Ask and answer the questions. Ask for more information and try to keep each 'mini-conversation' going for as long as possible.

Couple switch on after 37 years without power

An elderly couple are going to swap candles for light bulbs after 37 years without electricity at their Suffolk home. Pat Payne, 74, and his wife Margaret, 72, brought up their large family in their farmhouse in Whepstead, near Bury St Edmunds, without any modern appliances.

Their children left home years ago but now one of them has moved back and is paying £19,000 to have electricity put in the 200-year-old house next month. Mrs Payne said that she was looking forward to 'being modernized' but does not feel that she has missed much by not having electricity.

'It would have been nice to have been able to do the ironing or to have a vacuum cleaner instead of having to sweep the floor, but we got by,' she said. 'I think our children are more excited about us getting electricity than we are.'

The couple have mostly lived off the land. Mr Payne, a former farm labourer, grows vegetables in the garden. Without a fridge or freezer in the three-bedroom house, milk is delivered every other day and fresh meat is bought as needed. Water comes from a well.

Mrs Payne used to wash clothes by hand, and with nine children that was a lot of clothes, but she believes that not having electricity may have been a good thing for her children while they were growing up. 'Instead of watching television, they played together and used to make up games or read books,' she said.

The life also suited her and her husband. 'Neither of us has ever been seriously ill and we rarely get a cough or cold,' Mrs Payne said. 'With our fresh vegetables and not having central heating it's been a very healthy way to live.' The couple have 24 grandchildren and eight great-grandchildren.

5 READING

a You're going to read an article about a couple who lived without electricity for 37 years. Which **two** of these things do you think they missed most?

central heating	an iron
electric light	a TV
a freezer	a vacuum cleaner
a fridge	a washing machine

b Read the article once. Were you right? Do they regret living without electricity for so long?

c Read the article again. Then cover the text and say what the following numbers refer to.

37	74 and 72	19,000	200	3	9	24	8

d Answer the questions in pairs.

1 Do any of their children still live with them?
2 How does Mrs Payne feel about the house being modernized?
3 Was it a really big problem for her not having an iron or a vacuum cleaner?
4 Where did they get most of their food from?
5 Why does Mrs Payne think that not having electricity was good for the children?
6 How was it good for her and her husband?

e Match the highlighted phrasal verbs with their definitions. Write the infinitives in the chart.

Phrasal verbs	Meaning
1 _____ _____	to develop into an adult
2 _____ _____	to manage to live or do something with difficulty
3 _____ sth _____	to install something in your house, e.g. central heating
4 _____ _____	to return to live in a place where you lived before
5 _____ sth _____	to invent
6 _____ _____ sb / sth	to depend on sb or sth in order to live
7 _____ sb _____	look after a child until he / she is an adult

6 LISTENING

a **7.16** Listen to four people answering the question 'If you had to live without electricity for a week, what two things would you miss most?' Write the two answers for each person.

Claire 1 _____ 2 _____
Why? _____

Andy 1 _____ 2 _____
Why? _____

Julia 1 _____ 2 _____
Why? _____

Tyler 1 _____ 2 _____
Why? _____

b Listen again and write their reasons.

c In pairs, say what **two** things *you* would miss and why.

APOLOGIZING, GIVING EXCUSES

a **7.17** Cover the dialogue. Who does Allie apologize to? Why?

b Read the dialogue. In pairs, what do you think the missing words are? **Don't write them in yet.**

Mark	Mark Ryder.
Allie	Mark, can you come in?
Mark	Sure.
Allie	Thanks for the sales report.
Mark	I think there's something more important to talk about right now.
Allie	What do you mean?
Mark	That message you sent me. You hit 'reply to all'. You sent it to everyone in the office.
Allie	Oh no. You're joking. Oh, Mark. I'm _____ sorry. I did it without _____.
Mark	It's _____, Allie. It's an easy mistake to make.
Allie	How could I be so _____? I just wasn't _____.
Mark	Allie…
Allie	I'm _____ sorry.
Mark	Don't _____ about it. It doesn't _____. But I think we should talk to the others.
Allie	Yes, you're right. I'll do it. It was my _____.
Allie	Listen everybody. I just want to say that I'm _____ sorry. I haven't been honest with you. Erm, we… Mark and I…
Nicole	That's OK, Allie. We had already guessed. It wasn't really a surprise.

c Listen again and complete the dialogue.

d **7.18** Listen and repeat the highlighted phrases from the dialogue. Copy the rhythm.

e Look at the highlighted phrases in the dialogue. Put them in the right place in the chart.

Apologizing	Admitting responsibility/ Explaining	Responding to an apology
_____	*I did it without thinking.*	_____
_____	_____	_____
_____	_____	_____

f ➤ **Communication** *I'm so sorry! A p.118 B p.121.*

SOCIAL ENGLISH A walk by the Seine

a **7.19** Listen. How does the story end?

b Listen again and answer the questions.

1 According to Allie, how did the people in the office discover their secret?
2 Does Mark agree with her?
3 Is Mark sorry everybody knows? Why (not)?
4 Why doesn't Allie hear what Mark's saying?
5 What's the last thing Mark asks Allie to do?

USEFUL PHRASES

So if it w_____ me, it must have been you.
You're h_____ (at keeping secrets)!
Don't b_____ me.
But it's now or n_____.
I didn't hear a w_____ you said.
Can you c_____ that (in an email)?

c **7.20** Complete the USEFUL PHRASES. Listen and check.

d Listen again and repeat the phrases. How do you say them in your language?

a Read an article for a student magazine about the advantages and disadvantages of living without a TV. The computer has found <u>ten mistakes</u> (grammar, punctuation, or spelling). Can you correct them?

Living without a TV

ALMOST every family today [1]<u>have</u> a TV, in fact probably more than one, and people everywhere spend hours watching it. But a few families choose to live without a TV because they think there are advantages.

The first advantage is that families spend more time [2]<u>talk</u> to each other. Secondly, they spend more time doing more creative things like reading or painting. Thirdly, they spend more time outdoors, and are usually [3]<u>more fit</u>.

On the other hand, there are also disadvantages. For example, children who don't have a TV may feel [4]<u>differents</u> from [5]<u>there</u> school friends, and often won't know what they are talking about. Also it is not true that all TV [6]<u>programes</u> are bad. There are also good ones, like [7]<u>documentarys</u>, and people who live without a TV may know less about [8]<u>whats</u> happening in the world.

In conclusion, [9]<u>althought</u> living without a TV has some advantages, I think today it's unrealistic and that we should just try to turn the TV [10]<u>out</u> when there's nothing good on.

b Read the article again. Then cover it and in pairs answer the questions from memory.

1 What are the three advantages of life without a TV?
2 What are the two disadvantages?
3 Is the writer for or against having a TV?

c You are going to write a similar article about mobile phones. First, with a partner, make a list of the advantages and disadvantages.

d Now decide which are the three biggest advantages and number them 1–3 (1 = the biggest). Do the same with the disadvantages.

Useful language: writing about advantages and disadvantages

Listing advantages
First, / Firstly,… Secondly,… Thirdly,…

Listing disadvantages
On the other hand, there are also (some) disadvantages.
For instance,… / For example,…
Also,…

Conclusion
In conclusion / To sum up, I think…

WRITE an article called *Mobile phones – a great invention?*

Begin the article with this introduction:
Almost everybody has a mobile phone. But is it a great invention? I think there are both advantages and disadvantages.

Write three more paragraphs.

PLAN what you're going to write. Use the paragraph summaries below and the **Useful language** box to help you.

Paragraph 2 Write two or three advantages.
Paragraph 3 Write two or three disadvantages.
Paragraph 4 Conclusion – decide if you think mobiles are a great invention or not.

CHECK the article for mistakes (grammar , punctuation , and spelling).

GRAMMAR

a Choose a, b, or c.

1 If we hadn't gone to that meeting, we _____ each other.
   a wouldn't meet
   b hadn't met
   c wouldn't have met

2 Could you tell me what _____?
   a is your name
   b your name is
   c your name

3 Do you know _____ after lunch?
   a if the shop does open
   b if opens the shop
   c if the shop opens

4 You aren't coming tonight, _____?
   a are you
   b aren't you
   c you aren't

5 If you've finished watching TV, _____.
   a turn off it
   b turn it off
   c turn off

b Complete the second sentence with **two words** so that it means the same as the first.

1 We were late because we got lost.
   If we _____ _____ lost, we wouldn't have been late.

2 What time did you arrive home last night?
   Could you tell me what time _____ _____ home last night?

3 Does this train stop in Norwich?
   Do you know _____ this train _____ in Norwich?

4 I think the film finishes at 8.00.
   The film finishes at 8.00, _____ _____?

5 I'm excited about our holiday.
   I'm looking _____ _____ our holiday.

10

VOCABULARY

a Complete with an adjective or adverb from the **bold** noun.

1 He's very intelligent but _____ he's not very good-looking. **fortune**
2 He hates waiting. He's very _____. **patience**
3 Let's buy this sofa. It's definitely the most _____. **comfort**
4 I was very _____ in the exam. The questions were all on things I'd studied the night before. **luck**
5 He writes very _____ and makes a lot of spelling mistakes. **care**

b Complete the compound nouns.

1 Excuse me? Where's the nearest **police** _____?
2 **A** Do you like _____ **films**?
   B No. I don't enjoy feeling frightened!
3 My three-year-old has just started at _____ **school**.
4 Yesterday I had to pay a £50 **parking** _____.
5 When the banks are closed you can get money from a _____ **machine**.

c Complete the phrasal verbs.

1 He has to _____ **after** his father, as he's in his 90s.
2 Could you **turn** the music _____? It's really quiet.
3 Could you **give** me _____ my book, please!
4 My uncle has **set** _____ a small company.
5 I always feel nervous when planes _____ **off**.
6 _____ **down**, you're walking much too fast.
7 Do you _____ **on well with** your boss?
8 If you **carry** _____ watching TV, you'll get square eyes.
9 My grandmother **brought** _____ eight children without any help.
10 They _____ **up** last month, and now she's got a new boyfriend.

20

PRONUNCIATION

a Underline the word with a different sound.

1	lucky	comfortable	plug in	put on
2	patient	traffic jam	adverts	reality
3	down	show	soaps	slow
4	murder	birthday	careful	turn
5	channel	machine	chat	switch

b Underline the stressed syllable.

impatient   comfortable   documentary   cartoons   detective

10

What can you do?

CAN YOU UNDERSTAND THIS TEXT?

The man who missed the lottery bus

YESTERDAY bus driver Dennis Hassall was behind the wheel as usual, reflecting on his fate as one of the unluckiest men in Britain. Just six months earlier, he decided to give up playing the lottery with his 11 workmates after four years of paying every week but winning almost nothing.

But last Saturday night, his workmates, who had carried on playing, each received a cheque for £744,126. While they toasted their success with champagne, Mr Hassall worked his morning shift, driving a number 7 bus between Plymouth and Plymstock in Devon. He refused to talk to journalists.

The winners said they were very sorry for Dennis, but they were not going to share the money with him. 'He hasn't paid his contribution since last summer,' winner Chris Robinson said. 'He must be feeling pretty bad. But as far as I know, he has wished us all the best of luck.' All the winners are now planning to retire. For Les Read, aged 53, the win couldn't have come at a better time. Two weeks ago he failed an eyesight test and is no longer able to drive. 'If I hadn't won the lottery, I'd have been unemployed.' Fellow winner Ian Crampton, 46, the man who picked out the six winning numbers, has been off work for several weeks and is having chemotherapy and radiotherapy for a cancer-related illness. 'Now I don't have to worry about going back to work,' he said.

The leader of the lottery syndicate, Dave Mallet, said, 'We all feel very sorry for Dennis, but he knew the rules. It's OK if you don't pay for two weeks, but any more than that and you're out. It wouldn't be fair on the others. I haven't spoken to Dennis yet, but we will be inviting him to the party we're going to have at the social club. But I don't know if he'll turn up .'

Adapted from the British press

a Read the article and mark the sentences T (true), F (false), or DS (doesn't say).

1 Dennis stopped playing the lottery four years ago.
2 Dennis didn't drink champagne with the lottery winners.
3 He gave an interview to journalists.
4 He stopped playing the lottery because he was short of money.
5 Dennis is the only person who will continue working.
6 Two of the winners had health problems.
7 Dave Mallet feels bad about what has happened to Dennis.
8 Dennis doesn't want to go to the party.

b Look at the highlighted phrasal verbs. What do they mean?

CAN YOU UNDERSTAND THESE PEOPLE?

a 7.21 Listen and circle the correct answer, a, b, or c.

1 Had the man saved his article (on his computer)?
  a Yes.   b No.   c Some of it.
2 Why didn't the man wear his lucky T-shirt?
  a Because he didn't need it.
  b Because he had lost it.
  c Because he couldn't.
3 What kind of books does the woman usually read?
  a Several kinds.   b Science fiction.   c Detective novels.
4 Where does Gerald say he was last night?
  a At home and at the pub. b At home and at a shop.
  c At home and at a football match.
5 What time do the children normally go to bed?
  a 10.00   b 9.15   c 9.30

b 7.22 Listen and complete the missing information.

Time	Channel	Programme
8.00	BBC 2	*Eight-legged Wonders.* A documentary film about [1] _____
8.00	ITV	*The Silent* [2] _____, a new crime series
[3] _____	ITV	*Who wants to be a millionaire?* Quiz show
10.05	[4] _____	Cinema: All-time greats: *Fanny and Alexander*
10.30	ITV	[5] _____ _____ A tribute to John Miller

CAN YOU SAY THIS IN ENGLISH?

Can you…? Yes (✓)

☐ complete these three sentences in a logical way
  If I hadn't gone to bed so late,…
  If I had known it was your birthday,…
  I would have arrived on time if…
☐ ask your partner three polite questions and check three things you think you know about him / her
☐ talk about how much TV you watch and what kind of programmes

Communication

2B Are you hungry? Yes, I'm starving! **Student A**

a Say your sentences to **B**. He / she must respond with the phrase in brackets.

1 Is the water cold? *(Yes, it's freezing.)*
2 Was the film good? *(Yes, it was great.)*
3 Were you tired after the exam? *(Yes, I was exhausted.)*
4 Is the kitchen dirty? *(Yes, it's filthy.)*
5 Is it a big house? *(Yes, it's enormous.)*
6 Was the weather bad? *(Yes, it was awful.)*

b Respond to **B**'s questions. Say *Yes, it's / I'm*, etc. + the **strong** form of the adjective which **B** used in the question. Remember to <u>stress</u> the **strong** adjective.

c Repeat the exercise. Try to respond as quickly as possible.

3B Who do you think they are? **Students A + B**

a In pairs, look at the people. You will have to match them with one of the jobs in the list below.

| politician | boxer | violinist | university professor | comedian |

b Discuss person A with your partner.
   • Eliminate the jobs you think are impossible for that person. Use *He / She can't be a…* Say why.
   • Now say which jobs you think are possible. Use *He / She might be…*
   • Now make a final choice for person A. Use *He / She must be…* Say why.

c Now do the same for B–E.

d Finally, your teacher will tell you if you are right.

3C Guess the sentence **Student A**

a Look at sentences 1–5 and complete them with the correct form of *be able to* + a verb.

1 I've never _____ the guitar well.
2 I'm sorry I won't _____ to your party next weekend.
3 I used to _____ a little Japanese but I can't now.
4 I love _____ in bed late at the weekend.
5 Will you _____ all the work before Saturday?

b Read your sentence 1 to **B**. If it's not the same, try again until **B** tells you 'That's right'. Continue with 2–5.

c Now listen to **B** say sentence 6. If it's the same as your sentence 6 below, say 'That's right'. If not, say 'Try again' until **B** gets it right. Continue with 7–10.

6 I won't **be able to see** you tonight. I'm too busy.
7 It was the rush hour but luckily I **was able to park** near the cinema.
8 They haven't **been able to find** a flat yet. They're still looking.
9 It must be fantastic **to be able to speak** a lot of languages.
10 You must **be able to do** this exercise! It's very easy.

Practical English 3 How do I get there? **Student A**

a You are a tourist. You are near Marble Arch tube station. Ask **B** how to get to the following places. **B** will explain how to get to the nearest tube station. Draw the route on the map and write the name of the place next to the tube station.

The Science Museum
Madame Tussauds
The National Gallery
The British Museum

> Excuse me. What's the best way to get to The Science Museum?

> The best way is by tube. The nearest station is…

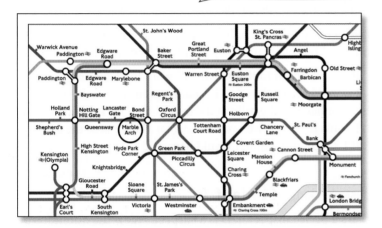

b Swap roles. You are a Londoner. **B** is a tourist. He / she is near Marble Arch tube station. **B** is going to ask you how to get to the four tourist attractions below. Look at the map to find the best route to the nearest tube station, and give **B** directions.

London Zoo (nearest tube station Regent's Park)
Harrods department store (nearest tube station Knightsbridge)
The Royal Opera House (nearest tube station Covent Garden)
The Tower of London (nearest tube station Monument)

4B What would you do if…? **Student A**

a Ask **B** your questions. Put the verbs in brackets in the past simple.

What would you do if you…?
(meet) your English teacher at a party
(find) a lot of extra money in your bank account
(get) a present from your partner that you really didn't like
(hit) somebody's car in a car park
(have) to sing at a karaoke evening
(be) invited to a really good concert by somebody you didn't like
(see) your best friend's personal diary open on a table

b Answer **B**'s questions. Ask *What about you?*

5C Test your memory **Student A**

a Ask **B** these questions. See if he / she can remember the answers.

1 What's the programme called? (*The Pretenders.*)
2 How many judges are there? (Three.)
3 What do the judges have to decide? (Who is pretending to be a professional.)
4 Where does Jessica work? (In her local library.)
5 How did Jessica react when the TV company phoned her? (She thought it was a joke and she said no.)
6 What job did she have to learn to do? (A political reporter.)
7 What did she have to do in her final test? (A live TV interview with the Minister of Education.)
8 What did she have to learn to do? (How to interview people / look more confident / speak clearly.)
9 How was she feeling before she started? (Nervous and terrified of being on TV.)

b Answer **B**'s questions. Who has the best memory?

Practical English 5 What do you think? **Student A**

a Ask **B** question number 1. Then say if you agree or disagree. If you disagree, say why. Use *I don't agree,…, Personally, I think…*, etc.

b Now answer **B**'s first question. Use *Personally, I think* or *In my opinion* Say why.

c Continue taking turns to ask questions and give your opinions.

1 What do you think is easier, to speak English or to write it?
2 Do you think that school holidays are too long?
3 Which do you think is the best sport for a young person to take up?
4 Do you think that people in your country are eating better or worse than they used to?
5 Who do you think are safer drivers, women or men?

Communication

6A I want to speak to the manager Student A

a Look at the situations and roleplay the conversations. Spend a few minutes preparing what you are going to say.

1 You're a **customer**. You bought something in a clothes shop in the sales yesterday (decide what) and there's a problem (decide what).
Go back to the shop. **B** is the shop assistant. You'd like to change it for another identical one. If you can't, you'd like a refund. If you aren't satisfied, ask the shop assistant to call the manager.

You start. Excuse me. I bought…

2 You're the **manager** of a restaurant. Your normal chef is off this week, and you have a temporary chef who is not very good. One of the waiters has had a problem with a customer, who would like to speak to you. When customers complain you usually offer them a free drink or a coffee. If it's absolutely necessary, you might give a 10% discount on their bill, but you would prefer not to. **B** is the customer.

B will start.

6C Relatives quiz Student A

a Complete the questions to describe the **bold** word. Begin with *who*, *which*, *that*, *whose*, *where* (or no relative pronoun when there is a new subject).

1 **selfish**
What do you call a person…?
2 **neighbours**
What do you call the people…?
3 **a boarding school**
What do you call a place…?
4 **a helmet**
What do you call the thing…?
5 **a boss**
What do you call the person…?
6 **traffic lights**
What do you call the things…?
7 **the butcher's**
What do you call the place…?
8 **a shop assistant**
What do you call a person…?

b Ask **B** the questions.

c Answer **B**'s questions.

7A Guess the conditional Student A

a Look at sentences 1–5 and think of the missing verb. Remember ⊞ = positive verb, ⊟ = negative verb.

1 If it had been cheaper, I _____ it. ⊞
2 If I _____ that it was your birthday, I would have made a cake. ⊞
3 I _____ so angry if you had told me the truth. ⊟
4 I would have written to you if I _____ your email address. ⊟
5 If you _____ to me, you wouldn't have married him. ⊞

b Read your sentence 1 to **B**. If it's not the same, try again until **B** tells you 'That's right'. Then write it in. Continue with 2–5.

c Listen to **B** say sentence 6. If it's the same as 6 below, say 'That's right'. If not, say 'Try again' until **B** gets it right. Continue with 7–10.

6 If I had listened to that CD first, I **wouldn't have bought** it.
7 I would have paid for her if I **hadn't paid** last time!
8 If you **had put** the milk in the fridge, it wouldn't have gone bad.
9 I would have gone with you last night if I **hadn't seen** the film before.
10 If I'd recognized him, I **would have said** hello.

7B Just checking Student A

a You are a police inspector. **B** is a suspect. Ask **B** the questions below but **don't write anything down**. Try to remember **B**'s answers.

What's your name?	Do you smoke?
Where do you live?	What car do you drive?
How old are you?	How long have you lived in this town?
Where were you born?	What did you do last night?
Are you married?	Where were you this morning at 7.00?
What do you do?	

b Now check the information with **B** using a question tag.

Your name's Angela, isn't it?   You live in Berlin, don't you?

c Change roles. Now you are the suspect and **B** is the detective. Answer his / her questions. You can invent the information if you want to.

d **A** will now check the information he / she has. Just say, 'Yes, that's right' or 'No, that's wrong.' Correct the wrong information.

Practical English 7 I'm so sorry! Student A

a **B** has done some very irritating things! You are going to tell **B** what he / she has done. **B** will apologize and make an excuse.

You forgot my birthday!	You took my dictionary home last night!
You've broken my glasses!	You didn't answer your mobile when
You've just eaten the last biscuit!	I called you last night!

b Now **B** is going to tell you about some things you've done. Apologize and make an excuse.

2B Are you hungry? Yes, I'm starving! **Student B**

a Respond to A's questions. Say *Yes, it's / I'm* etc. + the **strong** form of the adjective which A used in the question. Remember to <u>stress</u> the **strong** adjective.

b Say your sentences to A. He / she must respond with the phrase in brackets.

1 Are you afraid of flying? *(Yes, I'm terrified.)*
2 Is the soup hot? *(Yes, it's boiling.)*
3 Was the teacher angry? *(Yes, he / she was furious.)*
4 Is the bedroom small? *(Yes, it's tiny.)*
5 Are the children hungry? *(Yes, they're starving.)*
6 Is the chocolate cake nice? *(Yes, it's delicious.)*

c Repeat the exercise. Try to respond as quickly as possible.

Practical English 2 Requests **Students A + B**

a Look at the verbs below. Choose **one** thing you would like someone to do for you.

look after (my children, my dog, my cat, etc.)
lend me (some money, your car, a book, etc.)
give me a lift (home, to the centre, etc.)
help me (with my homework, to paint my flat, etc.)

b Ask as many other students as possible. Be polite, and explain why you want the favour. How many people agree to help you?

3C Guess the sentence **Student B**

a Look at sentences 6–10 and complete them with the correct form of *be able to* + a verb.

6 I won't _____ you tonight. I'm too busy.
7 It was the rush hour but luckily I _____ near the cinema.
8 They haven't _____ a flat yet. They're still looking.
9 It must be fantastic _____ a lot of languages.
10 You must _____ this exercise! It's very easy.

b Listen to A say sentence 1. If it's the same as your sentence 1 below, say 'That's right'. If not, say 'Try again' until A gets it right. Continue with 2–5.

1 I've never **been able to play** the guitar well.
2 I'm sorry I won't **be able to go** to your party next weekend.
3 I used to **be able to understand** a little Japanese but I can't now.
4 I love **being able to stay** in bed late at the weekend.
5 Will you **be able to finish** all the work before Saturday?

c Now read your sentence 6 to A. If it's not the same, try again until A tells you 'That's right'. Continue with 7–10.

Communication

Practical English 3   How do I get there?   **Student B**

a You are a Londoner. A is a tourist. He / she is near Marble Arch tube station. A is going to ask you how to get to the four tourist attractions below. Look at the map to find the best route to the nearest tube station, and give **A** directions.

The Science Museum (nearest tube station South Kensington)
Madame Tussauds (nearest tube station Baker Street)
The National Gallery (nearest tube station Charing Cross)
The British Museum (nearest tube station Russell Square)

Excuse me. What's the best way to get to The Science Museum?

The best way is by tube. The nearest station is…

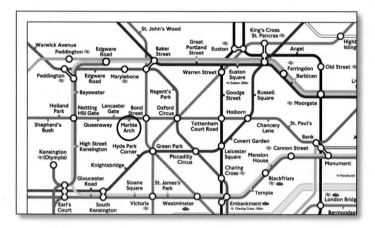

b Swap roles. You are a tourist. You are near Marble Arch tube station. Ask **A** how to get to the following places. A will explain how to get to the nearest tube station. Draw the route on the map and write the name of the place next to the tube station.

London Zoo
Harrods department store
The Royal Opera House
The Tower of London

4B   What would you do if…?   **Student B**

a Answer A's questions. Ask *What about you?*

b Ask A your questions. Put the verbs in the brackets in the past simple.

What would you do if you…?
(have) an exam the next day and somebody offered to sell you the answers
(be) offered a job in Australia
(wake up) and (see) a snake in your bedroom
(meet) your partner in the street with an ex-boyfriend / girlfriend
(get) too much change from a shop assistant
(see) somebody stealing something in a shop
(borrow) a friend's car and broke one of the lights

5C   Test your memory   **Student B**

a Answer A's questions.

b Now ask **A** these questions. See if he / she can remember the answers. Who has the best memory?

1 How long do the contestants have to learn to do the new job? (One month.)
2 What does the contestant have to do at the end of the month? (A test – they do the new job with three real professionals.)
3 How old is Jessica? (26.)
4 What did Jessica study at university? (English Literature.)
5 Why did she agree to be on the programme? (Her friends and family persuaded her.)
7 What was Jessica like before the programme? (Quiet and shy.)
8 Who were her teachers? (A political journalist and an ex-MP.)
9 What did she have to learn about? (The world of politics.)

Practical English 5   What do you think? Student B

a Answer A's first question. Use *Personally, I think* or *In my opinion* Say why.

b Ask **A** your question number 1. Then say if you agree or disagree with A. If you disagree, Use *I don't agree,…, Personally, I think…*, etc.

c Continue taking turns to ask questions and give your opinions.

1 Do you think it is easier to learn to drive or to learn to swim?
2 Do you think it's better to be an only child or have brothers or sisters?
3 Do you think that men are better cooks than women?
4 Which do you think is more dangerous, travelling by plane or travelling by car?
5 Do you think that it is a waste of money to buy designer clothes?

6A I want to speak to the manager Student B

a Look at the situations and roleplay the conversations. Spend a few minutes preparing what you are going to say.

1 You're a **shop assistant** in a clothes shop. **A** is going to come to you with a problem with something he / she bought in the sales yesterday. You can't change it for an identical one because there are no more in his / her size.
Try to persuade **A** to change it for something else, because you don't usually give refunds during the sales.

A will start.

2 You're a **customer** in a restaurant. You have just finished your meal and you didn't enjoy it at all (what was wrong with it?). You complained to the waiter but the waiter didn't solve the problems. You have asked the waiter to call the manager. Try to get at least a 50% discount on your meal. **A** is the manager.

You start.   Good evening. Are you the manager?

6C Relatives quiz Student B

a Complete the questions to describe the **bold** word. Begin with *who, which, that, whose, where* (or no relative pronoun when there is a new subject).

1 **shy**
   What do you call a person…?
2 **a referee**
   What do you call the person…?
3 **a classroom**
   What's the name of the place…?
4 **a trolley**
   What do you call the thing…?
5 **a dentist**
   What do you call a person…?
6 **a receipt**
   What do you call the piece of paper…?
7 **a taxi rank**
   What do you call the place…?
8 **a close friend**
   What do you call a person…?

b Answer **A**'s questions.

c Ask **A** your questions.

7A Guess the conditional Student B

a Look at sentences 6–10 and think of the missing verb. Remember ⊞ = positive verb, ⊟ = negative verb.

6 If I had listened to that CD first, I _____ it. ⊟
7 I would have paid for her if I _____ last time! ⊟
8 If you _____ the milk in the fridge, it wouldn't have gone bad. ⊞
9 I would have gone with you last night if I _____ the film before. ⊟
10 If I'd recognized him, I _____ hello. ⊞

b Listen to **A** say sentence 1. If it's the same as 1 below, say 'That's right.' If not, say 'Try again' until **A** gets it right. Continue with 2–5.

1 If it had been cheaper, I **would have bought** it.
2 If I **had known** that it was your birthday, I would have made a cake.
3 I **wouldn't have been** so angry if you had told me the truth.
4 I would have written to you if I **hadn't lost** your email address.
5 If you **had listened** to me, you wouldn't have married him.

c Read your sentence 6 to **A**. If it's not the same, try again until **A** tells you 'That's right.' Then write it in. Continue with 7–10.

7B Just checking Student B

a You are a suspect. **A** is a police inspector. Answer **A**'s questions. You can invent the information if you want to.

b **A** will now check the information he / she has. Just say, 'Yes, that's right' or 'No, that's wrong.' Correct the wrong information.

c Change roles. Now you are a police inspector and **A** is a suspect. Ask **A** the questions below but **don't write anything down**. Try to remember **A**'s answers.

What's your name?	Do you smoke?
Where do you live?	What car do you drive?
How old are you?	How long have you lived in this town?
Where were you born?	What did you do last night?
Are you married?	Where were you this morning at 7.00?
What do you do?	

d Now check the information with **A** using a question tag.

Your name's Angela, isn't it?   You live in Berlin, don't you?

Practical English 7 I'm so sorry! Student B

a **A** is going to tell you about some things you've done. Apologize and make an excuse.

b **A** has done some very irritating things! Tell **A** what he / she has done. **A** will apologize and make an excuse.

You didn't pay me back the money I lent you!
You haven't introduced me to your friend!
You're sitting in my seat!
You finished all the milk in the fridge!
You didn't reply to my email yesterday!

Listening

1.1

Interviewer Rumiko, what do you eat in a typical day?

Rumiko I don't usually have breakfast because I can't get up early enough to eat! I normally just buy a coffee and drink it in the office.
I usually have lunch in a restaurant near the office with people from work. When I was younger, I used to go to fast food restaurants and have pizza, or fried chicken and chips, but now I prefer eating something healthier, so I go to sushi restaurants or restaurants which serve organic food. And for dinner I eat out a lot too.

Interviewer Do you ever cook?

Rumiko Well, I like cooking, but I work very late every day and also my kitchen's too small. My boyfriend's a better cook anyway.

Interviewer Do you ever eat unhealthy food?

Rumiko Well, I don't eat a lot of sweet things but I drink a lot of coffee every day. I think I'm addicted to caffeine.

Interviewer Are you trying to cut down on anything at the moment?

Rumiko No. I eat healthily and I do exercise regularly, so I don't think I need to cut down on food.

Interviewer Are people's diets in your country getting better or worse?

Rumiko Oh, probably worse. I think the diet in Japan today is much more westernized than before and that's why some people are getting fatter. But personally I like the fact that there are more different kinds of food and restaurants now. I enjoy the variety, it makes eating out much more fun.

1.5

Interviewer Kevin, why did you decide to open a restaurant in Chile?

Kevin I'd always wanted to have my own restaurant and it would have been very expensive to do that in England. I'd visited Chile as a tourist and loved it, and I thought it would be a good place because Chileans are very pro-European, and are quite open to new things, new ideas. So I opened *Frederick's*.

Interviewer Right. Why did you call the restaurant *Frederick's*?

Kevin Because Frederick's my father's name. It's my second name too.

Interviewer What kind of food do you serve?

Kevin Mainly international dishes like pasta, steak and fries, risotto – but we also do several English dishes as well.

Interviewer Were Chilean people surprised when they heard that an English chef was going to open a restaurant here?

Kevin Yes, they were – very! I think people don't usually expect the English to be good cooks.

Interviewer Is your chef English?

Kevin No, he's Chilean – but I've taught him to make some English dishes.

Interviewer What kind of English dishes do you have on your menu?

Kevin Well, we're open in the morning, and we serve traditional English breakfasts, and then we have a lot of English desserts at lunchtime, for example trifle – that's a typical English dessert made with fruit and cake and cream. And we do proper English teas in the afternoon – tea with cakes or sandwiches.

Interviewer Are the English dishes popular?

Kevin Yes, especially the desserts and cakes. I think people here in Chile have a very sweet tooth.

Interviewer People who visit England always say that the food isn't very good, or that you have to spend a lot of money to eat well. Do you agree?

Kevin I think eating good food's never cheap. But I think that today, the best place for a tourist to eat in England is in a pub, especially the ones called gastropubs – pubs which are also restaurants. These pubs are beginning to serve really good food that's not too expensive.

Interviewer I see. You said earlier that your chef was a man. Do you have any women working in your kitchen?

Kevin Yes, one, but the rest are all men. In fact, I think that's typical all over the world – there are far more men than women in restaurant kitchens.

Interviewer Why do you think that is?

Kevin I think there are a lot of reasons. The most important reason is probably the unsocial hours. Most women don't want a job where you have to work until late at night. Then there's the atmosphere. Women don't like being shouted at, and there's a lot of shouting in restaurant kitchens. It's also usually incredibly hot and I think women don't like that either.

Interviewer And finally is there any English food that you really miss here?

Kevin The thing I miss most living in Chile is English cheese. I really miss Stilton – which is a wonderful English blue cheese. It's not as famous as some of the French cheeses like Roquefort but I think it should be. You should try it!

Interviewer I will! Kevin, thank you very much.

Kevin Thank you.

1.6

Interviewer What was the most exciting match you refereed?

Juan Antonio It's difficult to choose *one* match as the most exciting. I remember some of the Real Madrid–Barcelona matches, for example the first one I ever refereed. The atmosphere was incredible in the stadium. But really it's impossible to pick just one – there have been so many.

Interviewer Who was the best player you ever saw?

Juan Antonio During my career there have been many great players, like Johan Cruyff and Diego Maradona. It's very difficult to say who was the best but there's one player who stands out for me, not just for being a great footballer but also for being a great human being and that was the Brazilian international Mauro Silva, who used to play here in Spain, for Deportivo La Coruña.

Interviewer What was the worst experience you ever had as a referee?

Juan Antonio The worst? Well, that was something that happened very early in my career. I was only 16 and I was refereeing a match in a town in Spain and the home team lost. After the match, I was attacked and injured by the players of the home team and by the spectators. After all these years I can still remember a mother, who had a little baby in her arms, who was trying to hit me. She was so angry with me that she nearly dropped her baby. That was my worst moment, and it nearly made me stop being a referee.

Interviewer Do you think that there's more cheating in football than in the past?

Juan Antonio Yes, I think so.

Interviewer Why?

Juan Antonio I think it's because there's so much money in football today that it has become much more important to win. Also football is much faster than it used to be so it's more difficult for referees to detect cheating.

Interviewer How do footballers cheat?

Juan Antonio Oh, there are many ways, but for me the worst thing in football today is what we call 'simulation'. Simulation is when players pretend to have been fouled when they haven't been. For example, sometimes a player falls over in the penalty area when, in fact, nobody has touched him and this can result in the referee giving a penalty when it wasn't a penalty. In my opinion, when a player does this he's cheating not only the referee, not only the players of the other team, but also the spectators, because spectators pay money to see a fair contest.

Interviewer What's the most difficult thing about being a referee?

Juan Antonio Ah, the most difficult thing is to make the right decisions during a match. It's difficult because you have to make decisions when everything's happening so quickly – football today is very fast. Also important decisions often depend on the referee's *interpretation* of the rules. Things aren't black and white. And of course making decisions would be much easier if players didn't cheat.

Interviewer So, in your opinion, fair play doesn't exist any more.

Juan Antonio Not at all. I think fair play does exist – the players who cheat are still the exceptions.

1.9

1 **A** So what are you going to do next year, dear? Are you going to go to university?
B No, Gran. I've already told you three times. I'm not going to university. I'm going to look for a job. I want to earn some money.
A Oh, all right dear, you don't need to shout. I'm not deaf. What's the time now?
B Ten past five. Shall I make you a cup of tea?
A Oh yes, dear, that'd be lovely.
2 **A** See you tomorrow, then.
B Hold on a minute – where are you going?
A Out. It's Friday night, remember?
B What time are you coming back?
A I'm not coming back. I'm staying at Mum's tonight.
B I think you need a coat. It's going to be cold tonight.
A Dad – nobody wears coats any more! Bye!
3 **A** Can I use your car tonight?
B No.
A Why not?
B You'll crash it again.
A I won't. I'll be really careful. I'll drive slowly. I promise.
B OK. Here you are. But be careful.
A Thanks. See you later.

1.11

Continuity announcer It's eight o'clock and time for *Breakfast Time*.

Presenter Good morning, everyone. Our guest this morning is the American writer Norah Levy. Norah's here in Britain this week promoting her new book 'We are family', which is all about how our position in the family affects our personality. Welcome Norah.

Norah Thank you.

Presenter Now is this really true, Norah? That our position in the family affects our personality?

Norah Sure. OK, other factors can influence your personality too, but your position in the family is definitely one of the strongest.

Presenter So tell us a bit about the oldest children in a family – the first born.

Norah Well, the oldest children get maximum attention from their parents and the result is that they're usually quite self-confident people. They make good leaders. The famous Prime Minister, Winston Churchill, was a firstborn child. They're often ambitious and they're more likely to go to university than their brothers or sisters. They often get the top jobs too. Oldest children are also responsible people, because they often have to look after their younger brothers or sisters. The downside of this is that sometimes this means that when they're older they worry a lot about things. They can also be quite bossy, and even aggressive, especially when they don't get what they want.

Presenter What about the middle child?

Norah Well, middle children are usually independent and competitive.

Presenter Competitive?

Norah Yes, because they have to fight with their brothers and sisters for their parents' attention. And they're usually sociable, they like being with people, probably because they have always had other children to play with. However, on the negative side middle children are often jealous of their brothers and sisters and they can be moody.

Presenter And youngest children?

Norah If you're the youngest in a family, you'll probably be very charming, very affectionate, and probably quite a relaxed person. This is because parents are usually more relaxed when they have their last child. On the other hand, youngest children are often quite lazy. This is because they always have their older brothers and sisters to help them. And they can be quite manipulative – they use their charm to get what they want.

Presenter OK, that's all very interesting. Now, I'm an only child. People often have the idea that only children like me are spoilt. Is that true?

Norah Well, of course it's true! Only children are the only ones – they don't have to share with anyone – so they're often spoilt by their parents and their grandparents. As a result they can be quite selfish. They think of themselves more than of other people.

Presenter OK. Well, that sounds like a good description of me! Is there any good news?

Norah Yes, there is. On the positive side, only children are usually very organized and responsible, and they can be very imaginative too.

Presenter Well, thank you, Norah, and good luck with the book. And now it's time for the news headlines…

1.13

My name's Allie Gray and I'm from Cambridge in England. I met Mark about a year ago. He's from San Francisco. We both work for MTC, a music company. I was working in the London office and he came there on business. We got on really well and we really liked each other.

Anyway, at the end of his trip, he invited me to go to a conference in San Francisco. We had a great time again. And then something amazing happened. When I was in San Francisco, I was offered a job in our new office in Paris.

When I told Mark, he told me that he was going to work in the Paris office too!

There's just one little thing. His job is marketing director – but mine is managing director – so I'm going to be his boss. I've been in Paris for three weeks now, and I love it. Mark arrived from San Francisco yesterday. He's coming into the office this morning.

1.16

Allie What a lovely view! The river's beautiful, isn't it?

Mark Paris is so romantic. I can't believe we're here together at last.

Allie Yes, it's weird.

Mark Weird? It's wonderful. I really missed you.

Allie Me too.

Mark Why don't we sit down?

Allie So did you like the office?

Mark Yes, it's great. How do you get on with everyone?

Allie OK. But we'll see. I've only been here three weeks. What did you think of them?

Mark I thought Jacques was very nice, and Nicole …

Allie What about Nicole?

Mark She was very friendly.

Allie You know we have to keep things a secret.

Mark What things?

Allie You know, us. Our relationship. I don't want the people in the office to know we're together.

Mark No, of course not. But it isn't going to be easy.

Allie No, it isn't. How's the hotel?

Mark It's OK, I guess, but it's not like having my own place. I have to find an apartment.

Allie Don't worry. It won't take you long. What are you thinking?

Mark Do you really want to know? I was wondering what kind of a boss you'll be.

Allie Well, you'll find out tomorrow.

2.5

Good evening. I'm Peter Crane with the six o'clock news.

At least 17 people have been injured in the road accident that took place on the M1 near Leeds last night. The police said that the lorry which caused the accident was travelling at about 85 miles an hour, well over the 60 mile an hour speed limit for heavy goods vehicles.

2600 workers have walked out of the Peugeot car factory in Coventry in protest against the company's pay offer. The unions have asked for a rise of 8.5%. There'll be a meeting between their leaders and management later today.

The latest unemployment figures have been released for this year. They show an increase of 150,263 on last year's figures. This brings the total number of unemployed to approximately 1,490,000. The Employment Minister says this increase has been caused by the relocation of several factories from Britain to the Far East.

Estate agents are predicting that house prices will continue to rise this year, making it extremely difficult for first-time buyers to get onto the property ladder. It's estimated that house prices have increased by a third in the last five years. The average price of a three-bedroom house in south-east England is now £255,900.

And, the weather for the weekend…

2.6

Interviewer So, how long have you been living here?

Karen For about six months now.

Interviewer Why did you choose Beirut?

Karen Because, Mike – my husband – and I have always loved Arab culture and the language, Mike's an English teacher and he got a job here in a language school.

Interviewer Why did you want to take a year off?

Karen Basically I wanted a break from teaching. I love teaching children but I needed a change. Also I've been drawing and painting since I was little but I've never really had the chance to *study* drawing. So this seemed like the perfect opportunity to have a change and learn to draw properly.

Interviewer What have you been doing here since you arrived?

Karen Well, I found a fantastic art teacher, called Omayma, and I've been having classes with her since October. She's great and she speaks English, which is lucky because I don't know

much Arabic yet. But I am learning the language as quickly as I can.

Interviewer Is Arabic a difficult language to learn?

Karen Incredibly difficult! Especially the pronunciation. You have to learn to make a lot of new sounds. Also it takes a long time to learn to read and write in Arabic.

Interviewer You also teach belly dancing here.

Karen That's right.

Interviewer How did that happen?

Karen Well, I've been teaching belly dancing for about six years, and I love it so I wanted to continue doing it here. A lot of Lebanese women don't know how to belly dance and they want to learn. I give classes here in my living room. We have a lot of fun!

Interviewer Are your students surprised that an English person is teaching them belly dancing?

Karen Yes, very, but they're also really happy to find that a foreigner loves Arabic music and understands something from their culture.

Interviewer What's the best thing about living in Lebanon so far?

Karen The people. The hospitality of the people here is absolutely amazing.

2.11

1

A Hello?

B Hi Sharon. It's me… Kylie.

A Oh. Hi Kylie.

B Hey, you sound awful – what's been happening?

A Oh, nothing. Well, OK… Kenny and I have been arguing.

B What about? What's he been doing this time?

A He's been sending text messages to his ex-girlfriend again.

B No!

A I knew this holiday was a mistake. I shouldn't have come.

2

Wife You are so red! How long have you been sunbathing? All morning?

Husband I haven't been sunbathing. I've been reading.

Wife Yes, but in the sun! Didn't you put any suncream on?

Husband No.

Wife You'd better go and put some aftersun cream on now. You're going to feel terrible tonight…

3

Woman 1 You two look exhausted. What have you been doing?

Man We've been sightseeing in the town. We've been walking all afternoon.

Woman 2 Yes, my feet are killing me.

Woman 1 Well, come and sit down in the bar and have a nice cup of tea.

2.12

I set off at six. It was still dark when I put my suitcase in the car and drove off. I had a good journey through London because it was Saturday so there was no rush hour traffic.

Soon I was on the M20 motorway heading towards Folkestone on the south coast. I stopped at a service station for a cup of coffee and a sandwich. I didn't buy any petrol because it's much cheaper in France.

I arrived in Folkestone at 8.10. The problem with travelling by car from England to France is that Britain is an island. There are 35 kilometres of water between England and France. You can get across it by ferry, but there's a much better and quicker way – the Channel Tunnel!

The Channel Tunnel's only a train tunnel, not a road tunnel and so you have to put your car on a train. The journey takes an hour and a half, and drivers have

Listening

to sit in their cars because there are no seats on the train for passengers. I arrived at the terminal and joined the queue of cars waiting for the next train.

At 10.30 the train arrived in Calais and I drove my car off the train and onto the road – a French road. I had to remember to drive on the right, not on the left!

The traffic in Calais was quite bad. Finally I got out of Calais and onto the motorway to the South of France. The speed limit on French motorways is 130 kilometres an hour and the road was clear so now I could travel quickly. But first I stopped at a service station to fill up with petrol.

Petrol's cheaper in France than in Britain but on the other hand you have to pay to travel on French motorways. In Britain they're free.

It's 960 kilometres from Calais to Avignon, and the journey on the motorway was boring. I listened to my favourite music to pass the time and I stopped again for lunch.

At eight o'clock I finally arrived in Avignon. I found my hotel and I was looking forward to a lovely French meal.

2.15

TV host And this evening on *Behind the wheel* we talk to Brian Delaney, who's an expert on road safety. Brian, you did some tests to find out how dangerous it is to do other things when we're driving. According to your tests, what's the most dangerous thing to do?

Expert Well, the first thing I have to say is that doing any other things when you're driving is dangerous and can cause an accident. Because when you're driving you should concentrate 100% on controlling the car and anything else you do is a distraction.

The tests we did in a simulator showed that the most difficult and most dangerous thing is to try and open a packet of crisps or to open a can of drink. The reason is that most people actually need two hands to open a packet of crisps or a can of drink so they take both hands off the wheel for a second or two. And, of course, that's the most dangerous thing you can possibly do. In fact, one of the drivers in the simulator actually crashed when he did this.

TV host And which is the next most dangerous?

Expert The next dangerous thing is to select a specific CD from the passenger seat. This is extremely dangerous too because to do this you have to take your eyes off the road for one or two seconds.

TV host And number three?

Expert Number three was making a phone call on a mobile. What we found in the tests was that drivers drove more slowly when they did this, but that their control of the car got worse.

TV host Yes, I can believe that. And number 4?

Expert Number four was listening to our favourite music. In the tests most drivers drove more quickly and less safely when they were listening to music they already knew. If the music was fast and heavy, some drivers even drove more aggressively.

TV host So no heavy metal when you're driving.

Expert Absolutely not.

TV host And in fifth place?

Expert In fifth place was talking to other passengers. The problem when we talk to other people in the car is that we pay too much attention to what we're saying or what we're hearing and not enough attention to what's happening on the road.

TV host So the least dangerous is listening to music you *don't* know.

Expert That's right. The least dangerous of all these activities is listening to unfamiliar music on the radio or on a CD player. It seems that if we *don't know* the music then we're less distracted by it. In this part of the tests, all drivers drove safely and well.

2.18

Nicole Have you started looking for an apartment?
Mark No, I haven't had time yet.
Ben Anyway, it's best to get to know Paris first.
Mark Yeah – it's a big city.
Nicole Merci.
Ben Merci.
Mark Merci beaucoup.
Nicole Very good, Mark!
Mark Thanks. That's nearly all the French I know!
Ben Hi, Beatrice. … Yeah … just a minute. Sorry.
Nicole How do you like the office?
Mark Oh, it's great.
Nicole And the people?
Mark Really friendly! I like Ben a lot. He's amazing with computers. And Jacques's a really nice guy!
Nicole Oh, Jacques, he's very charming. Everybody likes him. And he has a lovely wife. She used to be a pop star when she was young. Have you heard of Isabelle?
Mark No, I'm sorry, I haven't.
Nicole She's very pretty. Allie is very attractive, too.
Mark Allie? Yeah, I guess.
Nicole Although her clothes are very English. And she's very formal. You know, today, I asked if I could have a day off, and she wanted me to send her an email!
Mark Well, the English have their funny ways.
Nicole Oh yeah. Oh, hello, Allie.
Allie Hi.
Mark Allie! Hi, let me get you a drink.
Allie Thanks. I'll have a Diet Coke.

3.2

1
I'm a shop assistant and I work in a clothes shop and what really makes me angry is when I'm serving somebody and suddenly their mobile rings and they answer the phone and start having a conversation. It's really annoying. I think that if you're in a shop and talking to a shop assistant, then you shouldn't answer the phone.
2
What most annoys me is people who use their phones on a plane. I mean everybody knows that you have to switch off your mobile on a plane and that you mustn't use it until you get off the plane. But some people switch on their phones the moment the plane lands and they start making calls. Why can't they wait another fifteen minutes?
3
I hate it when people talk very loudly on their mobile phone in a public place. The other day I was in the waiting room at the doctor's and there was a man there whose mobile rang about every two minutes and we all had to listen to him talking loudly to his wife, then to his boss, then to a garage mechanic… I think that if you're in a public place and someone calls you, you should talk really quietly or go somewhere else. And you don't have to shout – the other person can hear you perfectly well.
4
What really annoys me are people who use their phones a lot when they're with other people – like when you're out having a drink or a meal with someone and they spend the whole time talking on their mobiles or texting other people to arrange what they're doing the next day. I think it's really rude.

5
I hate people who use their mobiles in the car, even if they're hands free. Whenever you see someone driving badly, nine times out of ten they're on the phone.

3.4

László Well, I think sometimes yes. English people can be so polite that you don't really understand them. For example, I went to London with some other teachers from Hungary to do a training course for teachers of English. It was a special course for foreign teachers. During the course the tutors, the people who were teaching us, talked to us a lot about our progress – and we thought we were all doing really well. So we were very very surprised when some of us failed the course! What had happened was that the English tutors were so polite when they gave their opinion about our teaching that we didn't realize we were doing things badly. I think that's typically English. I think sometimes they need to say what they think, to be more direct.

Paula I think English people are so polite that it makes us Latin people think that they're cold. I mean we're very noisy and extrovert and so when they're quiet and polite we think that they don't like us, that they're being unfriendly. So maybe yes, they *can* be too polite. I think they need to relax more.

Melik I think the English are very polite, but I don't think they are too polite – I mean I don't think it's a bad thing, I think it's a good thing. In my job, I have met a lot of English people and I think they're much more polite than we are, both in the way they talk and also in the way they respect other people's opinions. And their manners in general are much better. OK, this isn't true about all English people. The football hooligans and some of the tourists that come here to Turkey and drink too much – they're not polite – but the majority are and I like it.

Renata Well, I went to London a few years ago and one day, surprise surprise, it was raining and I was walking along the street and everybody had an umbrella and every time someone went past me they hit me with their umbrella and then said, 'Oh sorry,' or 'I'm awfully sorry,' or 'I'm terribly sorry'. And after the tenth time this happened, I just said to the person who hit me, 'Please stop saying sorry and just be more careful!' So in answer to your question, I don't think English people are too polite. They say 'sorry' and 'thank you' a lot, but it doesn't really mean anything.

3.5

Policeman OK, ladies, now can you describe the man you saw in the bank?
Woman 1 Well, he was, er, sort of medium height, you know, not short – but not tall either. And quite skinny, you know thin.
Woman 2 Yes. And he had a beard and a little moustache.
Woman 1 No, he didn't. He had a moustache but not a beard. It's just that I think he hadn't shaved.
Woman 2 No, it was a beard, I'm sure.
Woman 1 And anyway, Doris, you weren't wearing your glasses so you can't have seen him very well.
Woman 2 I could see perfectly well.
Policeman Ladies, ladies, please. So, no moustache then.
Woman 1 No, he had a moustache but he didn't have a beard.
Policeman And what about his hair?
Woman 2 Dark.

Woman 1 Yes, short, dark hair.
Policeman Straight?
Woman 1 No, curly, I'd say. Wouldn't you say, Doris?
Woman 2 Yes, very curly.
Policeman So, dark, curly, hair?
Woman 1 Yes. That's what we said. Are you deaf or something?
Policeman And what time was it when…

3.8

Interviewer Rafael Lloyd. A Spanish first name and a British surname?
Rafael Yes. My mother was Spanish and my father's English.
Interviewer Is Rafael your real name then or your stage name?
Rafael It's my real name: my mother was from Cordoba in Spain and Rafael's the patron saint of Cordoba. But it's also my stage name.
Interviewer What nationality are you?
Rafael I'm British and Spanish. I was born in Spain and I was brought up there. I've spent a lot of time in Britain too. I've been living in Oxford for the last ten years.
Interviewer Oh, nice. Are you bilingual?
Rafael Yes, I am.
Interviewer And, it's a strange question, do you feel more Spanish than British or vice versa?
Rafael Well, I think I feel more Spanish in most respects, especially as a big part of my life revolves around Spanish culture. But I do like individuality, eccentricity, and tea. I must feel a little British too, I suppose!
Interviewer Do you think you look more Spanish than English?
Rafael Well, I think I look Spanish, but when I travel, people always think I'm from their country and people have stopped me in the street, for example in Cairo and in Rome, to ask me for help, so I must have an international face…maybe I should be a spy!
Interviewer When did you start learning to play the guitar?
Rafael I started when I was nine when my family lived in Madrid. A teacher used to come to our flat and give me lessons.
Interviewer I see, so how long have you been working professionally as a flamenco guitarist?
Rafael I started when I was 17, I mean that's when I started to get paid for my first concerts. I'm now 39, so that's, erm, 22 years.

3.9

Interviewer As a flamenco guitarist living in Britain, is it easy to make a living?
Rafael I think life as a musician is never easy. But I think it's easier here than in Spain, because there are fewer flamenco guitarists here.
Interviewer And where's flamenco popular, apart from in Spain?
Rafael Well, the biggest markets for flamenco outside Spain are really the USA, Germany, and Japan, but I've found that it's popular all over the world. It has a strong identity that people relate to in every corner of the planet.
Interviewer Now, you don't look like the stereotype of a flamenco guitarist. People imagine flamenco guitarists as having long dark hair…
Rafael That's true. I used to have really long hair, but I decided to cut my hair short.
Interviewer Are people in Britain surprised when they find out that you're a flamenco guitarist?
Rafael No, not really. That's one of the things I like about Britain: no one judges you on appearance.
Interviewer And what about in Spain?
Rafael Well, actually, in Spain people find it much harder to believe that I'm a flamenco guitarist. I

think Spanish people believe in stereotypes more than in Britain. And they judge you more on your appearance. But as soon as people hear me playing the guitar, then they know that I'm the real thing.
Interviewer Could you play something for us?
Rafael Of course.

3.13

Interviewer Hello and welcome to this week's edition of *All about you*. Today's programme's about taking up new activities, and how to succeed at them. With us is psychologist Dr Maggie Prior. Good afternoon.
Psychologist Good afternoon.
Interviewer Dr Prior, what tips can you give our listeners who are thinking of learning to do something new?
Psychologist Well, first of all I would say choose wisely. On the one hand, don't choose something completely unrealistic. For example, don't decide to take up sailing if you can't swim, or parachute jumping if you're afraid of heights. But, on the other hand, don't generalize and think that just because you aren't very good at one sport, you won't be able to do any sports at all. I mean, just because you were bad at gymnastics at school, doesn't mean that you might not love playing tennis.
Interviewer So think positive?
Psychologist Definitely. And never think you'll be bad at something before you've even tried it.
Interviewer OK, so, let's imagine I've started to learn to play tennis and I'm finding it very hard work.
Psychologist Well, first don't give up too quickly, carry on for at least a few months. It often takes time to begin to enjoy learning something new. Another thing that can help, if you're having problems learning something, is to give it a break and then try again, perhaps a month or two later.
Interviewer But what if I carry on and I find I really really don't have a talent for tennis?
Psychologist I think the important thing is not to be too ambitious. I mean if you've never done much sport and you decide to learn to play tennis, don't expect to become the next Wimbledon champion. Just aim to enjoy what you're doing, not to be the best in the world at it.
Interviewer But if, even after all this, I still feel I'm not getting anywhere?
Psychologist Well, sometimes you do have to accept it and say, 'OK, this really isn't my thing,' and you need to give it up. But why not try something else?
There are lots of other things you can learn to do. But remember that if you take up an activity that you're really interested in, even if you aren't very good at it, you'll make new friends, because you'll be meeting other people who have similar interests to you.
Interviewer So it might be good for my love life.
Psychologist Exactly.
Interviewer Dr Maggie Prior, thank you very much.

3.17

Landlady This is the apartment. *Je vous laisse visiter. Je serai en bas.*
Mark Merci, madame. Sorry, Nicole. What did she say?
Nicole She said that we can have a look at the flat. She's going to wait downstairs.
Mark Thanks. So, what do you think?
Nicole Well, it's a long way from the station. And it's on the fourth floor. It's a pity there isn't a lift.
Mark Who needs one? The stairs are good exercise. Look, there's a great view from here.
Nicole It's also very noisy.
Mark Sure, but it has character. It's just how I

imagined an apartment in Paris.
Nicole Everything's old, including the heating. It will be very cold in the winter.
Mark Oh, hi.
Allie Well, what's it like?
Mark Nice – really Parisian.
Allie Are you going to take it?
Mark I think so, yeah…
Allie I can't wait to see it!
Mark Yeah…
Allie Are you OK? Are you on your own?
Mark No, I'm with the woman who owns the apartment. I'll call you back.
Allie OK, speak later. Love you.
Mark Love you too, bye. Sorry about that. That was…that was my… my daughter.
Nicole Calling from America?
Mark You know. She's just taking an interest.
Nicole Taking an interest. That's nice.

4.3

Journalist What subjects did you take?
Charlotte Physics, chemistry, maths, and biology.
Journalist Do you think you've passed?
Charlotte I'm sure I've passed, but I'm worried about what grades I'll get.
Journalist Why?
Charlotte Because I want to study medicine at university – at Cambridge, and they won't give me a place unless I get three As and a B.
Journalist Do you think you'll get them?
Charlotte I don't know. I think I did OK, but I'm a bit worried about maths.
Journalist When will you get your results?
Charlotte Tomorrow, by post. I'm *really* nervous – and so are my parents!
As soon as the post comes, I'll take the letter upstairs and open it.
Journalist And how will you celebrate if you pass?
Charlotte I don't want to plan any celebrations, until I get the results.
Journalist And what will you do if you don't get the grades you need?
Charlotte I don't want to think about it. If I don't get into Cambridge, my parents will kill me. No, I'm joking. I suppose I'll do another year at school and take the exams again.
Journalist Well, good luck!
Charlotte Thanks.

4.4

Journalist What exam did you take?
Viktor FCE. First Certificate in English.
Journalist Do you think you've passed?
Viktor I think so. I'm quite optimistic. I think I did the exam quite well.
Journalist When will you get your result?
Viktor Tomorrow morning. I study at a language school and when I go to class tomorrow the grades will be on the notice board. My name will be the first on the list because my surname begins with A.
Journalist How will you celebrate if you pass?
Viktor I'll go and have a drink with the other people in my class. Well, with the people who have passed.
Journalist And what will you do if you pass? Will you carry on studying English?
Viktor Yes, I'd like to take the CAE exam next year.
Journalist And if you don't pass?
Viktor I'll take the exam again in June.

4.6

Journalist Charlotte – I can see from your face that the results, er, weren't exactly what you wanted – am I right?

Listening

Charlotte Yeah. I got an A in chemistry and biology but only a B in physics and a C in maths.

Journalist So what are you going to do now?

Charlotte Well, first I'll get in touch with the university. Perhaps they'll still accept me – but I don't think they will, so… I'll probably take my A levels again next year.

Journalist Were your parents angry?

Charlotte No, my Mum and Dad have been really nice – they know how disappointed I am.

Journalist Well, Viktor did you pass your FCE exam?

Viktor Yes, I passed – and I got a B. I'm very pleased. I didn't think I'd get a B. I thought I'd get a C.

Journalist And your friends?

Viktor They all passed except one. But he didn't expect to pass – he didn't do any work.

Journalist So are you going out to celebrate?

Viktor Oh yes. We're going to have champagne in a bar and then we're going to have dinner together.

4.7

Presenter Hello and welcome to our review of the week's TV. With me today is the television critic Michael Stein… Michael, what did you think was the best programme of the week?

Michael Well, I've chosen the last programme in the Channel 4 series *That'll Teach 'Em*. I must say I found the whole series absolutely fascinating. For those of you who didn't see it, what the programme did was to take a group of 30 16-year-old children and send them – as an experiment – to a boarding school for one month. But it wasn't a modern boarding school, it was a 1950s boarding school. They recreated exactly the same conditions as in the 1950s – the same food, the same discipline, the same exams. The idea was to compare education today with education in the 1950s.

Presenter I bet it was a shock for today's schoolchildren.

Michael Well, it was, of course. It wasn't just the classes – it was the whole atmosphere – I mean they had to wear the uniform from the 50s – horrible uncomfortable clothes – they hated them and they weren't allowed to leave the school once for the whole month, or watch TV, or use mobiles. And they had to have cold showers every morning, and go for cross country runs!

Presenter What was the worst thing for them?

Michael The food, definitely! Most of them hated it. They said it was cold and tasteless. And the girls didn't like the cold showers much either…

Presenter What about the classes?

Michael Well, of course the biggest difference for the kids was the discipline. It was silence all the time during the lessons – only the teacher spoke. And anyone who misbehaved had to go to the headmaster and was either – hit on the hand – or had to stay behind after class and do extra work. And of course they couldn't use computers or calculators, but curiously the kids didn't really mind that, and in fact most of them found the lessons interesting – some of them said they were more interesting than their normal lessons. They had to work very hard though.

Presenter So what happened in the end? Did they pass the 1950s exams?

Michael No. Most of them failed – although they were all really bright children. There was only one child who actually passed all the subjects.

Presenter So, do you think that means exams really used to be harder in the 1950s?

Michael No, I think the kids failed because exams in the 1950s were very different. The children in the programme will probably do very well in their own exams. On the other hand, 1950s children would probably find today's exams very difficult.

Presenter How did the kids themselves feel about the experiment?

Michael They were really positive. In general they had a good time and they all felt they learned a lot. I think it made them appreciate their own lifestyle more. Some of them actually said it was the best month of their lives. It was an interesting experiment and the programme was really well made. I very much enjoyed watching it.

4.9

1 When I retire, if I can afford it, I'd love to live in a cottage in a picturesque village somewhere in the country, not too remote. The most important thing for me would be the garden – I'd like a traditional English garden, with fruit trees and lots of flowers – not too big, though. I'd spend my life in the garden, especially in the spring and summer.

2 My dream house would be on the coast, by the sea, on a beautiful unspoilt beach. It'd be modern and quite simple, with wooden floors and big windows, and from every window you'd be able to see the sea. It'd be quite isolated, with no neighbours for miles and miles. Can you imagine – just the sound of the wind and the sea?

3 I'd love to have a big old town house in the centre of London, maybe one of those beautiful terraced houses with big rooms and high ceilings, and a lovely staircase going down to the hall. But the bathrooms and kitchens would have to be modern, because old ones are cold and a bit impractical. I'd need some help looking after it though, so…

4 If I won the lottery, which of course I won't, I'd buy a big penthouse flat near the river with a great view, a really hi-tech flat, you know, with one of those intelligent fridges which orders food from the supermarket all by itself when you're running out and a huge TV and music system – but all very stylish and minimalist.

4.11

Carol When Robert replied to my email I got really excited. He didn't actually say very much about himself. He just told me that he was now a teacher, which surprised me because he always used to say he would hate to teach. He also told me that he'd been married but was now divorced.

Anyway, I answered his email and we agreed to meet for lunch at a restaurant I like – it's a place where I often go at weekends.

When I got there I looked around to see if I could see him, but I couldn't, and I thought, 'Typical! Same old Robert,' because he always used to be late. So I sat down and ordered a drink. I was just sipping my wine when a man came over to my table and said, 'Carol, how are you?' I could hardly believe it – I mean I know neither of us is young any more, but I think I look good for my age. People usually say I look five years younger than I am. But Robert looked like an old man. His lovely long hair was all gone – in fact he was bald, with a few strands of hair sort of combed over his head – and he was wearing the most *hideous* jacket. Well, I know you shouldn't judge by appearances, so I smiled at him and we started talking, and well, I quite enjoyed the lunch and we talked a lot about the past – but I knew as soon as I saw him that we didn't have anything in common any more. And I was right. Instead of the rebel he used to be, he was, well, now much more conventional than me. In fact, he seemed just like the sort of teachers we used to hate when we were young.

4.12

Alex I got to the pub late because I couldn't find it, but when I walked in I saw a whole group of young people at a table and I thought that must be them, though I didn't really recognize anybody. So I went up and they all said hello. They all recognized me, which was great though it felt a bit strange. I must admit I was feeling quite nervous. Anyway, I sat down and we started talking. They told me lots of things that I used to do when I was at school, like play in the school football team – they said I used to be really good – and they told me about all sorts of other things: places we used to go to, things like that. Some of my friends had even brought photos and we looked at them. I'd completely forgotten that I used to wear these really awful big glasses – and I sort of relaxed and I felt that I was getting to know them again, and getting to know more about myself and my past. Anyway, since we met that evening, we've all been emailing each other and I've started going out with Anna – one of the girls who was at the pub that night. She says she used to really like me at school, but that I didn't use to take any notice of her then! I can't remember any of that, but I know I like her a lot now!

4.14

1 I don't agree at all. I think it's much easier. Today you can text, you can email, you can chat online on Messenger and things like that. I'm still in touch with some friends who I met on holiday last year even though they live miles away.

2 Actually, I think it's probably true. Because I know a lot of men who are still friends with people they went to primary school with, but I don't know many women who are. For example, my brother has a friend called Tim who he's known since they were three years old. But I think the reason why is because men's friendships are less intense, sort of less intimate than women's friendships. As men only ever talk about sport or superficial things, it doesn't matter if they've completely changed and don't have much in common any more – they can still talk about football.

3 You definitely shouldn't. I mean that's the quickest way to lose a friendship. If you don't like a friend's girlfriend, you should just keep quiet. You have to wait until they break up, and of course then you can say how awful you thought she was and your friend will agree and think you're being supportive. But if you say anything bad while they're still madly in love, it's a disaster. I know because it happened to me once with a friend of mine. I said something negative about his girlfriend. And now we're not friends any more.

4.17

Mark So … Scarlett. What would you like?

Scarlett Nothing.

Mark Aren't you hungry?

Scarlett Sure. But this food's really horrible.

Allie This is one of the finest restaurants in Paris.

Scarlett I can't eat this stuff. I never touch meat.

Allie The seafood looks good –

Scarlett Hey, fish have feelings, too.

Mark What about the mushroom risotto?

Scarlett Mushrooms? No way! Didn't they tell you guys about my allergies? I'm allergic to mushrooms, strawberries, nuts…

Mark Shall we go some place else?

Scarlett Whatever. I'm going to the restroom.

Allie Well, that was a disastrous morning. The boat trip made her feel sick and she wouldn't go up the Eiffel Tower. 'I can't stand heights.'

Mark It's a pity we didn't just take her shopping.

Allie She's so spoilt.

Mark Oh, come on, she's just a kid really.

Allie So, what are we going to do about lunch? Shall we leave now?

Mark No, hang on. I have an idea. Let me talk to the waiter.

Waiter Monsieur?

Mark Do you think you could possibly do me a favour?

Waiter Yes, of course, sir. What would you like?

Mark Well, I think this place is great. More wine, Allie?

Allie No, thanks.

Waiter Mademoiselle…

Scarlett What's this?

Mark It's your lunch, Scarlett.

Scarlett But I didn't order anything.

Waiter Voilà!

Scarlett Hey, pizza margherita! Cool!

5.3

Tip number 1. Eat breakfast sitting down. Most people stay in bed until the last minute and then have a coffee and a piece of toast standing up. This is really bad for you, because it means that you start the day in a hurry. Your body and mind are already moving too fast. So do yourself a favour. Get up ten minutes earlier every day and have breakfast – nice and slowly.

Tip number 2. Forget the gym, and do yoga instead. Many people go to the gym after work to do exercise because they think that this relaxes them, but it doesn't, believe me. I really think that a gym is a very stressful place. Exercising hard, for example doing aerobics, makes your heart beat more quickly, so it doesn't relax your body at all. In fact, it does the opposite. So, forget the gym and try doing yoga. Yoga will not only help you to get fit, but it will also slow your body down and help you to think more clearly.

Tip number 3. Go for a long walk. Walking is the most traditional form of exercise but many people have just forgotten how to do it. These days we all just get into our cars. The great thing about walking is that you can't walk very fast, so walking actually slows you down. And when we walk, we look around us at the birds, the trees, the shops, other people. It reminds us of the world we live in and it helps us to stop, and think, and relax.

Tip number 4. Spend 10 minutes each day in silence. Meditation isn't new. People have been doing it for thousands of years and now it is becoming really popular again. In the United States now you can find meditation rooms in companies, schools, airports, and even hospitals. Meditation is a fantastic way to teach your mind to slow down and to think more clearly. And spending time in silence every day will also benefit your general health.

And finally, tip number 5. Have a bath, not a shower. Having a shower is very quick and convenient but it is another part of our fast-living culture. When you come home from work, instead of having a shower, have a bath and spend half an hour there. A bath is one of the most relaxing things you can do and it will really help to slow you down at the end of a hard day.

5.8

Voice-over 1 The body polish

Joanna So? What did you think?

Stephen It was just horrible! Horrible. Fruit's for eating, not for putting on your body. It was hot and sticky and incredibly uncomfortable. And I felt so stupid. I'd never have that again. I give it zero out of ten.

Joanna Sticky? It was fruit for goodness' sake! I thought it was wonderful. It smells so good and it was incredibly relaxing. I mean how could anybody not like it? And the head massage was divine! That was one of my favourite spa treatments ever. Ten out of ten. OK, so now, the facial.

Stephen Hmm. How long is this one?

Joanna One hour 40 minutes.

Stephen Oh you're joking? That's too long.

Joanna Too long? It'll be heaven. See you later.

5.9

Voice-over 2 The facial

Stephen Oh that was so boring. It went on forever.

Joanna I loved it.

Stephen Well, I must admit my face feels different – much smoother. But I'm not sure I really want a smooth face. And it was nearly two hours and she used about 12 different creams and things. It normally only takes me a minute to wash my face – and I just use soap and water – the therapist said I ought to buy *five* different products!

Joanna Well, I enjoyed every second. My skin feels great – really healthy. I give it nine out of ten.

Stephen Hmm… I give it four.

Joanna Your problem was that you were hungry so you couldn't relax. We could have a fruit juice before the last treatment…

Stephen A fruit juice? Oh, OK then.

5.10

Voice-over 3 The foot treatment

Stephen Wow!

Joanna Don't tell me you liked it!

Stephen It was wonderful!

Joanna I must say, your feet look…well, better. Clean anyway.

Stephen Well, I've never liked my feet much to be honest, but now they look great. That was definitely worth the time and money. Nine out of ten. What do you think?

Joanna Yes, it was great. A real luxury. And I love the colour they painted my nails. I agree – nine out of ten. You see…

5.14

Voice-over Week one.

Jessica When I got to the studio on the first day, I was really nervous. I met my teachers, Adam and Sally, and they were very nice to me but I could see that they thought it was going to be impossible to teach me to be a reporter in just a month.

Adam The problem with Jessica at the beginning was that she was too shy and too nice. Political reporters need to be hard – almost aggressive sometimes – and I've never met anyone less aggressive than Jessica. And also she knew nothing about politics – she knew who the Prime Minister was but not much else!

Jessica I spent the first week watching lots of political interviews on TV, and Adam and Sally taught me how to speak more clearly and more confidently. In the evenings they made me read the political sections of all the newspapers. It was very boring. At the end of the week I was exhausted.

5.15

Voice-over Week two

Jessica Adam and Sally said I had to change my image for TV, so I had my hair cut and coloured, and I got new, smarter clothes. I must say I liked my new look.

I spent the week learning how to interview someone in front of a camera.

Adam Then came Jessica's first big challenge. The Prime Minister was arriving home after a visit to the USA. She had to wait outside number 10 Downing Street with the other journalists and try to ask him a question.

Jessica It was a disaster. I was so nervous I was shaking. There were a lot of other journalists pushing and shouting. They didn't let me get near the Prime Minister. I tried to ask my question, but he didn't hear me. I felt really stupid.

5.16

Voice-over Week three.

Adam Jessica was finally making some progress. She was more relaxed. This week she had to interview a politician from the Conservative party in the studio.

Jessica In the beginning it was fine. But then I made a stupid mistake.

Jessica *So could you tell us what the Labour party are going to do about…sorry, I mean the Conservative party*

I said the 'Labour party' instead of the 'Conservative party'. And after that I was really nervous again.

Adam We all make mistakes sometimes. Jessica just has to learn to carry on, and not lose her confidence.

5.17

Voice-over Week four.

Jessica I spent the last week preparing for the test. It was going to be a live interview with the Minister of Education. There would be three professional reporters and me, all asking him questions. I'd done lots of research so although I was nervous, I felt well prepared.

Jessica *Minister, many people think that the real reason why there aren't enough teachers is because their salaries are so low. Are you proposing to increase teachers' salaries?*

Minister *Well, let's not forget that salaries are much higher today than they were under the previous government.*

Jessica *Yes, but you haven't answered my question. Are you going to increase them?*

Minister *Well, we're planning to spend a lot more money on education in the next two years.*

Jessica *Is that a yes or a no?*

Minister *There are no immediate plans to increase teachers' salaries.*

Jessica *So it's a no then. Thank you Minister.*

Jessica When it was all over came the worst part. I had to wait while the judges decided which of us they thought *wasn't* a professional reporter.

Adam The judges gave their verdict – and incredibly *none* of the three realized that Jessica wasn't a professional! She did very very well.

Who knows, maybe one day soon you'll be seeing her on TV… and this time she'll be a real reporter, not pretending!

Jessica It was a great experience and I was pleased how I did, but actually I *wouldn't* like to change jobs. I'm much happier working in the library.

5.20

Allie It's great to be on our own again.

Mark Yeah.

Allie Is this the first time you've been to the Louvre?

Mark Uh huh.

Listening

Allie What's the matter? Is this about the meeting? Because I agreed with Jacques and not with you?

Mark Yeah, well, we knew it wouldn't be easy. Working together, I mean.

Allie It's difficult for me as well. But if I don't agree with you…

Mark I know, I know, you're the boss.

Allie And I have to do my job. I really thought that Jacques' idea was better. And so did Scarlett.

Mark It's not a big deal, Allie. I'm fine, really. So who exactly was the Mona Lisa?

Allie I'm not sure. I think she was the wife of a banker…

Mark Is that why she's smiling? Because her husband has a good salary?

Allie I also read somewhere that she was a self-portrait of Leonardo.

Mark A self-portrait? You're kidding. Now I don't know much about art, but Leonardo da Vinci was a man, right?

Allie Well, it's just a theory. Why do you think she's smiling?

Mark Well, in my opinion, she's the managing director of a music company.

Allie What?

Mark She lives in Paris, she's in love with her marketing director, and she has a lot of fun telling him what to do.

Allie That's really unfair!

Mark Hey, we're not in the office now – you can't tell me I'm wrong! Let's get a coffee.

Allie Good idea.

Mark Don't turn round!

Allie What is it?

Mark I've just seen Ben from the office.

Allie Where?

Mark I said don't look! I don't think he's seen us. Let's get out of here. Come on.

6.4

1 I was in a taxi in Greece, in Athens, and I was going into the centre to do some shopping and the taxi driver started chatting to me. He asked me where I was from. When I said I was English, he started getting really aggressive. He said that he didn't like the English and that all English people were football hooligans. He went on and on – he just wouldn't stop. I got really annoyed. I mean I thought, 'Why do I have to listen to all of this'. So I asked him to stop the taxi and let me get out. Luckily, he stopped and I got out – and of course, I didn't pay him anything.

2 This happened to me recently when I was travelling around France on business. I was really tired because I'd been working and travelling all day. Anyway, when I got to the hotel in Toulouse – it was the evening – I checked in and the receptionist gave me the key to my room. So I went up to my room and opened the door, but it was a complete mess! The bed wasn't made, there were dirty towels on the floor and the bathroom was *filthy*. I went downstairs and told the receptionist and he said that I would have to wait for half an hour while they prepared the room. But I was exhausted and needed to rest, so I told him to give me another room straightaway. Luckily he did.

3 This happened to me last week. I went to a restaurant in London with my family to celebrate my dad's birthday. Anyway, my dad ordered ravioli and when his dish arrived he saw that it had a long, black hair in it. So he asked the waitress to take it back and bring him another one. She brought him another plate of ravioli and it was fine, and we finished our meal. But when my dad asked for the bill, he saw that they had charged us for the ravioli. He didn't think that was right. He thought the ravioli should be free because he had found a hair in it. So he asked the waitress to take it off the bill. She went away and spoke to the manager, and he came and apologized and he took the ravioli off the bill.

6.6

Interviewer So how did you get involved in the film, Dagmara?

Dagmara Well, as you probably know, a lot of the film *Schindler's List* was shot in Krakow, in Poland, which is where I live. And before the actual shooting of the film started, the film company had an office in Krakow and I got a job there translating documents and parts of the script – things like that – I was a university student at the time.

Interviewer But how did you get the job as Spielberg's interpreter in the film?

Dagmara It's a funny story. I didn't think I would ever get to meet Spielberg or any of the actors. But then, just before the shooting started, there was a big party in one of the hotels in Krakow and I was invited.

At first, I wasn't going to go – I was tired after working all day, and I didn't think I had anything suitable to wear. But in the end, I borrowed a jacket from a friend and I went. But when I arrived at the party, the producer – who was Polish – came up to me and said, 'Dagmara, you're going to interpret for Steven Spielberg. You have to translate his opening speech, because the girl who was going to do it couldn't come.'

Interviewer How did you feel about that?

Dagmara I couldn't believe it! I was just a student – I had *no* experience of interpreting – and now I was going to have to speak in front of hundreds of people. I was nervous so I drank a couple glasses of champagne to give myself courage. But when I started speaking, I was *so* nervous that I confused the dates of the Second World War – but luckily I managed to get to the end without making any more mistakes.

And afterwards, during the party, Spielberg came up to speak to me to say thank you – he was really nice to me and said he was impressed by the way I had interpreted. And then he said, 'I'd like you to be my interpreter for the whole film.' I couldn't believe it. I had to pinch myself to believe that this was happening to me.

6.7

Interviewer So what exactly did you have to do?

Dagmara I had to go to the film set every day. A car came every day to pick me up from my house – I felt really important! And then what I had to do was to translate Spielberg's instructions to the Polish actors, as well as the extras. I had to make them understand what he wanted. It was really exciting – sometimes I felt as if I was a director myself.

Interviewer Was it a difficult job?

Dagmara Sometimes it was really difficult. The worst thing was when we kept having to shoot a scene again and again because Spielberg thought it wasn't exactly right. Some scenes were repeated as many as 16 times – and sometimes I would think that maybe it was my fault – that I hadn't translated properly what he wanted, so I'd get really nervous. I remember one scene where we just couldn't get it right and Spielberg started shouting at me because he was stressed. But in the end we got it right and then he apologized, and I cried a little, because I was also very stressed – and after that it was all right again.

Interviewer So, was Spielberg difficult to work with?

Dagmara Not at all. I mean he was very demanding – I had to do my best every day – but he was really nice to me. I felt he treated me like a daughter. For instance, he was always making sure that I wasn't cold –it was freezing on the set most of the time – and he would make sure I had a warm coat and gloves and things. It was hard work but it was fascinating – an amazing experience.

Interviewer What did you think of the finished film?

Dagmara I believe that *Schindler's List* is truly a great movie, a masterpiece. I think the actors were brilliant, especially Liam Neeson and Ben Kingsley – and I love the way it was shot in black and white, with colour in just one scene.

But, as you can imagine, I can't be very objective about it – I mean, I lived through nearly every scene. And when I watch it – and I've seen it a lot of times – I always remember exactly where I was at that moment. I can't help thinking, 'Oh there I am, hiding under the bed, or standing behind that door.'

6.8

It's 12.00 noon and so it's time for today's competition. Today the topic is 'Heroes and Icons'. As usual, the rules are very simple. I'm going to give you eight clues and you have to identify the people. If you know all the answers send them to me straightaway by email. The first person who sends me the correct answers wins a prize. Today's prize is two plane tickets to … the Big Apple, New York!

OK, so let's get started with those clues. I'll say each one twice only. And remember, I always give you the first letter or letters of the word I'm looking for. Today they are all people's names.

Let's start with an easy one. Two letters, B and G. It's a man who's probably the richest man in the world, the founder of Microsoft. That's BG, the man who started Microsoft.

Number 2. Two letters again, J and P, although this isn't the name he was born with. A man whose humanity made him an icon for millions of people all over the world. This religious leader was born in Poland but he died in Rome in 2005.

Number 3 begins with M, just one word. It's the name of a woman who has had a lot of different jobs. She's been an actress, she's even written children's books, but she's most famous as a singer. One word beginning with M.

And number 4. This time it's a man, and the letters are G and A, though many people just know him by his surname. He's an Italian designer whose clothes are considered among the most elegant in the world, and whose name is also on perfume bottles everywhere. G and A, for an Italian fashion designer.

On to number 5. Two letters, J and O. It's the name of a famous American woman, whose first husband was president of the USA and whose second husband was a Greek millionaire. Although she died in 1994, she is still admired for her style all over the world. Two letters, J and O.

And number 6. It's a woman again and the letters are M and N. She's the woman who changed the shape of women's tennis, and is possibly the greatest female player of all time. She was born in Prague but later became a US citizen. M and N for the greatest ever woman tennis player.

Number 7 is an American actor. He was born in Kentucky in 1961 and he is often called the most attractive male actor in Hollywood today. He first became famous in a TV hospital drama in which he played the part of a doctor. His first name begins with G and his surname with C. So that's a Hollywood actor, G and C.

And finally, number 8. Two letters. M and C. She was born in Greece and died in Paris, and she is the woman whose voice is familiar to lovers of opera all over the world. Nicknamed 'La Divina' her life was tragic, but her voice will never be forgotten. MC, la Divina.

So, if you think you've got the eight correct answers, email them to me now at this address, Guessthenames@BT.com, that's Guessthenames @BT.com. And the first person with the correct answers will win those two tickets to New York.

Time for some music.

6.13

Mark Dear all
Please find attached a copy of the latest sales report from the USA.
Mark.

Mark So, did you guys have a good weekend?
Ben Yes, fine.
Jacques Not bad. Very quiet.
Ben What about you, Mark?
Mark Oh, I spent most of the time at home… just being domestic, you know. The apartment's looking pretty nice, now. You must come round for a meal one evening.
Jacques That would be very nice.
Ben So didn't you go out at all?
Mark Oh sure. I went to the Louvre on Saturday. I felt like getting a bit of culture.
Jacques On your own?
Mark Yeah. I kind of prefer going to museums and galleries on my own. You can look at everything at your own pace.
Ben That's funny. I went to the Louvre on Saturday, too.
Mark Really? I didn't see you.
Ben Well, it's a big place. I didn't see you either.
Nicole I've just had an email from Allie.
Jacques So have I.
Mark Me, too…
Nicole Dear Mark, Thank you for the information. And thank you, darling, for a wonderful weekend. Allie.

7.1

Narrator Ian thought Amy had gone out for the evening and sat down to wait for her to come back. Tired after his long journey, he fell asleep. When he woke up, the phone was ringing. Ian answered the phone. It was Amy.
Ian I said, 'Where are you?' She said, 'Ian, I'm sitting in your flat in Australia.' At first I didn't believe her but then she gave the phone to Eddie, who lives in my flat in Sydney, and he told me it was true. I was so shocked I couldn't speak.
Narrator Amy had had the same idea as Ian. She had flown from London to Sydney via Singapore at exactly the same time Ian was flying in the opposite direction. Incredibly, both their planes stopped in Singapore at the same time. Ian and Amy were sitting in the same airport lounge but they didn't see each other.
Amy I had saved all my money to buy a ticket to Sydney. I wanted it to be a fantastic surprise for Ian. I couldn't wait to see his face when I arrived. You can't imagine how I felt when I arrived at his flat and his friend Eddie told me he had gone to England! I just couldn't believe it! When I spoke to Ian on the phone, he told me that he had flown back to England for a special reason and then he asked me to marry him. I didn't know whether to laugh or cry but I said 'yes'.
Ian It was just bad luck. If one of us had stayed at home, we would have met. It's as simple as that.

7.2

Narrator The cabin crew put out a desperate call to the passengers: 'If there's a doctor on the plane, could you please press your call bell.'

The cabin crew were hoping to hear this, but they didn't. They heard this. Incredibly, there were *fifteen* doctors on the plane, and *all* of them were cardiologists. They were from different countries and they were travelling to Florida for a medical conference.

Four of the doctors rushed to give emergency treatment to Mrs Fletcher. At one point, they thought she had died, but finally they managed to save her life.

The plane made an emergency landing in North Carolina and Mrs Fletcher was taken to hospital. After being in hospital for four days, she was able to go to her daughter's wedding.
Mrs Fletcher I was very lucky. If those doctors hadn't been on the plane, I would have died. I can't thank them enough.
Narrator But now that she's back in England, Mrs Fletcher has been less lucky with British hospitals.
Mrs Fletcher I had *fifteen* heart specialists on that plane, but I'll have to wait three months until I can see *one* in this country!

7.6

Interviewer Good morning and thank you for coming, Mr Morton – or should it be Inspector Morton – you were a detective with Scotland Yard, weren't you?
Ken Yes, that's right. For twenty-five years. I retired last year.
Interviewer People today are still fascinated by the identity of Jack the Ripper, more than a hundred years after the crimes were committed. It's incredible, isn't it?
Ken Well, it's not really that surprising. People are always interested in unsolved murders – and Jack the Ripper has become a sort of cult horror figure.
Interviewer Who are the main suspects?
Ken Well, there are a lot of them. But probably the best known are Prince Albert, Queen Victoria's grandson, the artist Walter Sickert, and a Liverpool cotton merchant called James Maybrick.
Interviewer Patricia Cornwell in her book 'Jack the Ripper – case closed?' says that she has identified the murderer. Who does she think it was?
Ken Well, she's convinced that Jack the Ripper was Walter Sickert, the painter.

7.7

Interviewer What evidence did she discover?
Ken Well, she mainly used DNA analysis. She actually bought a painting by Sickert at great expense and she cut it up to get the DNA from it – people in the art world were furious.
Interviewer I can imagine.
Ken And then she compared the DNA from the painting with DNA taken from the letters that Jack the Ripper sent to the police. Patricia Cornwell says that she's 99% certain that Walter Sickert was Jack the Ripper.
Interviewer But you don't think she's right, do you?
Ken No, I don't. I don't think her scientific evidence is completely reliable and there's a lot of evidence which says that Sickert was in France *not* London when some of the women were killed.
Interviewer There's been another recent theory, hasn't there? About James Maybrick? Do you think he was the murderer?
Ken Well, somebody found a diary which is supposed to be his, where he admits to being Jack the Ripper. But nobody has been able to prove

that the diary is genuine and, personally, I don't think he was the murderer.
Interviewer And Prince Albert, the Queen's grandson?
Ken This for me is the most ridiculous theory. I can't seriously believe that a member of the royal family could be a serial murderer. In any case, Prince Albert was in Scotland when at least two of the murders were committed.
Interviewer So, who do *you* think the murderer was?
Ken I can't tell you because I don't know.
Interviewer So you don't think we'll ever solve the mystery?
Ken No, I wouldn't say that. I think one day the mystery *will* be solved. Some new evidence will appear and we'll be able to say that the case of Jack the Ripper is finally closed. But at the moment it's still a mystery, and people like a good mystery.

7.16

Claire Well, it wouldn't be electric light because I love candles. And I could live without a washing machine for a week – I often do when I'm on holiday. I think I would miss a fridge though – I'd hate not to have cold drinks, and it would mean having to go shopping every day for food or it would go off. So a fridge would be one thing, and then probably my laptop. It has a battery, but I could only use it for three hours or so without charging it. So I wouldn't be able to do much work.
Andy Er well, it depends. I'd quite miss the TV, but I suppose I could live without it for a week if I had to. And, er, what else – oh no, my mobile. I wouldn't be able to charge it. I couldn't *live* without my mobile. I mean that's how I keep in touch with all my friends. And my MP3 player. I need my music. Yes, definitely those two.
Julia I think for me it would have to be first and foremost the dishwasher. Because with a family and so much washing up, I would just be over the sink for ever. It would be a nightmare for me to have no dishwasher and I've got so used to it. So that would be the first thing. And the second thing, probably again because of having a family, a young family, would be an iron, because there's so much ironing and if I had to go without that, everyone would look terrible. Nobody would look smart. So those would be my two things.
Tyler Well, I suppose the first thing I'd miss most would be my mobile phone, because I couldn't charge it up, so I couldn't use it, and I'd get very upset about that. There are some people's numbers that are only stored in the phone. I haven't got them written down, and I wouldn't be able to get in touch with those people. So mobile phone. And the other thing I'd miss would be, electricity, em if the electricity had gone, would be the lights, at this time of year especially, when the days are short, the mornings are dark, early afternoon, late afternoon's dark too. I'd miss lights as well. So mobile phone and lights.

1

1A present simple and continuous, action and non-action verbs

present simple: *I live, he works*, etc.

> They **work** in a bank.
> Where **do** you **live**?
> He **doesn't wear** glasses.
> She **usually has** cereal for breakfast.
> I**'m never** late for work.

- Use the present simple for things that are always true or happen regularly.
- Remember the spelling rules, e.g. *lives, studies, watches*.
- Use **ASI** (**a**uxiliary, **s**ubject, **i**nfinitive) or **QUASI** (**qu**estion word, **a**uxiliary, **s**ubject, **i**nfinitive) to help you with word order in questions.
- Put adverbs of frequency, e.g. *usually*, before the main verb and after *be*.

present continuous: *be* + verb + *-ing*

> **A** Who **are** you **waiting for**?
> **B** I**'m waiting** for a friend.
> **A** What **are** you **doing** after class?
> **B** I**'m going** to the café.

- Use the present continuous (not present simple) for actions in progress at the time of speaking or for future arrangements.
- Remember the spelling rules, e.g. *living, studying, getting*.

action and non-action verbs

> **A** What **are** you **cooking** tonight?
> **B** I**'m making** pasta.
> **A** Great! I really **like** pasta.

- Verbs which describe actions, e.g. *make, cook*, can be used in the present simple or continuous.
- Verbs which describe states or feelings (not actions), e.g. *like, want, be*, are <u>not</u> normally used in the present continuous.
- Common non-action verbs are **agree, be, believe, belong, depend, forget, hate, hear, know, like, love, matter, mean, need, prefer, realize, recognize, seem, suppose.**

> ⚠ A few verbs have an action and a non-action meaning. The most common is *have*.
> *I have a big flat.* = possession (non-action)
> *I can't talk now. I'm having lunch.*
> = an activity (action)

1B past tenses

past simple: *worked, stopped, went, had*, etc.

> They **got** married last year.
> What time **did** you **wake up** this morning?
> I **didn't have** time to do my homework.

- Use the past simple for finished past actions.

past continuous: *was / were* + verb + *-ing*

> **A** What **were** you **doing** at six o'clock last night?
> **B** I was watching TV. It was a cold night and it was raining.

- Use the past continuous to describe an action in progress at a specific time in the past.

past perfect: *had* + past participle

> When they turned on the TV, the match **had finished**.
> I **felt** nervous because I **hadn't flown** before.

- Use the past perfect when you are talking about the past and you want to talk about an earlier past action.

using narrative tenses together

> When John **arrived**, they **had** dinner. (first John arrived, <u>then</u> they had dinner)
> When John **arrived**, they **were having** dinner. (when John arrived they were <u>in the middle of</u> dinner)
> When John **arrived**, they **had had** dinner. (they had dinner <u>before</u> John arrived).

- Remember **Irregular verbs** p.156.

1C future forms

be going to + infinitive

> future plans and intentions
>
> My sister**'s going to adopt** a child.
> **Are** you **going to buy** a new car?
> I**'m not going to go** to New York next week.

> predictions
>
> I think they**'re going to win**. (They're playing very well.)
> It**'s going to rain**. (The sky is very dark.)

- Use *going to* NOT *will / won't* when you have already decided to do something.
- With the verb *go* you can leave out the infinitive.
  I'm not going (to go) to New York.

present continuous: *be* + verb + *-ing*

> future arrangements
>
> We**'re getting** married in October.
> They**'re meeting** at 10.00.
> She**'s leaving** on Friday.

- You can usually use present continuous <u>or</u> *going to* for future plans / arrangements.
- *going to* shows that you have made a decision.
  We're going to get married in the summer.
- Present continuous emphasizes that you have made the arrangements.
  We're getting married on July 12th (e.g. we've booked the church).

will / shall + infinitive

> I**'ll have** the steak. (instant decision)
> I **won't tell** anybody where you are. (promise)
> I**'ll carry** that bag for you. (offer)
> **Shall** I **help** you with your homework? (offer)
> **Shall** we **eat** out tonight? (suggestion)
> You**'ll love** the film! (prediction)

- Use *will / won't* (NOT the present simple) for instant decisions, promises, offers, and suggestions.
- Use *shall* (NOT *will*) with *I* and *we* for offers and suggestions when they are questions.
- Use *will* or *going to* for predictions.

1A

a Correct the mistakes in the highlighted phrases.

Ouch! You stand on my foot!   *You're standing*

1 They have always breakfast in bed on a Sunday morning.
2 She can't come to the phone now. She has a shower .
3 We are needing an answer from you before Wednesday.
4 I'm studing a lot now because I have exams next week.
5 She don't eat meat at all.
6 They always are late.
7 Do you go out tonight?
8 He never replys to my emails!
9 **A** Are you going to the park this afternoon?
   B I don't know. It's depending on the weather.

b Write questions in the present continuous or present simple.

A What *are you eating*? (you / eat)   **B** A cheese sandwich.

1 **A** Where _____ lunch today? (you / have)
   B At home. My mum's making pasta.
2 **A** What _____? (he / do)
   B He's an accountant.
3 **A** _____ this weekend? (you / go away)
   B No, we're staying here.
4 **A** _____ to eat out tonight? (you / want)
   B Yes, that would be nice. Where shall we go?
5 **A** What _____? (she / cook)
   B I don't know, but it smells good.

1B

a Combine the two sentences. Use the verb in **bold** in the past continuous or past perfect.

Sarah **had** a siesta from 3.00 to 5.00. Peter picked up the tickets at 4.00.
Peter picked up the tickets when Sarah *was having* a siesta.

1 They **watched** TV from 7.00 until 9.00. I arrived at 7.30.
   When I arrived, they _____ TV.
2 He **left** the office at 7.00. She phoned him at 8.00.
   When she phoned him, he _____ the office.
3 I **studied** for the exam the night before. The exam didn't go well.
   The exam didn't go well although I _____ the night before.
4 He **cycled** to work this morning. In the middle of his journey, he had an accident.
   When he _____ to work this morning, he had an accident.
5 He only **had** five lessons. He passed his driving test.
   When he passed his driving test, he _____ (only) five lessons.

b Complete with the past simple, past continuous, or past perfect.

We *didn't realize* that we *had been* there before.
(not realize, be)

1 **A** How _____? (the accident / happen)
   B He _____ back from Manchester when he _____ a tree. (drive, hit)
2 I _____ cooking the meal when they _____ me to say they couldn't come. (already / start, call)
3 When I got home I was really tired, so I _____ a shower and _____ to bed. (have, go)
4 I arrived too late. The concert _____ and my friends _____ home. (finish, go)
5 The driver _____ control of his car because he _____ on his mobile. (lose, talk)

1C

a Circle the correct form. Tick (✔) the sentence if both are possible.

(*I'm not going*)/ *I won't go* to work tomorrow because it's Saturday.

1 *I'm going to study* / *I'll study* English here next year.
2 **A** *Shall we* / *Will we* eat out tonight?
   B Good idea.
3 *We'll go* / *We're going* to Brazil next week. I can't wait.
4 What *are you going to wear* / *are you wearing* to the party?
5 Do you think *it will rain* / *it's going to rain* tomorrow?
6 **A** This is heavy.   **B** *I'll help* / *I help* you.
7 *I'm meeting* / *I meet* a friend this evening.
8 I'm really sorry. I promise *I won't do* / *I'm not going to do* it again.
9 *They're getting* / *They're going to get* married in May.

b Complete B's replies with a correct future form.

A Sorry, Ann's not in.
B OK. *I'll call back* later. (call back)

1 **A** There's no milk.
   B Don't worry, I _____ some. (get)
2 **A** Can we meet on Tuesday?
   B Sorry, I can't. I _____ to Brighton on Tuesday. (go)
3 **A** Can we have pizza for lunch?
   B No, we _____ chicken. I've already put it in the oven. (have)
4 **A** Is that the phone?
   B Yes, but don't get up. I _____ it. (answer)
5 **A** Jane's put on a lot of weight!
   B She's pregnant. She _____ a baby in August. (have)

2A present perfect and past simple

present perfect simple: *have / has* + **past participle** (*worked, seen,* etc.)

past experiences	recent past actions	with *yet* and *already* (for emphasis)
I've been to London, but I **haven't been** to Oxford. She's never **met** his ex-wife. **Have** you ever **lost** your credit card?	**I've cut** my finger! He's just **arrived** at the airport.	**I've** already **done** my homework. Can I watch TV? **Have** you **finished** yet? My brother **hasn't found** a new job yet.

- We often use *ever* and *never* when we ask or talk about past experiences. They go before the main verb.
- *just* and *already* go before the main verb in ⊞ sentences, *yet* goes at the end of the phrase in ⊟ sentences and ⍰.
- For irregular past participles see **Irregular verbs** p.156.

unfinished states (non-action verbs) which start in the past and are still true now
A They've **known** each other for 10 years. **B** How long **have** they **been** married? **A** Since 2004.

- Use *How long…?* + present perfect to ask about an unfinished period of time (from the past until now).
- Use *for* + a period of time, e.g. *for two weeks,* or *since* with a point of time, e.g. *since 1990.*

present perfect or past simple?

I've been to Madrid twice. (= in my life up to now)	**I went** there in 1998 and 2002. (= on two specific occasions)
How long **have** you **been** married to Alan? (= you are married to Alan now)	How long **were** you married to Jake? (= you are not married to Jake now)
I've (just) **bought** a new computer. (= I don't say exactly when)	I **bought** it on Saturday. (= I say when)

- Use the present perfect when there is a connection between the past and the present.
- Use the past simple to ask or talk about **finished** actions in the past, when the time is mentioned or understood. We often use a past time expression, e.g. *January, last week,* etc.

2B present perfect continuous

present perfect continuous for unfinished actions

How long **have** you **been learning** English? He's **been working** here since April. They've **been going out** together for three years.

- *have / has been* + verb + *-ing*
- Use the present perfect continuous with *for* and *since* with **action verbs** (e.g. *learn, go,* etc.).

⚠ With **non-action verbs** (e.g. *know, be,* etc.) use the present perfect simple NOT the present perfect continuous with *for* and *since*.
I've known her for ages. NOT *I've been knowing her for ages.*
With *live* and *work* you can use the present perfect simple or continuous with *for* and *since*.
I've been living here for six months.
I've lived here for six months.

present perfect continuous for recent continuous actions

A Your eyes are red. **Have** you **been crying**? **B** No, I've **been cutting** onions.

- Use the present perfect continuous for actions which have been going on very recently. They have usually just stopped.

2C comparatives and superlatives

comparing two things (or actions)

My sister is a bit **taller than** me. London is **more expensive than** Edinburgh. This test is **less difficult than** the last one.
Olive oil is **better** for you **than** butter. You drive **more slowly than** me. Liverpool played **worse** today **than** last week.
Flying isn't **as comfortable as** going by train. He doesn't smoke **as much as** she does. Her new car looks **the same as** the old one.

superlatives

He's **the tallest** player in the team. Oslo is **the most expensive** capital city in Europe. This book is **the least difficult** to understand. She's the **best student** in the class.
Who drives **the most carefully** in your family? That's **the worst** they've ever played.

- Form superlatives like comparatives but use *-est* instead or *-er* and *most / least* instead of *more / less.*
- You normally use *the* before superlatives, but you can also use possessive adjectives, e.g. *my best friend, their most famous song.*

- Regular comparative adjectives / adverbs:
  hard>harder, big>bigger, easy>easier, modern>more modern, difficult>more difficult, carefully>more carefully
- Irregular comparative adjectives / adverbs: *good / well>better, bad / badly>worse, far>further*
- After *than* or *as* we can use an object pronoun *me, him, her,* etc. or a subject pronoun (*I, he, she*) + auxiliary verb, e.g. *She's taller than me* OR *She's taller than I am* but NOT *She's taller than I.*

2A

a Correct the mistakes in the highlighted phrases.

I've never saw *Star Wars.*   *I've never seen*

1   He left quite early but he yet hasn't arrived .
2   We don't see each other since we left school.
3   Have you ever wrote a poem?
4   She have never been to Istanbul.
5   I've lent him €50 last week, but he hasn't paid me back yet.
6   I don't see them often but I've known them since ten years .
7   What year have you left school?
8   We're lost. We already have been down this road twice.
9   I sent her an email last week, but she doesn't reply yet .
10 They live in that house since 1980.

b Complete the dialogues with the past simple or present perfect.

I*'ve already seen* that film twice. (already / see)

1   **A** How long _____ at university? (you / be)
    B I _____ two years ago. I'm in my third year now. (start)
    A Do you live with your parents?
    B I _____ with them for the first two years but then I _____ into a student hostel last September and I _____ there since then. (live, move, live)
2   **A** _____ a job yet? (your brother / find)
    B Yes, he _____ work in a hotel. (just / start)
3   **A** _____ to Nobu – that new Japanese restaurant? (you / ever / be)
    B Yes, we _____ there for my birthday. (go)
    A What was it like?
    B The food _____ fantastic but it _____ a fortune! (be, cost)

2B

a Make sentences with the present perfect continuous (and *for* / *since* if necessary).

she / work there / 2003 ⊞
She's been working there since 2003.

1   how long / they / go out together ?
2   I / study English / two years ⊞
3   he / feel very well recently ⊟
4   you / read that book / months! ⊞
5   you / wait / a long time ?
6   we / spend much time together ⊟
7   how long / she / live there ?
8   I / rent this flat / three years. ⊞
9   the lift / work / 10 o'clock ⊟
10 she / work here / a long time ?

b Complete with a verb from the list in the present perfect continuous.

bark   cry   do   ~~eat~~   play   shop   not sleep   watch

A Your sister's lost a lot of weight!
B Yes. She *'s been eating* a lot less recently.

1   **A** Your eyes are red. _____ you _____?
    B Yes. I _____ a sad film.
2   **A** It's very late. Why aren't you in bed?
    B I can't sleep. That dog _____ for the last two hours.
3   **A** You look tired.
    B I know. I _____ well recently.
4   **A** Wow! You've bought a lot of things!
    B Yes, we _____ all day.
5   **A** You look hot! What _____ you _____?
    B I _____ in the garden with the children.

2C

a Complete with one word.

She's much *more* intelligent than her brother.

1   He's not as clever _____ he thinks he is.
2   It's _____ best book I've read for a long time.
3   The journey took longer _____ we expected.
4   I think it was the saddest film I've _____ seen.
5   Is Texas the biggest state _____ the USA?
6   He's the _____ selfish person I've ever met.
7   Your watch is the same _____ mine.
8   My father speaks _____ quickly than I do.
9   We don't go swimming _____ often as we did before.
10 Her brother's about 10 and she's a year younger than _____ .

b Complete with the comparative or superlative of the **bold** word.

Mexican food is much *spicier* than American food. **spicy**

1   It's _____ than it was this time last year.   **hot**
2   Jan's _____ of all my sisters.   **competitive**
3   He's _____ person in the office.   **lazy**
4   He looks much _____ with shorter hair.   **good**
5   I sat next to _____ person at the party!   **boring**
6   Could we meet a bit _____ tomorrow?   **early**
7   It was _____ film I've seen this year.   **bad**
8   Sue is _____ member of my family.   **ambitious**
9   The _____ way to travel is by train.   **safe**
10 The beach was _____ from the hotel than we expected.   **far**

3

3A   *must, have to, should* (obligation)

obligation / necessity: *have to* / *must* (+ infinitive)

You **have to** wear a seatbelt in a car.
Do you **have to** work on Saturdays?
I **had to** wear a uniform at my primary school.
I**'ll have to** get up early tomorrow. My interview is at 9.00.

I **must** remember to phone Emily tonight – it's her birthday.
You **must** be on time for class tomorrow – there's a test.

- *Must* and *have to* have a very similar meaning.
  Have to is more common for **general**, **external** obligations,
  for example rules and laws.
  Must is more common for **specific** (i.e. on one occasion)
  or **personal** obligations.
  Compare:
  I have to wear a shirt and tie at work (It's the rule in this company).
  I must buy a new shirt – this one is too old now (It's my own decision).
- *Have to* is a normal verb and it exists in all tenses.
- *Must* is a modal verb. The only forms are *must* and *mustn't*.
- You can also use *have to* or *must* for strong recommendations,
  e.g. *You have to / must see that film – it's fantastic.*

no obligation / necessity: *don't have to*

You **don't have to** pay for the tickets. They're free.
You **don't have to** go to the party if you don't want to.

prohibition: *mustn't* (+ infinitive)

You **mustn't** eat that cake – it's for the party.
You **mustn't** touch that. It's dangerous.

- *Don't have to* and *mustn't* are completely different.
  Compare:
  You mustn't drive along this street. = It's prohibited,
  against the law.
  You don't have to drive – we can get a train. = You can
  drive if you want to but it's not necessary / obligatory.
- You can often use *can't* or *not allowed to* instead of *mustn't*.
  *You mustn't park here. You can't park here. You're not
  allowed to park here.*

⚠ *Have got to* is often used instead of *have to* in spoken
English, e.g. *I've got to go now. It's very late.*

advice or opinion: *should* / *shouldn't* (+ infinitive)

You **should** take warm clothes with you to Dublin.
It might be cold at night.
I think the government **should** do something
about unemployment.

- *Should* is not as strong as *must* / *have to*. We use it to say if we think
  something is the right or wrong thing to do.
- *Should* is a modal verb. The only forms are *should* and *shouldn't*.
- You can also use *ought to* and *ought not to* instead of *should* / *shouldn't*.
  You should take an umbrella with you. You ought to take an umbrella with you.

3B   *must, may, might, can't* (deduction)

when you are sure something is true: *must*

They **must** be out. There aren't any lights on.
She **must** have a lot of money. She drives a Porsche.

when you think something is possibly true: *may* / *might*

His phone's switched off. He **might** be on the plane now.
She **might not** like that skirt. It's not her style.
She's not at home. She **may** be working.
He hasn't written. He **may not** have my address.

when you are sure something is impossible / not true: *can't*

He **can't** be ill. I saw him at the gym.
They **can't** be Italian. They're speaking to each other in Spanish.

- We often use *must*, *may* / *might*, and *can't* to say how sure
  or certain we are about something (based on the
  information we have).
- In this context, the opposite of *must* is *can't* NOT ~~mustn't~~.

3C   *can, could, be able to* (ability and possibility)

can / could

I **can** speak Spanish very well.
She **could** play the violin when she was three.
She **can't** come tonight. She's ill.
They **couldn't** wait because they were in a hurry.
Could you open that door, please?

- *Can* is a modal verb. It only has a present, past,
  and conditional form (but can also be used
  with a future meaning).
- For other tenses and forms use *be able to*.

be able to + infinitive

I **am able to** accept your invitation.
They **weren't able to** come.
I**'ll be able to** practise my English in London.
She **has been able to** speak French since she was a child.
I'd like **to be able to** ski.
I love **being able to** sleep late at weekends.

- You can use *be able to* in the present, past, future, present perfect,
  and as a gerund or infinitive.
- *be able to* in the present and past is more formal than *can* / *could*.

134

3A

a Circle the correct form.

You *shouldn't* / (*mustn't*) drink that water. It's not safe.

1 We *mustn't* / *don't have to* hurry. We have plenty of time.

2 You *must* / *should* remember to write the report. The boss will be furious if you forget.

3 The exhibition was free so I *hadn't to* / *didn't have to* pay.

4 *Do you have to* / *Should you* wear a uniform at your school?

5 We *must* / *had to* wait two hours at security and nearly missed our flight.

6 *Had you to* / *Did you have to* do a lot of homework when you were at school?

7 I think people who live in flats *mustn't* / *shouldn't* have dogs.

8 She's allergic to dairy products so she *mustn't* / *doesn't have to* eat anything made from milk.

b Complete the second sentence with **two** or **three** words so it means the same as the first.

Smoking is prohibited here.   You *mustn't smoke* here.

1 It isn't a good idea to go swimming after a big meal.
You _____ swimming after a big meal.

2 Was it necessary for them to pay cash?
Did _____ pay cash?

3 The meeting isn't obligatory.
You _____ go to the meeting.

4 It's bad manners to talk loudly on a mobile on a train.
People _____ quietly on their mobile on a train.

5 Lorries are not allowed to go on this road.
Lorries _____ on this road.

3B

a Match the sentences.

1 He must be over 70. *I*
2 He can't be at university.
3 He may not remember me.
4 He might like this book.
5 He must be very shy.
6 He can't be serious.
7 He may be in bed already.
8 He might not be at home yet.
9 He must have a computer.
10 He can't be a good footballer.

A He hasn't seen me for ages.
B He sometimes sends me emails.
C He must be joking.
D He's interested in history.
E He sometimes works late.
F He gets up very early.
G He's only 16.
H He's not fit enough.
I He retired 10 years ago.
J He never opens his mouth.

b Complete with *might (not)*, *must*, or *can't*.

This sauce is really spicy. It ___*must*___ have chilli in it.

1 **A** What music is this?
   B I'm not sure but it _____ be Mozart.

2 She looks very young. She _____ be more than 16.

3 I'm not sure why she hasn't phoned. She _____ have my new number.

4 They _____ have a lot of money. They live in an enormous house.

5 He _____ be away. His car is outside his house.

6 I _____ be a size 44! I'm usually a 40 or 42.

7 It _____ be true! I saw it on the news.

3C

a Complete with the correct form of *be able to*.

‑ I' *ve* never *been able to* learn to swim.

1 ‑ I _____ send any emails since lunchtime.

2 + She used to _____ speak German really well.

3 ‑ I _____ do my homework until tomorrow.

4 + I'd really like _____ dance well.

5 ? _____ you _____ come to our wedding? It's on May 10th.

6 + If I spoke better English, I _____ get a job in a hotel.

7 + When I've saved another €1000, I _____ buy a new car.

8 ‑ She hates _____ do what she wants.

b Complete with *can* / *can't*, or *could* / *couldn't* where possible. If not, use a form of *be able to*.

They told me that they ___*couldn't*___ do anything about the noise.

1 I _____ talk to you now. I'm too busy.

2 When I lived in Rome I _____ speak Italian quite well.

3 I would love _____ play tennis very well.

4 If we don't hurry up, we _____ catch the last train.

5 My mother _____ see much better now with her new glasses.

6 To do this job you need _____ speak at least two languages.

7 I _____ help you tonight if you want.

8 They _____ find a flat yet. They're still looking.

4

4A first conditional and future time clauses + *when, until*, etc.

first conditional sentences: *if* (or *unless*) + present simple, *will* / *won't* + infinitive

> If you **don't do** more work, you**'ll fail** the exam.
> He**'ll be** late for work if he **doesn't hurry up**.
> She won't get into university unless she **gets** good grades.

- Use the present tense (NOT the future) after *if* in first conditional sentences.
- *unless = if…not*
  I won't go unless she invites me. = I won't go if she doesn't invite me.
- You can also use an imperative instead of the *will* clause, e.g. *Come and see us next week if you have time.*

future time clauses

> As soon as you **get** your exam results, **call** me.
> We**'ll have** dinner when your father **gets** home.
> I **won't go** to bed until you **come** home.
> I**'ll have** lunch before I **leave**.
> After I **finish** university, I**'ll** probably **take** a year off and travel.

- Use the present simple (NOT the future) after *when, as soon as, until, before,* and *after* to talk about the future.
- *as soon as* = at the moment when, e.g. *I'll call you as soon as I arrive.*

4B second conditional

second conditional sentences: *if* + past simple, *would* / *wouldn't* + infinitive

> If I **had** more money, I**'d buy** a bigger house.
> If he **spoke** English, he **could get** a job in a hotel.
> I **would get on** better with my parents if I **didn't live** with them.
> I **wouldn't do** that job unless they **paid** me a really good salary.
> If I **were** you, I**'d buy** a new computer.

- Use the second conditional to talk about a hypothetical / imaginary situation in the present or future and its consequence. Compare:
  I don't have much money, so I can't buy a bigger house (real situation).
  If I had more money, I'd buy a bigger house (hypothetical / imaginary situation).
- Use second conditionals beginning *If I were you, I'd…* to give advice. Here you can't use *If I was you*.

would / wouldn't + infinitive

> My ideal holiday **would be** a week in the Bahamas.
> I**'d** never **buy** a car as big as yours.

- You can also use *would / wouldn't* + infinitive (without an *if* clause) when you talk about imaginary situations.
- The contraction of *would* is **'d**.

> ⚠ Remember the difference between first and second conditionals.
> *If I have time, I'll help you.*
> = a possible situation. I may have time.
> *If I had time, I'd help you.*
> = an imaginary / hypothetical situation. I don't / won't have time.

4C *usually* and *used to*

present habits and states

> I usually **get up** at 8.00 on school days.
> I **don't** usually **go out** during the week.
> Houses in the suburbs usually **have** gardens.
> **Do** you usually **walk** to work?

past habits and states

> We **used to be** close friends but we don't see each other any more.
> I **used to go out** with that girl when I was at school.
> **Did** you **use to wear** glasses?
> She **didn't use to have** fair hair. She had dark hair before.

- For present habits use *usually* or *normally* + present simple.
- For past habits use *used to / didn't use to* + infinitive. *Used to* does not exist in the present tense.
- We use *used to* for things that were true over a period of time in the past. It usually refers to something which is not true now.
  I used to smoke. = I smoked for a period time in the past but now I don't.
- *Used to / didn't use to* can be used with action verbs (e.g. *wear, go out*) and non-action verbs (e.g. *be, have*).
- We often use *not…any more / any longer* (= not now) with the present simple to contrast with *used to*.
  I used to go to the gym but I don't any more / any longer.

4A

a Complete with a word or expression from the list.

after   as soon as   before   if   unless   until   when

___After___ we have dinner, we could go for a drink.

1 I must write the date in my diary _____ I forget it.
2 Let's wait under the tree _____ it stops raining.
3 This job is very urgent so please do it _____ you can.
4 We won't get a table in the restaurant _____ we don't book.
5 I'll pay you back _____ I get my first salary.
6 I can't go _____ you pay for my ticket. I'm broke.
7 They'll be really happy _____ they hear your news.
8 I want to go on working _____ I'm 60. Then I'll retire.
9 I must renew my passport _____ I go to New York.
10 _____ you work harder, you won't pass the final exam.

b Complete with the present simple or *will*.

I'll give him your message when I ___see___ him. (see)

1 Don't forget to turn off the lights before you _____. (leave)
2 Go to bed when the film _____. (finish)
3 They _____ married until they find a place to live. (not get)
4 If I see Emma, I _____ her you are looking for her. (tell)
5 I'll call you as soon as I _____ at the hotel. (arrive)
6 You won't be able to park unless you _____ there early. (get)
7 As soon it stops raining, we _____ out. (go)
8 She won't like curry if she _____ spicy food. (not like)
9 Don't write anything until I _____ you. (tell)
10 When she finds out what he's done, she _____ furious. (be)

4B

a Write second conditional sentences.

If you / speak to your boss, I'm sure he / understand.
If you spoke to your boss, I'm sure he would understand.

1 It / be better for me if we / meet tomorrow.
2 She / not treat him like that if she really / love him.
3 If I / can live anywhere in the world, I / live in New Zealand.
4 The kitchen / look bigger if we / paint it white.
5 I / not buy that house if I / be you.
6 He / be more attractive if he / wear nicer clothes.
7 If we / not have children, we / travel more.
8 What / you do in this situation if you / be me?

b First or second conditional? Complete the sentences.

If you tell her anything, she *'ll tell* everybody in the office. (tell)
We'd have a dog if we ___had___ a garden. (have)

1 It'll be quicker if we _____ a taxi to the airport. (get)
2 If you stopped smoking, you _____ better. (feel)
3 What would you do if you _____ your job? (lose)
4 If you buy the food, I _____ tonight. (cook)
5 I think he'd be happier if he _____ alone. (not live)
6 I'll be very surprised if Marina _____ coming here. (not get lost)
7 Where will he live if he _____ the job in Moscow? (get)
8 If she didn't have to look after her mother, she _____ life more. (enjoy)

4C

a Correct the mistakes in the highlighted phrases.

She wasn't use to be so shy. *She didn't use to be*

1 I use to get up at 6.30, but I don't any more.
2 Did she always used to have long hair?
3 Do you use to have breakfast before you go to work?
4 They didn't used to have a car, they used to cycle everywhere.
5 He doesn't like coffee, so he use to drink tea in the morning.
6 He used be a teacher , but now he works for *Greenpeace*.
7 Do usually you wear trousers or skirts?
8 Last year we used to go to Prague in August.
9 Does she use to live near you when you were children?
10 At school we don't use to wear a uniform. We wore what we liked.

b Complete with *used to* in +, −, or ? and a verb from the list.

argue   be (x2)   go   have (x2)   like   live   play   work

− I *didn't use to go* to the theatre much but now I go twice a month.

1 + Kirsty _____ in Bristol but she moved to London last year.
2 ? _____ you _____ a moustache? You look different.
3 − I _____ my boss but now we get on quite well.
4 + We _____ really close but now we hardly ever meet.
5 ? Where _____ you _____ before you started with this company?
6 + She _____ tennis professionally but she retired last year.
7 + When I lived in Paris, I always _____ breakfast in a café.
8 ? _____ you _____ with your parents when you were a teenager?
9 − He _____ so slim. In fact, he was quite overweight before.

5

5A   quantifiers

large quantities

> They have **a lot of money**.
> She has **lots of friends**.
> He eats **a lot**.
> There aren't **many cafés** near here.
> Do you watch **much TV?**
> Don't run. We have **plenty of time**.

- Use *a lot of / lots of* in ⊞ sentences.
- Use *a lot* when there is no noun, e.g. *He talks a lot*.
- *Much / many* are normally used in ⊟ sentences and ⍰, but *a lot of* can also be used.
- Use *plenty of* in ⊞ sentences to mean *as much as we need or more*.

small quantities

> **A** Do you want some ice cream? **B** Just **a little**.
> The town only has **a few cinemas**.
> Hurry up. We have **very little time**.
> I have **very few close friends**.

- Use *little* + uncountable nouns, *few* + plural countable nouns.
- *a little* and *a few* = some, but not a lot,
- *very little* and *very few* = not much / many.

zero quantity

> There **isn't any** room in the car.
> There**'s no** room in the car.
> **A** How much money do you have?
> **B None**.

- Use *any* for zero quantity with a ⊟ verb. Use *no* with a ⊞ verb.
- Use *none* (without a noun) in short answers.

more than you need or want

> I don't like this city. It's **too big**.
> There's **too much traffic**.
> There are **too many tourists**.

less than you need

> There aren't **enough parks**.
> The buses aren't **frequent enough**.

- Use *too* + adjective, *too much* + uncountable noun, *too many* + plural countable nouns.
- Use *enough* before a noun but after an adjective.

5B   articles: *a / an*, *the*, no article

Use *a / an* with singular countable nouns

– the first time you mention a thing / person.	I saw **an old man** with **a dog**.
– when you say what something is.	It's **a nice house**.
– when you say what somebody does.	She's **a lawyer**.
– in exclamations with *What…!*	What **an awful day!**
– in expressions like …	three times **a week**

Use *the*

– when we talk about something we've already mentioned.	I saw an old man with a dog, and **the dog** was barking.
– when there's only one of something.	**The moon** goes round **the sun**.
– when it's clear what you're referring to.	He opened **the door**.
– with places in a town, e.g. *cinema* and *theatre*.	I'm going to **the cinema**.
– with superlatives.	It's **the best** restaurant in town.

Don't use *the*

- when you are speaking in general (with plural and uncountable nouns). **Women** talk more than **men**. **Love** is more important than **money**.

- with some nouns (e.g. *home*, *work*, *school*, *church*) after *at / to / from*, She's not **at home** today. I get back **from work** at 5.30.

- before meals, days, and months. I never have **breakfast** on **Sunday**.

- before *next / last* + days, week, etc. See you **next Friday**.

5C   gerunds and infinitives

Use the gerund (verb + *-ing*)

1 after prepositions and phrasal verbs.	I'm very good **at remembering** names. She's **given up smoking**.
2 as the subject of a sentence.	**Eating out** is quite cheap here.
3 after some verbs, e.g. *hate, spend, don't mind*.	I **don't mind getting up** early.

Common verbs which take the gerund include: **enjoy**, **hate**, **finish**, **like**, **love**, **mind**, **practise**, **spend**, **stop**, **suggest** and phrasal verbs, e.g. **give up**, **go on**, etc.

Use the infinitive (+ *to*)

1 after adjectives.	My flat is **easy to find**.
2 to express a reason or purpose.	He's saving money **to buy** a new car.
3 after some verbs, e.g. *want, need, learn*.	She's never **learnt to drive**. **Try not to make** a noise.

Common verbs which take the infinitive (with *to*) include: **(can't) afford**, **agree**, **decide**, **expect**, **forget**, **help**, **hope**, **learn**, **need**, **offer**, **plan**, **pretend**, **promise**, **refuse**, **remember**, **seem**, **try**, **want**, **would like**

Use the infinitive (without *to*)

1 after most modal and auxiliary verbs.	I **can't** drive. We **must** hurry.
2 after *make* and *let*.	My parents don't **let** me **go** out much. She always **makes** me **laugh**.

- Gerunds and infinitives form the negative with *not*, e.g. *not to be, not being*.
- More verbs take the infinitive than the gerund.
- These common verbs can take either the gerund or infinitive with no difference in meaning: **begin**, **continue**, **prefer**, **start**.

⚠ These verbs can take a gerund or an infinitive but the meaning is different.

Try to be on time.
= make an effort to be on time.

Try doing yoga.
= do it to see if you like it.

***Remember** to phone him.*
= Don't forget to do it.

*I **remember** meeting him years ago.*
= I have a memory of it.

5A

a Circle the correct answer. Tick (✔) if both are possible.

I think this restaurant is (too)/ *too much* expensive.

1 There are *too much* / *too many* people in my salsa class.
2 Nobody likes him. He has *very little* / *very few* friends.
3 We've had *a lot of* / *lots of* rain recently.
4 There aren't *enough car parks* / *car parks enough* in the city centre.
5 *I have no* / *I don't have any* time.
6 He works *a lot* / *much*. At least ten hours a day.
7 **A** Do you speak French? **B** Yes, *a little* / *a few*.
8 I don't have *no time* / *any time* for myself.

b Right (✔) or wrong (✘). Correct the wrong sentences.

She drives too much fast . *too fast*

1 Slow down! We have plenty time .
2 We have too many work at the moment.
3 I think I made a few mistakes in the letter.
4 He isn't enough old to understand.
5 We can't go tomorrow. We're too busy .
6 We have very little time to do this.
7 **A** How many eggs are there? **B** Any .
8 He's retired so he has much free time .

5B

a Circle the correct answer.

Did you see *news* /(the news) on TV last night?

1 Did you lock *door* / *the door* when you left *a house* / *the house*?
2 My brother is married to *Russian* / *a Russian*. She's *lawyer* / *a lawyer*.
3 We go to *theatre* / *the theatre* about once *a month* / *the month*.
4 What *beautiful* / *a beautiful day*! Let's have breakfast on *a terrace* / *the terrace*.
5 I love *classical music* / *the classical music* and *Italian food* / *the Italian food*.
6 Who is *a girl* / *the girl* by *a window* / *the window*?
7 I leave *home* / *the home* at 8.00 and get to *work* / *the work* at 9.00.
8 *Men* / *The men* aren't normally as sensitive as *women* / *the women*.
9 We usually have *dinner* / *the dinner* at 8.00 and go to *bed* / *the bed* at about 11.30.
10 She has *a lovely face* / *the lovely face* and *the attractive eyes* / *attractive eyes*.

b Complete with *a* / *an*, *the*, or – (= no article).

Can you give me __a__ lift to __the__ station?
I want to catch __the__ 6.00 train.

1 We went to _____ cinema _____ last night. We saw _____ great film.
2 **A** Do you like _____ sport? **B** It depends. I hate _____ football. I think _____ footballers earn too much money.
3 He always wears _____ expensive clothes and drives _____ expensive car.
4 Jake's _____ musician and _____ artist.
5 They've changed _____ date of _____ meeting. It's _____ next Tuesday now.
6 We walked to _____ city centre but we got _____ taxi back to _____ hotel.

5C

a Complete with the gerund or infinitive.

__Smoking__ is banned in all public places. (smoke)

1 It's very expensive _____ a flat in the centre. (rent)
2 Are you afraid of _____? (fly)
3 I called the restaurant _____ a table for tonight. (book)
4 Be careful _____ a noise when you come home tonight. (not make)
5 She's worried about _____ the exam. (fail)
6 Everybody went on _____ until after midnight. (dance)
7 _____ an only child is a bit boring. (be)
8 It's easy _____ the way if you look at the map. (find)
9 He's terrible at _____ languages. (learn)
10 **A** Why are you learning Spanish?
   B _____ talk to my in-laws. They're Argentinian, and they don't speak English. (be able to)

b Complete the sentences with *work*, *to work*, or *working*.

I regret not __working__ harder when I was at school.

1 I spent all weekend _____ on the computer.
2 I've decided _____ abroad next year.
3 You must _____ harder if you want to get promoted.
4 My boss often makes me _____ late.
5 He isn't very good at _____ in a team.
6 I don't mind _____ on Saturdays if I can have a day off during the week.
7 He's gone to the UK _____ in his uncle's shop.
8 _____ with members of your family can be quite difficult.
9 My husband promised not _____ on my birthday.
10 I used _____ in a restaurant when I was a student.

6

6A   reported speech: statements and questions

direct statements	reported statements
'**I like** shopping.'	She said (that) **she liked** shopping.
'**I'm** going **tomorrow**.'	He told her **he was** going **the next day**.
'**I'll** always love **you**.'	He said **he would** always love **me**.
'**I passed** the exam!'	She told him **she had passed** the exam.
'**I've forgotten my** keys.'	He said **he had forgotten his** keys.
'**I can't** come.'	She said **she couldn't** come.
'**I may** be late.'	He said **he might** be late.
'**I must** go.'	She said **she had to** go.

- Tenses usually change like this: **present>past; will>would; past simple / present perfect>past perfect**
- Some modal verbs change, e.g. **can>could, may>might, must>had to**. Other modal verbs stay the same, e.g. *could, might, should*, etc.

direct questions	reported questions
'**Are you** married?'	She asked him **if he was** married.
'**Did** she **phone**?'	He asked me **whether** she **had phoned**.
'What**'s** your name?'	I asked him **what** his name **was**.
'Where **do you live**?'	They asked me **where** **I lived**.

⚠ • *Must* changes to *had to* BUT *mustn't* stays the same. *'You mustn't touch it.'* She said I mustn't touch it.

- You usually have to change the pronouns. 'I like…'>She said **she** liked…
- Using **that** after *said* and *told* is optional.
- If you report what someone said on a different day or in a different place, some time and place words can change, e.g. **tomorrow>the next day, here>there, this>that**, etc. *'I'll meet you here tomorrow'.>He said he'd meet me there the next day.*

⚠ After *said* don't use a person or object pronoun. *He said he was tired* NOT He said me… After *told* you must use a person or pronoun. *He told me he was tired.* NOT He told he was…

- When you report a question, the tenses change as in reported statements.
- When a question begins with a verb (not a question word), add *if* (or *whether*).
- You also have to change the word order to subject + verb, and not use *do / did*.

reported speech: commands

direct speech	reported speech
'**Go** away.'	She told him **to go** away.
'**Don't worry**.'	The doctor told me **not to worry**.
'**Can / Could you help** me?'	I asked the shop assistant **to help** me.

⚠ You can't use *said* in these sentences. NOT She said him to go away.

- To report an imperative or request, use *told* or *asked* + person + the infinitive with *to*.
- To report a negative imperative, use a negative infinitive (e.g. **not to do**).

6B   the passive: *be* + past participle

A lot of films **are shot** on location.	My bike **has been stolen**.	
My car **is being repaired** today.	You**'ll be picked up** at the airport.	
Death in Venice **was directed by** Visconti.	This bill **has to be paid** tomorrow.	
She died when **the film was being made**.		

- We often use the passive when it's not clear or important who does an action, e.g. *My bike has been stolen* (= Somebody has stolen my bike. I don't know who.)
- If you want to say who did the action, use *by*.

6C   relative clauses

defining relative clauses

Julia's the woman **who / that** works with me.
It's a book **which / that** tells you how to relax.
That's the house **where** I was born.
That's the boy **whose** father plays for Real Madrid.
He's the man (**who / that**) I met on the plane.

- To give important information about a person, place, or thing use a relative clause (= a relative pronoun + subject + verb).
- Use the relative pronouns *who* for people, *which* for things, and *where* for places. Use *whose* to mean 'of who / of which'.
- You can use *that* instead of *who* or *which*.
- *Who, which*, and *that* can be omitted when the verbs in the main clause and the relative clause **have a different subject**, e.g. *He's the man I met on the plane.* (The subject of *met* is *I*, so it's not necessary to put *who*.)

non-defining relative clauses

This painting, **which** was painted in 1860, is worth £2 million.
Last week I visited my aunt, **who's** nearly 90 years old.
Burford, **where** my mother was born, is a beautiful town.
My neighbour, **whose** son goes to my son's school, has just re-married.

- If a relative clause gives extra, non-essential information (the sentence makes sense without it), you must put it between commas (or a comma and a full stop).
- In these clauses, you can't leave out the relative pronoun (*who, which*, etc.).
- In these clauses, you can't use *that* instead of *who / which*.

6A

a Complete the sentences using reported speech.

'The hotel is full.' The receptionist told me the hotel _was full_ .

1 'I'll call the manager.' The waiter said _____ .
2 'I've passed all my exams.' Jack said _____ .
3 'You should get to the airport early.' They said that we _____ .
4 'I may be late.' Jack said _____ .
5 'I didn't tell anybody!' Mary said _____ .
6 'Can you help me?' She asked us _____ .
7 'Do you want to dance?' He asked me _____ .
8 'Have you been here before?' I asked her _____ .
9 'What music do you like?' She asked me _____ .
10 'Where's the nearest bank?' I asked her _____ .

b Complete the reported imperatives and requests.

'Don't stop here.' The traffic warden told us _not to stop there_ .

1 'Be quiet!' The teacher told us _____ .
2 'Please don't smoke!' I asked the taxi driver _____ .
3 'Open your mouth.' The dentist told me _____ .
4 'Don't tell anyone!' Melinda told us _____ .
5 'Could you show me your driving licence?' The policeman asked me _____ .
6 'Please switch off your mobiles.' The flight attendant told us _____ .
7 'Don't eat with your mouth open!' I told my daughter _____ .
8 'Can you bring me the bill, please?' He asked the waiter _____ .
9 'Get off at the next stop.' The bus driver told me _____ .
10 'Don't wait.' Our friends told us _____ .

6B

a Correct the mistakes in the highlighted phrases.

Lada cars made in Russia . _are made in Russia._

1 A new motorway is being build at the moment.
2 The film based on a famous novel.
3 This programme were watched by millions of people.
4 My bag was stole when I was in Florida.
5 The Harry Potter books were written for JK Rowling.
6 I couldn't send you an email because my computer was repairing .
7 You will taken to your hotel by taxi.
8 Oh no! Our flight has being cancelled .
9 English is spoke in this restaurant.
10 Seat belts must wear at all times.

b Rewrite the sentences with the passive.

They sell cold drinks here. Cold drinks _are sold here_ .

1 They subtitle a lot of foreign films.
   A lot of foreign films _____ .
2 Someone threw the letters away by mistake.
   The letters _____ .
3 Some people are painting my house.
   My house _____ .
4 They have sold all the tickets for the concert.
   All the tickets for the concert _____ .
5 They will play the match tomorrow.
   The match _____ .
6 Somebody must pay this bill tomorrow.
   This bill _____ .

6C

a Complete with *who*, *which*, *where*, or *whose*.

The man _whose_ car I crashed into is taking me to court.

1 We drove past the house _____ we used to live.
2 The girl _____ was talking to you is the boss's daughter.
3 Look! That's the man _____ son plays for Chelsea.
4 The car was an invention _____ changed the world.
5 That's the restaurant _____ I told you about.
6 Is this the shop _____ you bought your camera?
7 What was the name of your friend _____ wife is an actress?
8 The woman _____ called this morning didn't leave a message.
9 It's the film _____ won all the Oscars last year.
10 This is the book _____ everybody is reading at the moment.

b Tick (✔) the sentences in **a** where you could leave out the relative pronoun.

c Are the highlighted phrases right (✔) or wrong (✘)? Correct the wrong ones.

After Rome we went to Venice, that we loved . ✘
   which we loved

1 Is that the girl you used to go out with ?
2 My brother, that you met at my wedding , is getting divorced.
3 It's a machine that makes sweets .
4 He lives in Valencia, that is on the east coast of Spain .
5 Our neighbour, who garden is smaller than ours , has an enormous dog.
6 Jerry, who I work with , is completely bilingual.
7 The film I saw last night was fantastic.
8 I met some people who they come from the same village as me .

7A third conditional

third conditional sentences: *if* + *had* + past participle, *would* + *have* + past participle.

> If I**'d known** about the meeting, I **would have gone**.
> If I **hadn't gone** to that party, I **wouldn't have met** my wife.
> You **wouldn't have been** late if you**'d got up** earlier.
> We **would have arrived** at 6.00 if we **hadn't got** lost.

- The contraction of *had* is *'d*.

- Use third conditional sentences to talk about a hypothetical / imaginary situation in the past (which didn't happen) and its consequence. Compare:
  Yesterday I got up late and missed my train (= the real situation).
  If I hadn't got up late yesterday, I wouldn't have missed my train (= the hypothetical / imaginary situation).
- To make a third conditional, use *if* + past perfect and *would have* + past participle.

7B question tags, indirect questions

question tags

positive verb, negative tag	negative verb, positive tag
It**'s** cold today, **isn't it**?	She **isn't** here today, **is she**?
You**'re** Polish, **aren't you**?	You **aren't** happy, **are you**?
They **live** in Ankara, **don't they**?	They **don't** smoke, **do they**?
The match **finishes** at 8.00, **doesn't it**?	She **doesn't** eat meat, **does she**?
She **worked** in a bank, **didn't she**?	You **didn't** like the film, **did you**?
We**'ve met** before, **haven't we**?	She **hasn't been** to Rome before, **has she**?
You**'ll be** OK, **won't you**?	You **won't tell** anyone, **will you**?

- Question tags are often used to check something you already think is true.
  Your name's Maria, isn't it?
- To form a question tag use:
  – the correct auxiliary verb, e.g. *do / does* for the present, *will / won't* for the future, etc.
  – a pronoun, e.g. *he, it, they*, etc.
  – a negative tag if the sentence is positive, and a positive tag if the sentence is negative.

indirect questions

direct question	indirect question
Where**'s** the bank?	Could you tell me where **the bank is**?
What time **do the shops close**?	Do you know what time **the shops close**?
Is there a bus stop near here?	Do you know **if there's a bus stop** near here?
Does this train go to Victoria?	Could you tell me **if this train goes** to Victoria?

- To make a question more polite we often begin *Could you tell me…?* or *Do you know…?* The word order changes to subject + verb, e.g. *Do you know where the post office is?* NOT *Do you know where is, the post office?*

- If the question begins with an auxiliary verb, add *if* (or *whether*) after *Could you tell me…? / Do you know…?*
- We also use this structure after *Can you remember…?*, e.g. *Can you remember where he lives?*

7C phrasal verbs

group 1: no object – verb and *up, on*, etc. can't be separated.

> **Come on**! **Hurry up**! We're late.
> The plane **took off** two hours late.
> **Go away** and never **come back**!

group 2: with object – verb and *up, on*, etc. can't be separated.

> I'm **looking for** my keys. NOT *I'm looking my keys for.*
> I **asked for** chicken, not steak.
> Please **look after** the baby.
> I don't **get on with** my sister.
> I'm **looking forward to** the party.

group 3: with object – verb and *up, on*, etc. can be separated.

> Please **switch off** your phone. / Please **switch** your phone **off**.
> Can you **fill in** this form, please? / Can you **fill** this form **in**, please?
> They've **set up** a new company. / They've **set** a new company **up**.
> Don't **throw away** those papers. / Don't **throw** those papers **away**.

- A phrasal verb is a verb combined with a particle (= an adverb or preposition).
- Sometimes the meaning of the phrasal verb is obvious from the verb and the particle, e.g. *sit down, come back*.
- Sometimes the meaning is not obvious, e.g. *give up smoking* (= stop smoking), *carry on talking* (= continue talking).
- In group 3, where the verb and particle can be separated, if the object is a pronoun, it must go between the verb and particle.
  Switch it off. NOT *Switch off it.*
  Throw them away. NOT *Throw away them.*

⚠ Sometimes a phrasal verb has more than one meaning, e.g. *The plane took off. He took off his shoes.*

7A

a Match the phrases.

1 If you hadn't reminded me, *I*
2 This wouldn't have happened
3 If they hadn't worn their seat belts,
4 We wouldn't have been late
5 We would have gone to the beach
6 If you hadn't told me it was him,
7 You would have laughed
8 I wouldn't have bought it
9 If you'd arrived two minutes earlier,
10 If you hadn't forgotten the map,
11 It would have been cheaper

A if you'd seen what happened.
B we wouldn't have got lost.
C if it hadn't rained.
D you would have seen them.
E if I'd known you didn't like it.
F if we'd bought tickets on the Internet.
G if you'd been more careful.
H they would have been killed.
I I would have forgotten.
J I wouldn't have recognized him.
K if we hadn't missed the bus.

b Cover A–K. Look at 1–9 and try to remember the end of the sentence.

c Complete the third conditional sentences with the correct form of the verbs.

If you *hadn't helped* me, I *wouldn't have finished* on time. (not help, not finish)

1 We _____ if our best player _____ injured. (win, not be)
2 If she _____ he was so mean, she _____ him. (know, not marry)
3 I _____ you some money if you _____ me. (lend, ask)
4 If we _____ more time, we _____ another day in London. (have, spend)
5 I _____ to help you if you _____ me about it earlier. (be able, tell)
6 If you _____ me yesterday, I _____ my plans. (ask, change)
7 You _____ the weekend if you _____ with us. (enjoy, come)

7B

a Complete with a question tag (*are you?*, *isn't it?*, etc.)

Your name's Mark, *isn't it*?

1 You don't take sugar in your coffee, _____?
2 They're on holiday this week, _____?
3 He can't be serious, _____?
4 She eats meat, _____?
5 You won't be late, _____?
6 She was married to Tom Cruise, _____?
7 We've seen this film before, _____?
8 You didn't tell anybody, _____?
9 You would like to come, _____?
10 It's hot today, _____?

b Make indirect questions.

Where's the station? Could you tell me *where the station is?*

1 Where do they live? Do you know _____?
2 Is there a bank near here? Can you tell me _____?
3 Where can I buy some stamps? Do you know _____?
4 Does this bus go to the castle? Could you tell me _____?
5 What time do the shops open? Do you know _____?
6 Where are the toilets? Could you tell me _____?
7 Is Susan at work today? Do you know _____?
8 Did Milan win last night? Do you know _____?
9 Where did we park the car? Can you remember _____?
10 What's the time? Could you tell me _____?

7C

a Complete with the right particle (*in*, *on*, etc.).

What time did you get *up* this morning?

1 Could you turn _____ the radio? I can't hear it.
2 I'm in a meeting. Could you call _____ later, say in half an hour?
3 Hurry _____! We'll be late.
4 The match is _____! Brazil have won.
5 How long has she been going _____ with him?
6 Are we having dinner at home or are we eating _____?
7 Athletes always warm _____ before a race.
8 I didn't wake _____ until 8.30 this morning.
9 If you don't know the word, look it _____ in a dictionary.
10 I went online to find _____ what time the trains were.

b Rewrite the sentences. Replace the *object* with a pronoun. Change the word order where necessary.

Turn on *the TV*. *Turn it on.*

1 Take off *your shoes*.
2 Could you look after *the children*?
3 Do you get on with *your sister*?
4 Switch off *your mobiles*.
5 I'm looking for *my glasses*.
6 Please pick up *that towel*.
7 Turn down *the music*!
8 I'm really looking forward to *the trip*.
9 Can I try on *this dress*?
10 Don't throw away *that letter*!

Food and restaurants

1 Food

a Put two food words in each column. Use your dictionary to help you.

beans	duck	lettuce /ˈletɪs/
peaches	prawns /prɔːnz/	salmon /ˈsæmən/
sausages /ˈsɒsɪdʒɪz/		strawberries /ˈstrɔːbəriz/

meat	fish / seafood	fruit	vegetables

b Add three more words to each column.

2 Food adjectives

Complete the adjective column with a word from the box.

fresh   frozen   home-made   low-fat   raw /rɔː/   spicy /ˈspaɪsi/   sweet   takeaway

	Adjective
1 I love my mum's cooking. ▨▨▨ food is always the best.	_____
2 Indian food like curry is very ▨▨▨.	_____
3 Sushi is made with ▨▨▨ fish.	_____
4 Food which is kept very cold is ▨▨▨.	_____
5 ▨▨▨ food is food you buy at a restaurant and take home to eat.	_____
6 People on a diet often try to eat ▨▨▨ food.	_____
7 These eggs are ▨▨▨, I bought them today.	_____
8 This tea's very ▨▨▨. You've put too much sugar in it!	_____

3 Restaurants and cooking

a Match the words and pictures.

- ▨ knife /naɪf/ pl /naɪvz/
- ▨ fork
- ▨ desserts /dɪˈzɜːts/
- ▨ spoon
- ▨ plate
- ▨ glass
- ▨ main courses /meɪn kɔːsɪz/
- ▨ napkin (serviette)
- ▨ salt and pepper
- ▨ starters

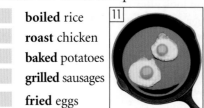

Today's menu

Prawn cocktail
Onion soup
~
Grilled steak
and chips
Salmon with
boiled potatoes
~
Strawberries
and cream
Tiramisu

8

9

10

b Match the words and pictures.

- ▨ **boiled** rice
- ▨ **roast** chicken
- ▨ **baked** potatoes
- ▨ **grilled** sausages
- ▨ **fried** eggs
- ▨ **steamed** vegetables

⟳ p.6

Can you remember the words on this page? Test yourself or a partner.

144

Study Link MultiROM www.oup.com/elt/englishfile/intermediate

Sport

1 People and places

a Match the words and pictures.

▢	captain /ˈkæptɪn/	▢	spectators
▢	coach	▢	team
▢	fans	▢	stadium
▢	players	▢	sports hall
▢	referee		

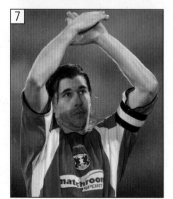

b Match the places and sports.

circuit /ˈsɜːkɪt/   court /kɔːt/   course
pitch   pool   slope   track

1 tennis / basketball _____
2 football / rugby / hockey _____
3 swimming / diving _____
4 athletics _____
5 Formula 1 / motorcycling _____
6 golf _____
7 ski _____

2 Verbs

a Complete with the past tense and past participles.

beat _____ _____
win _____ _____
lose _____ _____
draw /drɔː/ _____ _____

b Complete the **Verb** column with the past tense of a verb from **a**.

	Verb
1 Milan ▨ Chelsea 3-0.	_____
2 The Chicago Bulls ▨ 78-91 (to Celtics).	_____
3 Spain ▨ (with Brazil) 2-2.	_____
4 Milan ▨ (the match) 3-0.	_____

⚠ You *win* a match, competition, medal, or trophy. You *beat* another team or person NOT ~~Milan won Chelsea~~.

c Complete the **Verb** column.

do   get fit   get injured /ˈɪndʒəd/   go   play
score   train   warm up

	Verb
1 Players usually ▨ before a match starts.	_____
2 Professional sportspeople have to ▨ every day.	_____
3 It's dangerous to play tennis on a wet court. You might ▨.	_____
4 I've started going to the gym, because I want to ▨.	_____
5 He's a good player. I think he's going to ▨ a lot of goals.	_____
6 Would you like to ▨ swimming this afternoon?	_____
7 I ▨ basketball twice a week.	_____
8 My brothers ▨ yoga and tai-chi.	_____

Can you remember the words on this page? Test yourself or a partner.

⟲ **p.10**

Personality

1 What are they like?

a Complete the sentences with the personality adjectives.

affectionate /əˈfekʃənət/	aggressive	ambitious	bossy	charming	competitive	independent	jealous /ˈdʒeləs/	
manipulative	moody	reliable /riˈlaɪəbl/	selfish	sensible	sensitive	sociable /ˈsəʊʃəbl/	spoilt	

1 ___*Spoilt*___ children behave badly because they are given everything they want.
2 _____ people always want to win.
3 _____ people think about themselves and not about other people.
4 _____ people get angry quickly and like fighting and arguing.
5 _____ people have an attractive personality that makes people like them.
6 _____ people have common sense and are practical.
7 _____ people are friendly and enjoy being with other people.
8 _____ people are good at influencing other people to do what they want.
9 _____ people are happy one minute and sad the next, and are often bad-tempered.
10 _____ people like doing things on their own, without help.
11 _____ people like giving orders to other people.
12 _____ people show that they love or like people very much.
13 _____ people are people you can trust or depend on.
14 _____ people understand other people's feelings or are easily hurt or offended.
15 _____ people want to be successful in life.
16 _____ people think that someone loves another person more than them, or wants what other people have.

b With a partner, look at the adjectives again. Are they positive, negative, or neutral characteristics?

2 Opposite adjectives

Match the adjectives and their opposites.

extrovert	hard-working	mean
self-confident	stupid	talkative

clever _____   lazy _____
generous _____   quiet _____
insecure _____   shy _____

3 Negative prefixes

Which negative prefix do you use with these adjectives?
Put them in the correct column.

~~ambitious~~	friendly	honest /ˈɒnɪst/	imaginative
kind	organized	patient /ˈpeɪʃnt/	reliable
responsible	selfish	sensitive	sociable	tidy /ˈtaɪdi/

un-	dis-	in- / im- / ir-
unambitious		

Can you remember the words on this page?
Test yourself or a partner.

p.15

'Are we there yet? Are we there yet? Are we there yet?'

Study Link MultiROM   www.oup.com/elt/englishfile/intermediate

Money

1 Verbs

Complete with a verb in the correct tense.

be worth /wɜːθ/	borrow	can't afford /əˈfɔːd/	charge	cost	earn
inherit	invest	lend	owe /əʊ/	save	take out	waste /weɪst/

1 My uncle died and left me £2000.   I _____ £2000 from my uncle.
2 I put some money aside every week for my next holiday.   I _____ money every week.
3 I asked my brother to give me €10 until next week.   I _____ €10 from him.
4 My brother gave me €10 until next week.   He _____ me €10.
5 I often spend money on stupid things.   I often _____ money.
6 I don't have enough money to buy that car.   I _____ to buy that car.
7 I had to pay the mechanic £100 to repair my car.   The mechanic _____ me £100.
8 I went to the cash machine and got €200.   I _____ €200 from the cash machine.
9 I bought a book. It was $25.   The book _____ (me) $25.
10 Jim gave me £100. I haven't paid it back yet.   I _____ Jim £100.
11 I bought some shares in British Telecom.   I _____ some money.
12 I work in a supermarket. They pay me €2000 a month.   I _____ €2000 a month.
13 I could sell my house for about €200,000.   My house _____ about €200,000.

2 Prepositions

Complete the **Preposition** column.

Preposition

1 I paid _____ the dinner last night.   _____
2 When can you pay me _____ the money I lent you?   _____
3 Would you like to pay _____ cash or _____ credit card?   _____ , _____
4 I spent €50 _____ books yesterday.   _____
5 I don't like lending money _____ friends.   _____
6 I borrowed a lot of money _____ the bank.   _____
7 They charged us €60 _____ a bottle of wine.   _____

3 Nouns

Match the words and definitions.

cash machine /ˈkæʃ məʃiːn/	coin	loan
mortgage /ˈmɔːɡɪdʒ/	note	salary	tax

1 _____ A piece of paper money.
2 _____ A piece of money made of metal.
3 _____ Money a person gets for the work he / she does.
4 _____ Money that you pay to the government.
5 _____ Money that somebody (or a bank) lends you.
6 _____ Money that you borrow from a bank to buy a house.
7 _____ A machine inside or outside a bank where you can get money.

Can you remember the words on this page?
Test yourself or a partner.

◯ p.21

Transport and travel

1 Plane

Match the words and pictures.

land (vb)	take off (vb)
check-in desk	gate
luggage /ˈlʌgɪdʒ/	(suit)case
boarding card/pass	aisle /aɪl/
baggage reclaim	

2 Train

Match the words and pictures.

railway station
platform
carriage /ˈkærɪdʒ/
ticket office
the underground

3 Road

a Match the words and pictures.

coach	bike
lorry	car
van	scooter
motorbike	tram
helmet	motorway

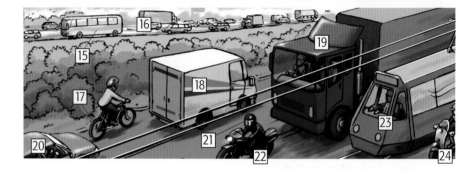

b Complete the compound nouns.

area	belt	crash	fine	hour	jam	lane	lights
limit	park	rank	station	transport	works		

1 petrol _____   a place where you can get petrol, often with a shop or café
2 traffic _____ 🚦
3 seat _____
4 rush _____   the time of day when there is a lot of traffic
5 car _____   when two or more cars hit each other
6 parking _____   money you have to pay for parking illegally
7 traffic _____   when there is so much traffic that cars can't move
8 speed _____ (50)
9 public _____   buses, trams, trains, etc.
10 pedestrian _____   a place where you can't drive
11 cycle _____   a narrow part of the road for bicycles only
12 road _____ ⚠️
13 taxi _____   where taxis park when they are waiting for customers
14 car _____   a place where you can leave your car

4 Travel

flight	journey /ˈdʒɜːni/
trip	travel

1 A _____ is when you travel from one place to another by car, train, plane, etc.
2 _____ is normally used as a verb, e.g. I _____ a lot.
3 A _____ is when you go somewhere by plane.
4 A _____ is when you go somewhere, either for a holiday or on business, stay there, and come back again.

Can you remember the words on this page? Test yourself or a partner.

◑ p.30

Describing people

1 Age

Complete the phrases.

mid-	early	about	late	forties

1 He's _____ 20.   = 19, 20, or 21
2 He's in his _____.   = between 41 and 49
3 She's in her _____ thirties.   = between 34 and 36
4 She's in her _____ sixties.   = between 67 and 69
5 He's in his _____ seventies.   = between 71 and 73

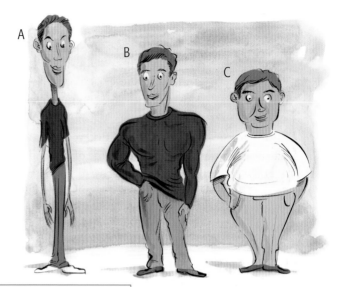

2 Height and build

Match the sentences and pictures A–C.

1 [ ] He's **tall** and **slim**.
2 [ ] He's **short** and a bit **overweight** /əʊvə'weɪt/.
3 [ ] He's **medium height** /'miːdiəm 'haɪt/ and **well built**.

⚠ *Thin* and *slim* are both the opposite of *fat*, but *slim* = thin in an attractive way.

3 Hair

Match the sentences and pictures.

1 [ ] She has **fair** (or **blonde**) hair and a **ponytail**.
2 [ ] She has **long wavy** hair.
3 [ ] He has **grey hair** and a **beard** /bɪəd/.
4 [ ] She has **short brown curly** hair.
5 [ ] She has **red shoulder-length** hair.
6 [ ] He's **bald** /bɔːld/ and has a **moustache** /mə'stɑːʃ/.
7 [ ] She has **straight dark** hair and a **fringe**.

4 General adjectives

a Are these adjectives ⊞ or ⊟? Are they used for men, women, or both? Write M, W, or B.

	⊞ or ⊟	M, W, or B
attractive		
beautiful		
good-looking		
handsome /'hænsəm/		
plain		
pretty /'prɪti/		
ugly		

⚠ *What does he / she look like?* = Can you describe his / her appearance?
What is he / she like? = Can you describe his / her personality?

Can you remember the words on this page? Test yourself or a partner.

⬅ p.41

Education

1 Verbs

Complete the **Verb** column.

behave	cheat	do	fail	learn	leave	pass	revise	start	<u>study</u>	take

Verb

1 When she was at school, she used to ▨▨▨ for hours every evening.   _study_ _____

2 I must ▨▨▨ tonight. I have an exam tomorrow.   _____

3 Our history teacher was terrible. We didn't ▨▨▨ anything.   _____

4 If you don't ▨▨▨ your homework, you can't watch TV later.   _____

5 The teacher was angry because some of the pupils had tried to ▨▨▨ in the exam.   _____

6 If you want to be a doctor, you have to ▨▨▨ a lot of exams.   _____ (or _do_)

7 In the UK children ▨▨▨ school when they are four and can't ▨▨▨ before they are 16.   _____ _____

8 I hope I'm going to ▨▨▨ my exams. My parents will be furious if I ▨▨▨.   _____ _____

9 He was a rebel at school. He used to ▨▨▨ very badly.   _____

2 Places and people

Match the words and definitions.

boarding school /'bɔːdɪŋ/	graduate /'grædʒuət/	head teacher	nursery school	primary school	private school

pupil /'pjuːpl/   professor   religious school /rɪ'lɪdʒəs/   secondary school   state school   student

1 _____ A school paid for by the government which gives free education.

2 _____ A non-government school where you have to pay.

3 _____ A school for very young children, e.g. 1–4.

4 _____ A school for young children, e.g. from 4–11.

5 _____ A school for older children, e.g. 11–18.

6 _____ A school where pupils live, eat, and sleep.

7 _____ A school where the teachers are often priests or nuns.

8 _____ The 'boss' of a school.

9 _____ A senior university teacher.

10 _____ A person who is studying at a college or university.

11 _____ A child who is at school.

12 _____ A person who has finished university and has a degree (e.g. in economics).

3 School life

Match the sentences and pictures.

1 ▨ We have to wear a horrible **uniform**!

2 ▨ The **discipline** here is very **strict**.

3 ▨ My **timetable's** terrible this **term**!

4 ▨ I love **maths**. It's my favourite **subject**.

5 ▨ Look! The **exam results** are on the notice board.

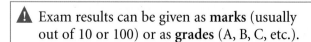

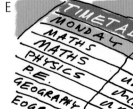

⚠ Exam results can be given as **marks** (usually out of 10 or 100) or as **grades** (A, B, C, etc.).

Can you remember the words on this page? Test yourself or a partner.

🔵 p.52

1 Types of houses

Match the words and pictures.

- [ ] block of flats
  (US apartment building)
- [ ] cottage /ˈkɒtɪdʒ/
- [ ] detached house
- [ ] terraced house

2 Where people live

Match the sentences.

1 I live in the **country**. [ ]
2 I live in the **city centre**. [ ]
3 I live in the **suburbs**. [ ]
4 I live in a **village** /ˈvɪlɪdʒ/. [ ]
5 I live in a **small town**. [ ]
6 I live in a **residential area**. [ ]
7 I live on the **second floor**. [ ]

a It has 20,000 inhabitants.
b It's very small, with only 800 inhabitants.
c There are a lot of houses but no offices or big shops.
d It's right in the middle of the city.
e It's the area outside the central part of town.
f There are two floors below me.
g There are fields and trees all around me.

3 Parts of a house

Match the words and pictures.

- [ ] balcony
- [ ] chimney
- [ ] garage /ˈgærɑːʒ/
- [ ] garden
- [ ] gate
- [ ] path
- [ ] roof
- [ ] steps
- [ ] terrace /ˈterəs/
- [ ] wall

4 Furniture

a Put two words in each column.
Use your dictionary to help you.

washbasin   sink   shower
bedside table   dishwasher
coffee table   armchair
chest of drawers

bathroom	kitchen	living room	bedroom

b Add two more words to each column.

Can you remember the words on this page? Test yourself or a partner.

◐ p.58

Work

1 Describing your job

a Read the texts and match them to the pictures. What are the jobs?

1 I only work part-time – four mornings a week. and I sometimes do overtime on a Saturday morning. I don't earn a big salary. It's a temporary job and I only have a six-month contract at the moment. But the working hours suit me as I have very young children. When they go to school I would like to find a permanent job and work full-time. What I like most about my job is working in complete silence! The only noise you can hear is of people turning pages and whispering.

2 I did a six-month training course at Technical College to get my qualifications and then I worked for a local company to get some experience. I worked long hours for a low salary and so I resigned last year and became self-employed. I prefer working for myself. I don't work regular hours (sometimes people call me in the middle of the night) but you can earn a lot of money in this job, especially in the winter. If I'm lucky, I'll be able to retire when I'm 60!

b Match the highlighted words in the texts to definitions.

1	a written legal agreement	_contract_
2	the knowledge you get from doing a job	_____
3	a series of lessons to learn to do a job	_____
4	the time you spend doing a job	_____
5	working for yourself, not for a company	_____
6	to stop working when you reach a certain age, e.g. 65	_____
7	left a job because you wanted to	_____
8	lasting for a short time	_____ (opposite _____)
9	for only a part of the day or the week	_____ (opposite _____)
10	exams you've passed or courses you've done	_____

2 Saying what you do

Complete the **Prepositions** column.

Prepositions

1 I **work** ▨▨▨ a multinational company. _____
2 I **work** ▨▨▨ a manager. _____
3 I'm ▨▨▨ **charge** ▨▨▨ the marketing department. _____ , _____
4 I **work** ▨▨▨ a factory. _____
5 I'm **responsible** ▨▨▨ customer loans. _____
6 I'm ▨▨▨ **school / university**. _____
7 I'm ▨▨▨ **my third year**. _____

3 People

Write two more jobs in each column.

-er	-or	-ist	-ian	others
lawyer /ˈlɔːjə/	actor	psychologist	electrician	accountant
plumber	conductor	scientist	librarian	chef /ʃef/

> ⚠ An **employer** is a person or company that employs other people. An **employee** is a person who works for somebody.

Can you remember the words on this page? Test yourself or a partner.

◐ p.76

1 Places

a Match the words and pictures.

- [ ] department store
- [ ] supermarket
- [ ] street market
- [ ] shopping centre (US mall)

b Match the shops and pictures of what you can buy there.

- [ ] baker's
- [ ] bookshop
- [ ] butcher's /'bʊtʃəz/
- [ ] chemist's / pharmacy
- [ ] newsagent's
- [ ] stationer's
- [ ] travel agent's
- [ ] shoe shop

2 In the shop

Match the words and definitions or pictures.

bargain /'bɑːgən/	basket	customer	discount	manager	receipt /rɪ'siːt/
refund	sales	shop assistant	trolley /'trɒli/	shop window	till

1 _____ a time when shops sell things at lower prices than usual

2 _____ something that you buy for what you think is a good price

3 _____ a place at the front of a shop where you can see the products

4 _____ a piece of paper which shows you have paid for something

5 _____ a reduction in the price

6 _____ a person who works in a shop

7 _____

8 _____ money that is paid back to you when you are unhappy with something you buy

9 _____

10 _____ a person who buys things in a shop

11 _____ the person who is in charge of a shop, hotel, etc.

12 _____

3 Verbs and phrases

Match the sentences.

1 I often **buy** books **online**.
2 This shop **sells** books.
3 I'm going to **buy** the dishwasher **on credit**.
4 I went back to the shop to **complain**.
5 I had to **queue** /kjuː/ for ages in the bank.
6 I want to **try on** this dress.
7 I'm **just looking**.
8 I had to **pay** 16% **VAT**.

a I had to wait behind lots of other people.
b I don't need any help at the moment.
c I buy books on the Internet.
d I'm going to pay for it over 12 months.
e I want to see what I look like in it.
f I had to pay tax on it.
g You can buy books in this shop.
h I went there to tell them I wasn't happy.

🡒 p.85   **Can you remember the words on this page? Test yourself or a partner.**

Cinema

1 Kinds of film

Match the films and film types.

action film

comedy

horror film

musical

science fiction

thriller

western

2 People and things

Match the words and definitions.

audience /ˈɔːdiəns/	~~cast~~	~~director~~	extra	plot	scene /siːn/	script
sequel /ˈsiːkwəl/	~~soundtrack~~	special effects	star	subtitles		

1 _cast_ all the people who act in a film
2 _____ the most important actor or actress in a film
3 _director_ the person who makes a film
4 _soundtrack_ the music of a film
5 _____ the story of a film
6 _____ a part of a film happening in one place
7 _____ the people who watch a film in a cinema
8 _____ a film which continues the story of an earlier film
9 _____ images, often created by a computer
10 _____ the words of the film
11 _____ person in a film who has a small, unimportant part, e.g. in a crowd scene
12 _____ transcription (usually translation) of the dialogue of a film that appears at the bottom of the screen

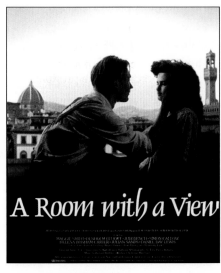

A Room with a View

MAGGIE SMITH · DENHOLM ELLIOTT · JUDI DENCH · SIMON CALLOW
HELENA BONHAM-CARTER · JULIAN SANDS · DANIEL DAY-LEWIS

3 Verbs and phrases

Match the sentences 1–6 with the sentences a–f.

1 The film **was set** in 19th century Italy and England.
2 It **was based on** a novel by EM Forster.
3 It was **filmed / shot on location** in Florence.
4 It **was directed** by James Ivory.
5 Helena Bonham-Carter **played the part** of Lucy.
6 It **was dubbed** into other languages.

a He was the director.
b It was situated in that place at that time.
c This was her role in the film.
d The actors originally spoke in English.
e It was an adaptation of the book.
f It was filmed in the real place, not in a studio.

Can you remember the words on this page? Test yourself or a partner.

⟳ p.90

Phrasal verbs

---

a The phrasal verbs below are all from Files 1–7. Cover the **Particle** column and look at sentence 1. Try to remember the phrasal verb.

b Uncover to check. Then do the same for the other sentences.

#	Sentence	Particle
1	When I go to a restaurant I always **ask** ⬚ something low fat.	for
2	I often **eat** ⬚ with friends at local restaurants.	out
3	Players usually **warm** ⬚ before a match starts.	up
4	When we have an argument we always **make** ⬚ quickly.	up
5	How do you **get** ⬚ ⬚ your brothers and sisters?	on with
6	**Take** the camera ⬚ to the shop and **get** your money ⬚.	back, back
7	I **took** some money ⬚ of a cash machine.	out
8	A German woman **gave** ⬚ all her money to charity.	away
9	I organized a school reunion but nobody **turned** ⬚.	up
10	She works in an animal sanctuary. She **looks** ⬚ apes.	after
11	We **set** ⬚ early and caught the 6.00 a.m. train.	off
12	The plane **took** ⬚ and soon I was looking down on London.	off
13	I **picked** ⬚ my suitcase and followed the 'Exit' signs.	up
14	A taxi **picked** me ⬚ and took me to the airport.	up
15	I **checked** ⬚ at the airport and got my boarding pass.	in
16	We were talking on the phone but suddenly she **hung** ⬚.	up
17	If he's not at home, I'll **call** ⬚ later.	back
18	I think people should **switch** ⬚ their mobiles in restaurants.	off
19	I tried to learn to dance salsa but I **gave** ⬚. I was terrible at it.	up
20	I want to **take** ⬚ a water sport like scuba-diving.	up
21	If I like this course, I'll **carry** ⬚ next year.	on
22	Bethany has written a book which is going to be **made** ⬚ a film.	into
23	*The Sunday Times* decided to **find** ⬚ if school is easier than it used to be.	out
24	The teacher told me to **do** ⬚ the button of my shirt.	up
25	Carol's parents didn't like her boyfriend so they **went** ⬚ together in secret.	out
26	After a year she **broke** ⬚ with her boyfriend.	up
27	If you have something you never use, **throw** it ⬚.	away
28	**Slow** ⬚! You're driving too fast.	down
29	I complained and the company tried to **sort** ⬚ the problem.	out
30	Aung San Suu-kyi didn't see her sons **grow** ⬚. She was under house arrest.	up
31	Bill and Melinda Gates **set** ⬚ a foundation to provide vaccinations.	up
32	You're very nervous. You need to **calm** ⬚.	down
33	I **bumped** ⬚ an old friend in the street yesterday.	into
34	He was **looking** ⬚ ⬚ having dinner with his friends.	forward to
35	**Look** ⬚! There's a car coming!	out
36	Her grandmother **passed** ⬚ last year at the age of 93.	away
37	We can't go to the concert. It's **sold** ⬚.	out
38	**Turn** ⬚ the TV. There's a programme I want to watch.	on
39	**Turn** ⬚ the radio. It's too loud.	down
40	Where can I **plug** ⬚ my computer?	in

Nobody turned up.

Do it up!

Look out!

> ⚠ Some phrasal verbs have more than one meaning:
> I was hot so I **took off** my jacket. The plane **took off**.

○ p.110   **Can you remember the words on this page? Test yourself or a partner.**

155

Irregular verbs

Infinitive	Past simple	Past participle
be	was	been
beat	beat	beaten
become	became	become
begin	began	begun
bite	bit	bitten
blow	blew /bluː/	blown
break	broke	broken
bring	brought /brɔːt/	brought
build	built /bɪlt/	built
buy	bought /bɔːt/	bought
can	could /cʊd/	–
catch	caught /kɔːt/	caught
choose	chose	chosen
come	came	come
cost	cost	cost
cut	cut	cut
do	did	done
draw	drew	drawn
dream	dreamt	dreamt
drink	drank	drunk
drive	drove	driven
eat	ate	eaten
fall	fell	fallen
feel	felt	felt
fight	fought /fɔːt/	fought
find	found	found
fly	flew /fluː/	flown
forget	forgot	forgotten
get	got	got
give	gave	given
go	went	gone
grow	grew /gruː/	grown
hang	hung	hung
have	had	had
hear	heard /hɜːd/	heard
hide	hid /hɪd/	hidden
hit	hit	hit
hold	held	held
hurt	hurt	hurt
keep	kept	kept
know	knew /njuː/	known

Infinitive	Past simple	Past participle
learn	learnt	learnt
leave	left	left
lend	lent	lent
let	let	let
lie	lay /leɪ/	lain /leɪn/
lose	lost	lost
make	made	made
mean	meant /ment/	meant
meet	met	met
pay	paid	paid
put	put /pʊt/	put
read	read /red/	read /red/
ride	rode /rəʊd/	ridden
ring	rang	rung
run	ran	run
say	said /sed/	said
see	saw /sɔː/	seen
sell	sold	sold
send	sent	sent
set	set	set
shine	shone /ʃɒn/	shone
show	showed	shown /ʃəʊn/
shut	shut	shut
sing	sang	sung
sit	sat	sat
sleep	slept	slept
speak	spoke	spoken
spend	spent	spent
stand	stood /stʊd/	stood
steal	stole	stolen
swim	swam	swum
take	took /tʊk/	taken
teach	taught	taught
tell	told	told
think	thought /θɔːt/	thought
throw	threw /θruː/	thrown /θrəʊn/
understand	understood	understood
wake	woke	woken
wear	wore	worn
win	won /wʌn/	won
write	wrote	written

■ short vowels
■ long vowels
■ diphthongs

■ voiced
■ unvoiced

1 fish /fɪʃ/	11 egg /eg/	21 parrot /ˈpærət/	33 thumb /θʌm/
2 tree /triː/	12 up /ʌp/	22 bag /bæg/	34 mother /ˈmʌðə/
3 cat /kæt/	13 train /treɪn/	23 key /kiː/	35 chess /tʃes/
4 car /kɑː/	14 phone /fəʊn/	24 girl /gɜːl/	36 jazz /dʒæz/
5 clock /klɒk/	15 bike /baɪk/	25 flower /ˈflaʊə/	37 leg /leg/
6 horse /hɔːs/	16 owl /aʊl/	26 vase /vɑːz/	38 right /raɪt/
7 bull /bʊl/	17 boy /bɔɪ/	27 tie /taɪ/	39 witch /wɪtʃ/
8 boot /buːt/	18 ear /ɪə/	28 dog /dɒg/	40 yacht /jɒt/
9 computer /kəmpˈjuːtə/	19 chair /tʃeə/	29 snake /sneɪk/	41 monkey /ˈmʌŋki/
10 bird /bɜːd/	20 tourist /ˈtʊərɪst/	30 zebra /ˈzebrə/	42 nose /nəʊz/
		31 shower /ˈʃaʊə/	43 singer /ˈsɪŋə/
		32 television /ˈtelɪvɪʒn/	44 house /haʊs/

Sounds and spelling – vowels

		usual spelling		⚠ but also
fish	**i**	dish bill pitch fit ticket since		pretty women busy decided village physics
tree	**ee** **ea** **e**	speed sweet peach team refund medium		people magazine key niece receipt
cat	**a**	fan tram crash tax carry land		
car	**ar** **a**	garden charge starter path glass cast		aunt laugh heart
clock	**o**	lorry cost plot bossy off on		watch want sausage because
horse	**or** **al** **aw**	score floor bald wall prawns draw		warm course thought caught audience board
bull	**u** **oo**	full butcher's cook book look good		could should would woman
boot	**oo** **u*** **ew**	pool moody true student few interview		suitcase juice shoe move soup through queue
bird	**er** **ir** **ur**	term prefer dirty third curly turn		learn work world worse journey
computer	Many different spellings, always unstressed. other nervous about complain director information			

		usual spelling		⚠ but also
egg	**e**	menu lend text spend plenty cent		friendly already healthy many said
up	**u**	public subject ugly duck hurry cup		money worried someone enough country tough
train	**a*** **ai** **ay**	save gate railway plain may say		break steak great weight they grey
phone	**o*** **oa**	broke stone frozen mobile roast coach		owe slow although shoulders
bike	**i*** **y** **igh**	fine resign shy cycle flight frightened		buy eyes height
owl	**ou** **ow**	hour lounge proud ground town brown		
boy	**oi** **oy**	boiled noisy spoilt coin enjoy employer		
ear	**eer** **ere** **ear**	beer engineer here we're beard appearance		really idea serious
chair	**air** **are**	airport upstairs fair hair rare careful		their there wear pear area
tourist	A very unusual sound. euro furious sure plural			
/i/	A sound between /ɪ/ and /iː/. Consonant + **y** at the end of words is pronounced /i/. happy angry thirsty			
/u/	An unusual sound. education usually situation			

* especially before consonant + **e**

Sounds and spelling – consonants

	usual spelling	⚠ but also
parrot	**p** plate pupil transport trip **pp** shopping apply	
bag	**b** beans bill probably job **bb** rabbit dubbed	
keys	**c** court script **k** kind basket **ck** track lucky	chemist's school mechanic queue
girl	**g** golf grilled burger forget **gg** aggressive luggage	
flower	**f** food roof **ph** photo nephew **ff** traffic affectionate	enough laugh
vase	**v** van vegetables travel invest private behave	of
tie	**t** try tidy stupid strict **tt** attractive cottage	worked passed
dog	**d** director afford comedy confident **dd** address middle	failed bored
snake	**s** steps likes **ss** boss assistant **ce/ci** twice city	science scene
zebra	**z** lazy freezing **s** lose cosy loves trousers	
shower	**sh** short dishwasher selfish cash **ti** ambitious station (+ vowel) **ci** special sociable (+ vowel)	sugar sure chef moustache
television	An unusual sound. revision decision confusion usually garage	

	usual spelling	⚠ but also
thumb	**th** thin thriller healthy path maths both	
mother	**th** the that with further whether	
chess	**ch** change cheat **tch** pitch match **t (+ure)** picture future	
jazz	**j** jealous just **g** generous manager **dge** fridge judge	
leg	**l** lettuce salary until reliable **ll** sell trolley	
right	**r** result referee primary fried **rr** borrow carriage	written wrong
witch	**w** wear waste western motorway **wh** white which	one once
yacht	**y** yet year yoghurt yourself before **u** university argue	
monkey	**m** mean slim romantic charming **mm** summer swimming	lamb
nose	**n** napkin honest none spoon **nn** tennis thinner	knife knew
singer	**ng** cooking going spring bring	think bank
house	**h** handsome helmet hard inherit unhappy perhaps	who whose whole

OXFORD
UNIVERSITY PRESS

Great Clarendon Street, Oxford OX2 6DP

Oxford University Press is a department of the University of Oxford. It furthers the University's objective of excellence in research, scholarship, and education by publishing worldwide in

Oxford New York

Auckland Cape Town Dar es Salaam
Hong Kong Karachi Kuala Lumpur Madrid
Melbourne Mexico City Nairobi New Delhi
Shanghai Taipei Toronto

With offices in

Argentina Austria Brazil Chile Czech Republic
France Greece Guatemala Hungary Italy Japan
Poland Portugal Singapore South Korea
Switzerland Thailand Turkey Ukraine Vietnam

OXFORD and OXFORD ENGLISH are registered trade marks of Oxford University Press in the UK and in certain other countries

© Oxford University Press 2006

ACKNOWLEDGEMENTS

Design and composition by: Stephen Strong

The authors would like to thank all the teachers and students round the world whose feedback has helped us to shape New English File. We would also like to thank: Kevin Poulter, Juan Antonio Fernandez Marín, Karen Wade, Rafael Lloyd, and Dagmara Walkowicz, *for agreeing to be interviewed, and Qarie and Victoria (Mark and Allie). The authors would also like to thank all those at Oxford University Press (both in Oxford and around the world), and the design team.*

Finally, very special thanks from Clive to Maria Angeles, Lucia, and Eric, and from Christina to Cristina, for all their help and encouragement. Christina would also like to thank her children Joaquin, Marco, and Krysia for their constant inspiration.

The authors would like to dedicate this book to Krzysztof Dabrowski.

The publisher and authors would also like to thank the following for their invaluable feedback on the materials: Beatriz Martín, Michael O'Brien, Wendy Armstrong, Tim Banks, Brian Brennan, Jane Hudson, Elena Ruiz, Maria Sonsoles de Haro Brito, and Gaye Wilkinson.

The authors and publisher are grateful to those who have given permission to reproduce the following extracts and adaptations of copyright material: p.19 adapted extracts from 'Jam today…tomorrow…yesterday…the day before that… the 11 years before that' by Sam Coates from *The Times* 23rd June 2004 © The Times 2004, p.20 lyrics from 'Ka-ching!' words and music by Shania Twain and Robert John Lange © 2002 Loon Echo Incorporated/ Out of Pocket Productions Limited. Universal Music Publishing Limited (50%)/ Zomba Music Publishers Limited (50%). All Rights Reserved. International Copyright Secured, p.22 translated and abridged extracts from 'Pobre por vocacion' by Ana Alonso Montes from *El Mundo* 24th March 2002. Reproduced by kind permission of El Mundo, p.26 adapted extracts from 'A holiday can change your life' by Mark Hodson from *The Sunday Times* 27th April 2003 © The Times 2003, p.35 adapted extracts from 'Why I didn't want to be a millionaire' by Kira Cochrane from *The Sunday Times* 11th January 2004. Reproduced by kind permission of the author, p.38 adapted extracts from 'Grin and bear it' by Miranda Ingram from *The Times* 16th June 2004 © The Times 2004, p.40 adapted extracts from 'A passport to embarrassment' by John Crowley from *The Daily Telegraph* 8th August 2003 © Daily Telegraph 2003, p.43 abridged extracts from 'Match the woman to the life' from *Marie Claire* June 2003 © Fanny Johnstone/Charlie Gray/Neil Cooper/Marie Claire/ IPC+ Syndication, p.51 adapted extracts from 'The best day of my life!' by Ray Connolly from *The Daily Mail* Weekend Magazine 8th December 2001 © The Daily Mail 2001, p.53 abridged extracts from 'Homework…old habits die hard so I decide to forget' by Damian Whitworth from *The Times* 30th November 2004 © The Times 2004, p.56 adapted extracts from 'Getting personal – Joaquin Cortes' by Carolyn Asome from *The Times* 16th September 2004 © The Times 2004, p.56 adapted extracts from 'Getting personal – Isabella Rossellini' by Carolyn Asome from *The Times* 11th November 2004 © The Times 2004, p.62 adapted extracts from 'Is it time to edit your friends?' by Julie Myerson from *Red Magazine* November 2001. Reproduced by kind permission of the author, p.73 adapted extracts from 'A gossip with the girls?' by Peter Markham from *The Daily Mail* 18th October 2001 © The Daily Mail 2001, p.100 adapted extracts from 'Missed you!' from *The Daily Mail* 26th July 2001 © The Daily Mail 2001, p.102 adapted extracts from 'Cheat your way to luck' by Richard Wiseman from *The Daily Mail* 13th January 2003. Reproduced by kind permission of the author, p.106 extract from 'A Venetian Reckoning' by Donna Leon. Reproduced by kind permission of Macmillan, London, UK.

The publisher would like to thank the following for their kind permission to reproduce photographs and other copyright material: AKG pp.15 (Archie Miles Collection), 154 (Lucasfilm/20th Century Fox/Star Wars); Alamy pp.7 (Food Features/Cheese, trifle); Albanpix p19 (Rob Howarth); Allstar pp.97 (Miramax); Anthony Blake Photo Library pp.7 (pub exterior), 144 (chicken); Apex p.115; Aviation Picture Library p.101; Bubbles p.73 (Chris Rout/ girls); Camera Press pp.51 (Charles Hopkinson), 56 (Gamma/Rossellini), 93 (Chris Ashford/ Gael Garcia Bernal); Catherine Blackie pp.38, 60 (graduation) 61; Geoff Cloake p.89 (landscape); Cittislow Ludlow p.71(logo); Corbis pp.17 (Zefa/A Inden), 33 (Alexandra Winkler), 52(Tom Wagner), 54 (Zefa/K Mitchell/girl, John-Francis Bourke/man), 56 (Reuters/ Andrea Comas/Cortes), 65 (Zefa/Theo Allofs/house) 70–71 (Bo Zanders/tree), 88 (Sygma/ Leonardo Di Caprio), 93 (Howard Yanes/Aleidita Guevara), 94 (Elvis Barukcic/Bernard Koucher, Stephanie Cardinale/ Queen Rania) 95 (Emmanuel Dunand/Aung Sang Suu-Kyi), 104 (Hulton-Deutsch Collection/misty scene), 105 (Bettmann/ D of Clarence, Hulton/Walter Sickert); Daily Telegraph pp.40/41 (Michael Winner/ Eddie Mulholland, Toby Young/John Taylor); Dorling Kindersly p.144 (potatoes, veg); David Elkington p.60 (hockey); Easyjet p28; Empics pp.7 (AP/Bebeto Matthews kitchen), 8 (Lorz, Onischenko), 9 (DPA/Fred Lorz, Sports Photo Agency/

Boris Onischenko), 11 (Bertil Ericson/ Beckenbauer, Maddalone Minto/Jordan, Gary Jones/ Ali, Dubreul Corinne Abaca/McEnroe), 20 (AP/Susannah Ireland/Sale), 28 (Eurostar), 47 (Lucy Pemani/ Hamilton), 54 (PA/Martin Rickett/ results), 92 (PA/flag), 93 (Adam Davy), 116 (PA/ David Cheskin/Glenda Jackson, PA/Mathew Fearn/Rik Mayall, Abaca/Olivier Doulier/ Laila Ali), 145 (PA/ Sean Dempsey/few players, PA/Phil Noble/fans, Sean Dempsey/spectators, Matthew Ashton/team, Adam Davy/captain, Nick Potts/Stadium, John Giustina/ Sportshall), 147 (AP/Mark Lennihan/visa cards, Reporter Press Agency/coins); Alison Findlay p.116 (Professor); For Life Charity p.35; Getty Images pp.4 (Image Bank), 14 (Time Life/Wilson children), 20 (Andreas Rentz/till), 28 (car), 50 (Cheese Images), 55, 60 (Image Bank/Jason Homa/two women), 65 (Photonica/ flats), 69 (Taxi/David Oliver/tennis, Jasper James/man), 73 (Taxi/John Booth/ men), 81(David Sacks), 102 (Stone/clover, Iconica/Angelo Cavelli/horseshoe), 106 (Sean Gallup/Donna Leon), 153 AFP/Sinead Lynch); *The Guardian* p.79 (Dan Chung/ journalists); Sally Guke p.26 (Sunday Times Travel/ S Guke); Robert Harding Picture Library p.28 (Avignon), 88 (Thailand); Nigel Hillier p.74; Hunter House Publishers p.83; Icon Photo Media p.67 (Robin Hammond); *The Independent* p.36 (Mark Chilvers); IPC pp.42, 58; Kobal Collection pp.88 (Universal/Meryl Streep), 89 (New Line/Saul Zaentz/ Wing Nut/Elilah Woods, 154 Stanley Kramer/United /High Noon, Lucasfilm Ltd/Paramount/Indian Jones, Miramax/ Chicago, Hammer/Dracula, Warner Brothers/ Dial M for Murder, Hal Roach/Laurel & Hardy); Ben Lack p.100 (Ian and Amy); Rafael Lloyd p.43; Juan Antonio Marin p.145; Masons News Service p.111(Duncan Miner); Museo Anahuacalli p.59 (Museum); NHPA p.26 (Andy Rouse/ orang-utan), 88 (giraffes); Network pp.75, 153 (Focus/ Peter Dammann); Pompidou Centre p.59 (The Frame); Kevin Poulter p.7 (Kevin Poulter and Frederick's); Punchstock pp.5 (sushi/Digital Vision), 49, 90, 144 (rice, sausages, eggs), 153 (Harrods); Rex Features pp.8 (Maradona), 14 (Wilson adults), 22 (Action Press), 24 (Beirut/Mika Minetti), 40 (Ruth England), 92 (C.Focus/ Everett/motorbike, 93 (Angelo Vavalli/ Alberto Korda), 94 (Sipa/Bono, Ken McKay/Thierry Henri), 99 (Sipa), 104 (20th C. Fox/Everett/Johnny Depp), 105 (James Maybrick, letter), 108 (ABC Inc/Everett/Who wants to be a Millionaire and All My Children, 20th C. Fox/ Futurama), 116 (Karl Schoendorfer/Nigel Kennedy), 145 (coach), 151 (Ilpo Musto/terraced houses, Clive Postlewaite/cottage, Rick Colls/flats, Andrew Drysdale/ detached house, 153 (Stuart Clarke/Shopping centre), 154 (Everett/ A Room with a View); Slow Food/Fiona Richmond p.70 (Logo, Maurizio Milanesio/market); Victoria Smith p.26 (*Sunday Times Travel*/V Smith); Solo Syndication, p.100 (Danny Howell/Dorothy Fletcher); Take 3 Management p.41 (Ruth England passport); Throckmorton Fine Art p.59 (Diego and Frida); *The Times* p.47 (Gill Allen/Natalie du Toit); Transport for London pp.117, 120 (copyright TFL); Karen Wade p.24 (Painting lessons); Dagmara Walkowicz p.91, Matt Writtle p.53. The painting on page 59 is *The Frame* © 2006 Banco de México Diego Rivera & Frida Kahlo Museums Trust. Av. Cinco de Mayo No. 2, Col. Centro, Del. Cuauhtémoc 06059, México, D.F.

Commissioned Photography by: Gareth Boden: pp. 23, 78, 79 (Jessica), 144 (table), Rob Judges: 16, 32, 48, 52 (whiteboard), 64, 80 (meeting), 96, 112, Mark Mason: pp.41, 68, 85, 102 (cat), 106 (book)

Illustrations by: Cartoonstock p.63 (Jerry King), 146 (Mark Guthrie); Stephen Conlin p.58; Bob Dewar pp.18, 34, 66, 82, 98, 113, 152;Phil Disley pp.6, 7, 10, 12, 21, 25, 29, 30, 31, 37, 46, 62, 76, 107, 109, 110,149; Ellis Nadler pronunciation symbols; Leo Hartas pp.148, 151; Neil Gower pp.28, 100, 153; LPG/Martyn Ford p.38; Andy Parker pp.41, 84, Kath Walker pp.9, 27, 39, 44, 54, 61, 72, 86, 87, 146, 150, 155; Annabel Wright p.56, 57, 103.

Thanks to Paul Seligson and Carmen Dolz for the English Sounds chart.